AF599332

TIME for KiDS

2027 ALMANAC

by Rachel Buchholz

PENGUIN YOUNG READERS LICENSES
An imprint of Penguin Random House LLC
1745 Broadway, New York, NY 10019
penguinrandomhouse.com

Produced by WonderLab Group, LLC
Design by Fan Works Design, LLC

Library of Congress Cataloging-in-Publication Data is available.

First published in the United States of America by
Penguin Young Readers Licenses, 2026

Manufactured in Malaysia
VIV

ISBN 9798217141821
10 9 8 7 6 5 4 3 2 1

The authorized representative in the EU for product safety and compliance is
Penguin Random House Ireland, Morrison Chambers, 32 Nassau Street,
Dublin D02 YH68, Ireland, https://eu-contact.penguin.ie.

CONTENTS

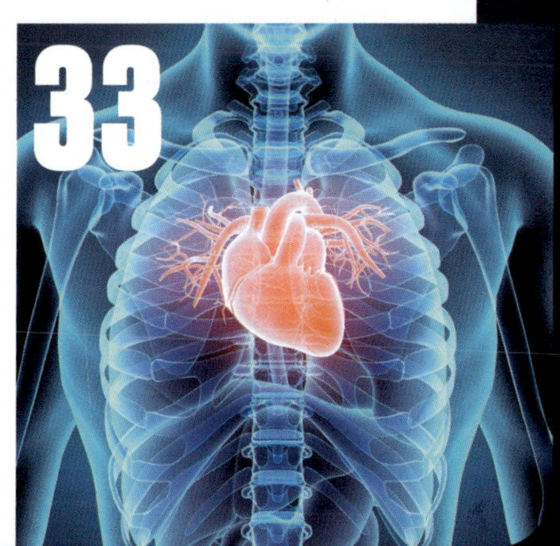

CALENDARS AND HOLIDAYS 39

TECHNOLOGY AND INVENTIONS 49

COUNTRIES OF THE WORLD 59

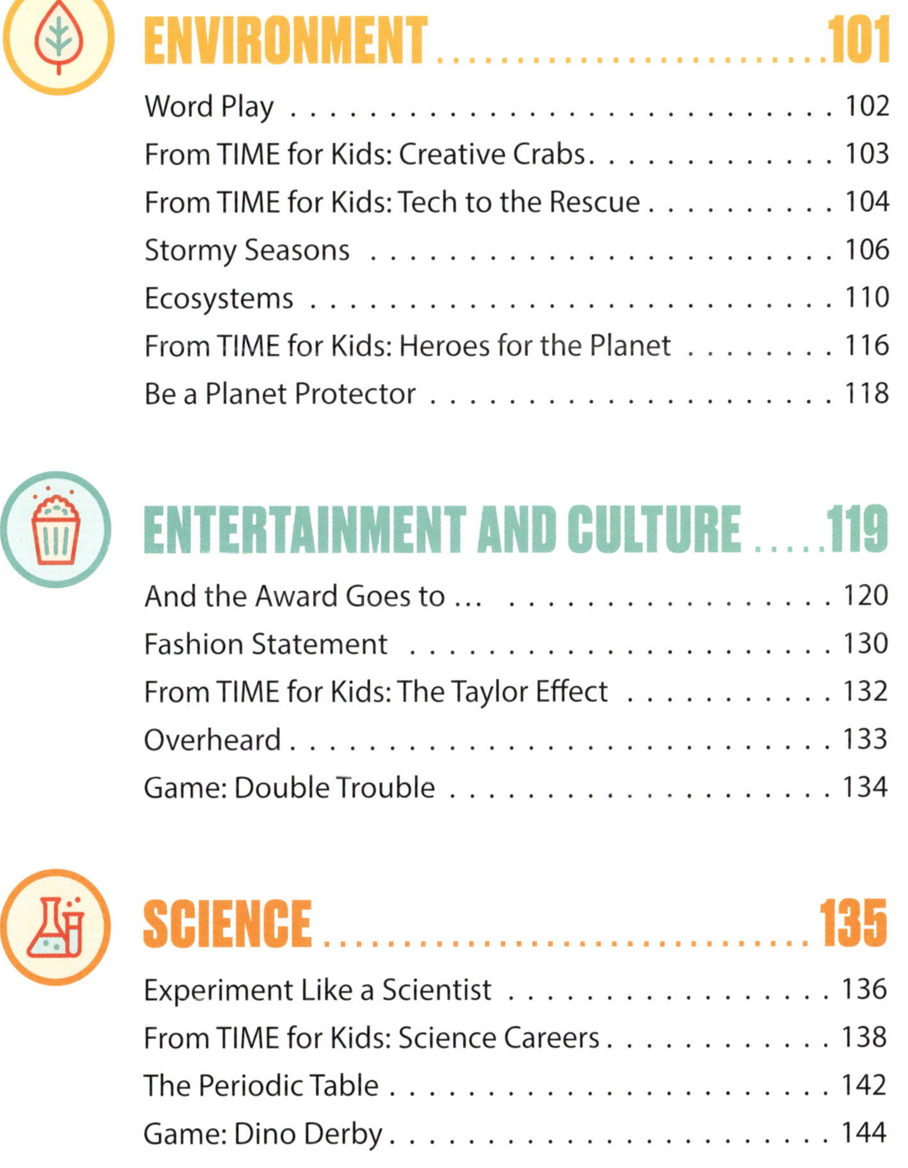

ENVIRONMENT 101

ENTERTAINMENT AND CULTURE 119

SCIENCE 135

145

155

165

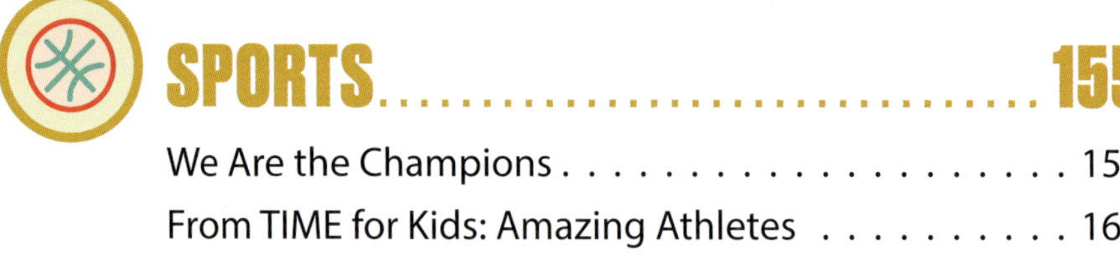

CHAPTER 1

HELLO, 2027!

GOTTA GO FAST!
Sonic the Hedgehog 4 is scheduled to be in movie theaters in 2027.

Next Stop: The Moon

Not since 1972 has a human walked on the moon. But the time has come to return to the lunar surface!

In 2027, NASA hopes to launch Artemis III, the first mission to the moon in more than 50 years. Four astronauts will blast off in the *Orion* spacecraft from Florida's Kennedy Space Center and enter the moon's orbit a few days later. Once the craft is near the moon's south pole, two astronauts will descend to the surface for about a week.

There, the astronauts will take pictures and video, collect samples, and conduct experiments. They'll wear super-advanced space suits to explore more of the surface; headlamps will help them see better on the dark, shadowy surface of the south pole. (Previous moon landings have been on the moon's equator.)

If the launch goes as planned, scientists hope to learn more about this part of the moon, which could play an important role as researchers plan future human-crewed trips to Mars. The sky—and the universe—is the limit.

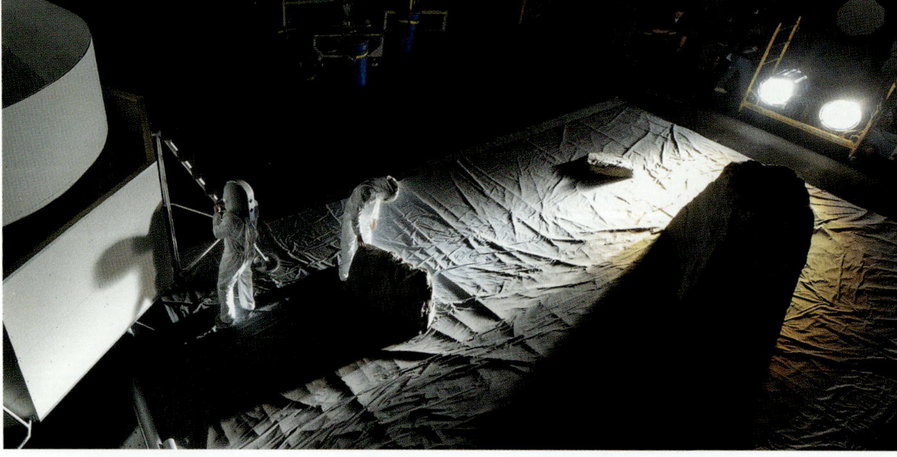

NASA engineers create a simulation to prepare for the Artemis III landing (left). The *Orion* spacecraft is getting ready for the 2027 launch (right).

WILL AN ASTEROID HIT EARTH?

Scientists will be keeping a close watch on a giant asteroid as big as the Empire State Building in 2027.

Named after the Egyptian god of chaos, Apophis is scheduled to harmlessly pass within 20,000 miles (32,000 km) of Earth in April 2029. (That's super close in space distance.) But there's a teeny-tiny chance that another asteroid might nudge the asteroid off its course—and toward Earth.

The year 2027 will be the first time in about six years that astronomers will be able to see the asteroid. So using high-powered telescopes, they'll make sure that Apophis is just passing by.

NASA scientists aren't worried. One researcher published a paper in the *Planetary Science Journal* saying that even if Apophis *has* been pushed off course, the chance of it actually hitting Earth is still only about one in a billion. (To compare, just 71 people out of 8.2 billion were bitten by sharks in 2024. That's a 1 in 155 million chance.)

POINT BRAZIL

Brazil has scored an important goal: For the first time ever, the country will host the FIFA Women's World Cup soccer tournament. It's also the first time the tournament will be held in South America, and officials are hoping the event will bring more attention to women's soccer on the continent.

Although men's soccer is very popular in South America, women's soccer is still pretty new. In fact, women in Brazil were banned from playing sports, including soccer, for nearly 40 years, until 1979. But now, from June 24 through July 25, 2027, 32 of the best women's soccer teams will compete for the World Cup title in Brazil.

Spain was the 2023 World Cup champion, and countries like the United States, Germany, Sweden, and Japan are expected to field strong teams. But officials have high hopes for Brazil's team, which will be playing in front of its home crowd. Let's go, team!

SPECIAL ATHLETES HEAD TO CHILE

You've probably watched Summer Olympic sports like gymnastics, weightlifting, and swimming. But at the 2027 Special Olympics World Games, athletes will also compete in sports such as bocce, bowling, and roller-skating.

The upcoming games, which happen every two years and alternate between summer and winter sports, will be held in Santiago, Chile—the first time the games will take place in the Southern Hemisphere. More than 6,000 athletes with intellectual disabilities will compete in 22 events.

As part of hosting the games, Chile's government has committed to creating more school programs that include children of all abilities. It will also expand Special Olympics into all 16 regions of the country to help fight discrimination against those with intellectual disabilities. That's good news for athletes—and for Chile.

AN IMPORTANT DIARY

Otto Frank made an important decision 80 years ago, in 1947. He knew that publishing the diary written by his daughter Anne would be painful. But he also knew that the world should know what her life was like hiding in Amsterdam, Netherlands, until the family was captured by the Nazis in 1944. Anne, her sister, and their mother died in German concentration camps in 1945.

Today, *Anne Frank: The Diary of a Young Girl* has sold more than 30 million copies in 67 languages. (The diary that Frank originally published in 1947 was called *The Secret Annex.*) It shows readers a true story about the Holocaust, in which six million Jewish people were killed. But more importantly, it shows the importance of choosing kindness over cruelty.

RETURN OF THE SEQUELS

What's better than your favorite movie? Your favorite movie's sequel!

A sequel continues the story of a movie, book, or game—and 2027 will be a big year for these. *Sonic the Hedgehog 4,* the live-action *How to Train Your Dragon 2,* and *Frozen III* are just a few of the sequels scheduled to be released in 2027.

Movie studios know that if the original film is popular with audiences and has great characters with new stories to tell, there's a good chance people will pay to see a sequel. They're often right: According to Box Office Mojo, *Frozen II* made $143 million more than the 2013 original; by spring 2025, *Inside Out 2* had become the top-grossing animated movie of all time. ("Gross" is how much money a movie makes before subtracting expenses, like actor salaries and special effects.)

Movies are delayed and rescheduled all the time. But even if these sequels don't hit theaters in 2027, you can be sure other sequels will.

SCIENCE

MEET THE WOOLLY MOUSE

This little cutie is sort of like a cousin to the woolly mammoth—and the mouse might help scientists bring back the extinct creature in just a year or two.

A company called Colossal Biosciences is trying to slightly change, or edit, Asian elephant **genes** to create a woolly mammoth. (Asian elephants and mammoths share 99.6 percent of the same **DNA**.) Scientists think that the edited genes would result in an elephant-like creature that has more blubber and longer, thicker hair—much like the original woolly mammoth, which lived in cold tundra habitats until about 4,000 years ago.

In 2025, scientists tried their technique on mice and were excited to see that the animals grew shaggy, mammoth-like hair. Ben Lamm, the company's cofounder, said in a statement that it was an important step toward bringing back the woolly mammoth.

Later in 2025, scientists had similar success using the technique to create an animal much like a dire wolf, which went extinct 10,000 years ago. If the gene-editing technique continues to work, scientists could bring back many extinct or endangered animals to their original habitats. That would definitely be one mammoth goal.

POWER WORDS

genes *(noun):* the information inside a cell that helps determine what a living thing looks like

DNA *(noun):* made from genes; the chemical that carries the recipe for a living thing

GAMING

LET THE (VIDEO) GAMES BEGIN

In 2027, some video-game players might be considered Olympic athletes.

Esports are video-game competitions in which gamers participate on teams or by themselves. Tournaments can attract millions of viewers on platforms like YouTube, and competitors can make millions of dollars.

But in 2027, players will be able to represent their countries at the Olympic Esports Games in Riyadh, Saudi Arabia. Created by the International Olympic Committee, the games aim to combine traditional and virtual sports with an esporting event vibe.

The 2025 Esports World Cup, which is a partner for the Olympic event, featured a mixture of virtual sports like the *EA Sports FC* soccer game and traditional player games like *League of Legends*. A race-car gaming developer is also partnering with the Olympic event.

So warm up those fingers—you just might be headed to the Olympics.

TECHNOLOGY

HAPPY BIRTHDAY, iPHONE!

What if you had to use different devices to play all your songs, another to watch movies, one more to play games, and yet another to make phone calls? Before the iPhone, most people did.

Released 20 years ago in 2007, the iPhone was the first mobile phone with a touch screen, with which users could use their fingers to make calls and open apps. People also loved the variety of apps they could choose to download on their phones.

Over the years, the iPhone has gotten thinner, longer, and faster. It's added features like a front-facing camera for selfies, a voice-command "assistant" named Siri, and even artificial intelligence.

Experts think that Apple will release a special phone in 2027 for its 20th anniversary, but the company is usually very secretive about upcoming changes. Maybe Siri knows? *Hey, Siri ...*

Jin, J-Hope, Jungkook, V, and RM of BTS

LIVE, IN CONCERT

Fans of K-pop—catchy, dance-worthy music played by South Korean bands—will now have another place to watch acts like BTS, BLACKPINK, and Stray Kids besides YouTube and TikTok. In 2027, the music genre will have its very own concert venue.

Located in and named after the country's capital city, Seoul Arena will be dedicated to K-pop music to help boost its popularity in South Korea. Even though the music comes from that country, more K-pop videos were streamed in Japan, the United States, and Indonesia than in South Korea in 2023, according to a music analysis company called Luminate.

When it opens, the main concert hall will hold 28,000 people. That'll mean plenty of fans to dance in sync with the stars onstage.

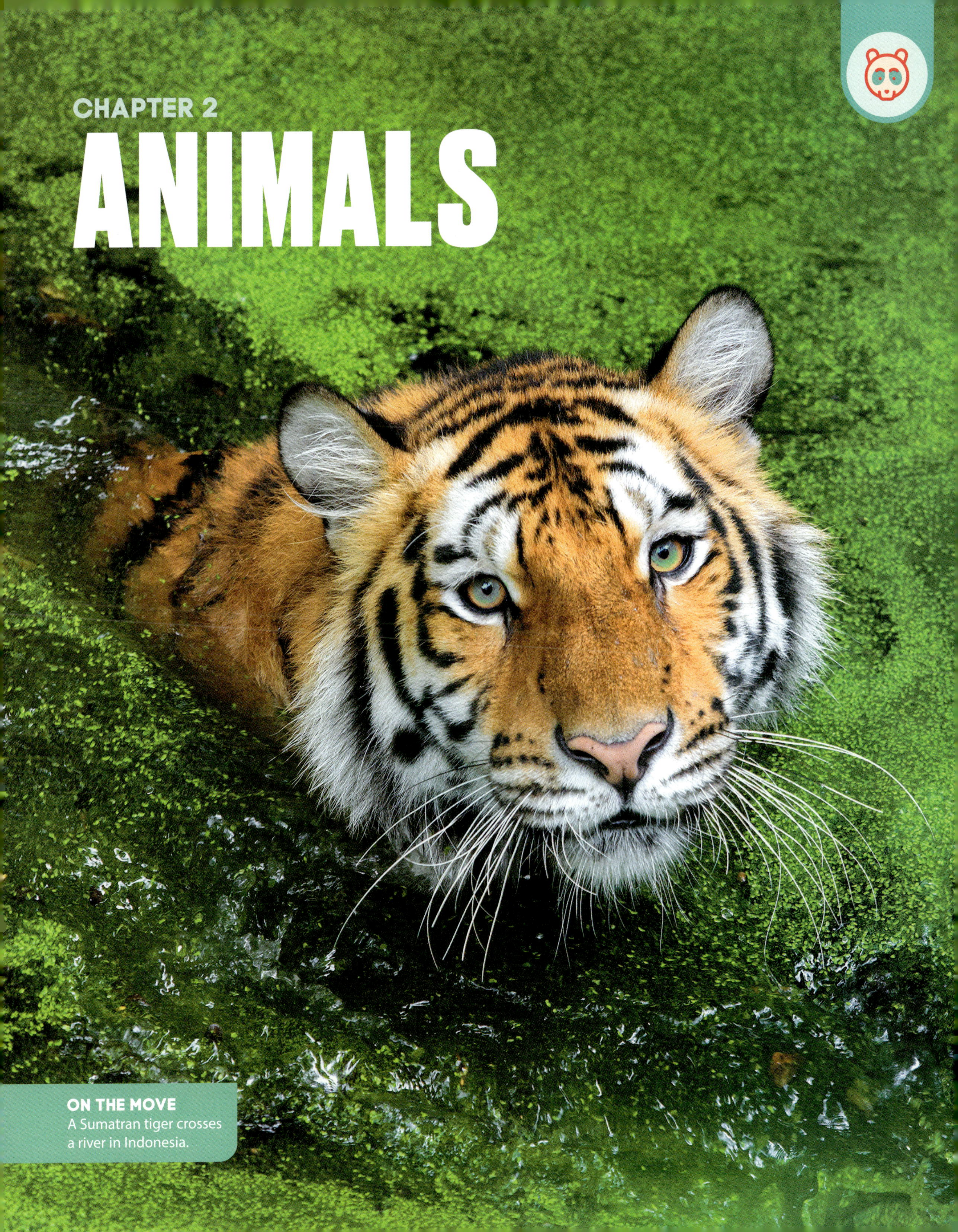

CHAPTER 2

ANIMALS

ON THE MOVE
A Sumatran tiger crosses a river in Indonesia.

FROM THE PAGES OF

Saving Sea Turtles

Grace Buschiazzo is a sea turtle biologist. She helps the animals from rescue to release.

In October 2023, a tiny green sea turtle was admitted to the South Carolina Aquarium's Sea Turtle Care Center. The patient, which was given the name Ricotta, had gotten tangled in fishing line and was missing a front flipper and part of its beak. More fishing line was found in the turtle's digestive tract. It took two surgeries to remove it. A long road to recovery was ahead.

Ricotta was a memorable patient, says Grace Buschiazzo, a marine biologist at the Sea Turtle Care Center. But Ricotta's story is not unique. Since the care center opened in 2000, workers there have seen many turtles affected by entanglement. Other injuries have been caused by boat strikes, **cold-stunning**, and animal bites.

Buschiazzo is part of a team of biologists, veterinarians, and technicians who care for sea turtles around the clock. "The best part about my job is that every single day is different," Buschiazzo told TIME for Kids. "We like to joke that [sea turtle biologists] are part-time janitors, part-time plumbers, part-time sushi chefs, and part-time nurses. So, basically, whatever the sea turtles need from me, I'm going to do it."

FINDING HER WAY

Buschiazzo was in fourth grade when she decided she wanted to become a marine biologist one day. Then at 15, she went to Panama, a country in Central America, with the Girl Scouts. She volunteered for a nesting project that helped protect leatherback sea turtle eggs from **poachers**. That's when she fell in love with sea turtles.

Buschiazzo pursued a degree in marine science at Coastal Carolina University, in South Carolina. While there, she volunteered for more nesting projects. After college, she interned at wildlife hospitals before winding up at the South Carolina Aquarium.

Buschiazzo recommends that kids interested in a similar career path should volunteer, like she did. "You can do it at an aquarium or at a zoo," she says. "You could do it at a local animal shelter. There are lots of ways to help animals."

A DAY IN THE LIFE

As a sea turtle biologist, Buschiazzo works directly with veterinarians. "They're going to prescribe the medicine for the turtles and tell me what the turtles need," she says. "And it's my job to make sure the turtles are getting it."

Buschiazzo assists the vets with medical procedures. She makes the turtles' meals and monitors their nutrition. She plans enrichment activities that simulate life in the wild. She does everything she can to prepare the turtles to thrive once they're released back into the ocean.

Since 2000, the team at the Sea Turtle Care Center has successfully treated and released more than 400 sea turtles. Ricotta eventually joined the list of patients who have recovered and made it back to the sea. "I was there," Buschiazzo says. "I got to watch it, and it was fantastic."

—By TFK Kid Reporter Milo Bhushan

A sea turtle "hunts" a plastic bag. To the turtle, it looks like a jellyfish to eat.

Turtle Anatomy

A sea turtle's throat is lined with spiny projections called esophageal papillae. They help keep food down while the esophagus pushes water back out. The papillae help prevent the turtle from ingesting too much of the salt in seawater. Unfortunately, they also prevent it from coughing up plastics and fishhooks. If a sea turtle accidentally swallows something like this, it can get stuck in the turtle's body, causing harm.

POWER WORDS

cold-stunning *noun:* a condition in which sea turtles become weak from exposure to cold temperatures

poacher *noun:* someone who hunts illegally

Newsmakers, Animal Style!

Check out these critters' claims to fame.

WORLD'S OLDEST BIRD LAYS EGG

A Laysan albatross named Wisdom surprised scientists in November 2024 after she laid an egg at 74 years old. The oldest known wild bird, Wisdom has been laying eggs—50 or 60 of them—since 1956 at the Midway Atoll National Wildlife Refuge, about 1,200 miles (1,900 km) northwest of Hawai'i. Scientists say the bird's parenting ability is quite rare at her age. In fact, the next oldest known bird is about 30 years younger than Wisdom!

FAST FACT
An albatross can soar for hours without flapping its wings.

BABY BOOM

Babies are born every day. But cute animals born at zoos often turn into news-making events.

Take Moo Deng, a pygmy hippo born July 10, 2024, at the Khao Kheow Open Zoo in Thailand. The rosy, playful calf quickly made headlines and was featured on news shows and in magazines. There's also Pesto the king penguin, who at nine months old already weighed 50 pounds (23 kg). And don't forget Tupi, an adorable capybara born at Texas's San Antonio Zoo.

Animal newbies become famous mostly because of social media: Moo Deng quickly went viral on her zoo's TikTok account, which at the time had 2.5 million followers, according to Forbes; Australia's SEA LIFE Melbourne Aquarium says that Pesto racked up a social audience of five billion in less than a year.

And the zoos love their social media stars. They bring people to the parks as well as raise awareness about these species. Looks like being famous is a good thing for the animals!

FAST FACT
Native to Africa, a pygmy hippo weighs about 10 times less than a hippopotamus.

WHAT'S YOUR NAME?

Scientists have discovered that African elephants might have names. How do they know? First, researchers at Kenya's Amboseli National Park and Samburu and Buffalo Springs National Reserves recorded 469 elephant calls and analyzed which elephants the calls were made to. Then they played those calls back. The scientists published their findings in a nature journal in 2024. The findings showed that certain elephants approached the caller more quickly than others, leading scientists to think they were responding to a name.

FAST FACT
To greet each other, elephants might wrap their trunks together.

Comeback Critters

By working together, conservationists and local people are helping protect threatened animals.

PARROT PATROL

Little green-and-red birds squawk like laughing kids in the chilly mountain forest. These thick-billed parrots once soared from South America to Arizona. But because of logging and the illegal pet trade, the endangered birds are now found only in northern Mexico.

That could be changing. In November 2024, the Mexican government announced that with help from organizations and local people, the parrot population in protected areas has increased 10 percent, from about 2,273 to 2,500 birds.

Working together, groups placed backpack-like trackers on the birds to understand flight patterns and how to better protect that habitat. Others trained local people to fight wildfires to protect the parrots' trees, and some organizations installed artificial nesting boxes to give the birds more breeding places.

With these actions, conservationists hope the parrot population will continue to soar.

CONGRATS, LYNX!

Congratulations, Iberian lynx—you're no longer an endangered species!

The Iberian lynx once prowled throughout the Iberian Peninsula, which includes Spain and Portugal. But because of habitat loss and poaching, only 62 adult lynx remained by 2001.

Conservationists sprang into action. First, they increased the population of the lynx's favorite food, the European rabbit, by restoring the hoppers' habitat and reintroducing animals from other parts of Europe. They also protected their habitat and paid farmers when lynx attacked cattle so the farmers wouldn't harm the wild cats.

The result? A jump to more than 2,000 Iberian lynx by June 2024!

The Iberian lynx is still listed as vulnerable, but conservationists are hopeful that by continuing to protect rabbits and prevent poaching, the wild cats will be around for a very long time.

REEF RECOVERY

The coral reef system off Indonesia's Pulau Bontosua island was colorless, flat, and silent, with no animals swimming nearby. Forty years ago, "blast fishing," in which fishers use explosives to stun or kill their catch, had nearly destroyed the reef—and it wasn't recovering on its own.

Coral reefs form when tiny animals called coral polyps attach to hard surfaces and wait for other polyps to attach to their rocklike skeletons. But that wasn't happening quickly enough at this reef system, and scientists wanted to see if humans could speed up the restoration of the unhealthy reef.

Working with local people, conservationists attached healthy polyps to "reef stars," six-sided, sand-covered steel frames that were then installed at the unhealthy reef site. What happened amazed them: In March 2024, scientists announced that in just four years, the amount of coral production tripled—just like what would happen at a healthy reef.

Scientists now have hope that, soon, animals like sea turtles and whale sharks will swim through this reef once again—and that similar projects can help unhealthy reefs quickly recover all over the world.

25 Fast Facts

Check out these bite-size nibbles about pets.

1 Cats give some dogs allergies.

2 Guppies are one of the few types of fish that give live birth instead of hatching eggs. The babies are called "fry."

3 There are more than 470 million pet dogs and nearly 375 million pet cats around the world.

4 A cat can sprint up to 30 miles an hour (48 km/h). That's speedier than the fastest person in the world!

5 Bearded dragons "talk" by changing the colors of their beards as well as bobbing their heads.

6 Most kittens are born with blue eyes. This is because their young cells haven't produced enough of the pigment (or color) that their eyes will become.

7 Researchers think that classical music might help dogs relax.

8 A cockatiel's beak is so strong it can crack nuts.

9 In the wild, guinea pigs live in social groups called herds. That's why as pets, these critters do best with a friend.

10 The corn snake is thought to be named for its belly markings, which look like a type of corn that has red, black, and yellow kernels.

11 A dog might yawn in response to a human or another dog to show it's aware of the other critter's feelings.

12 A rabbit's teeth never stop growing. That's why they love to chew on things like sticks and logs to keep their chompers healthy.

13 The Greenland dog is one of the world's oldest dog breeds. It's thought to be descended from a canine that lived with people migrating from Siberia 2,000 years ago.

14 A hamster's cheeks can nearly triple in size when stuffed with food like seeds, nuts, and even baby carrots.

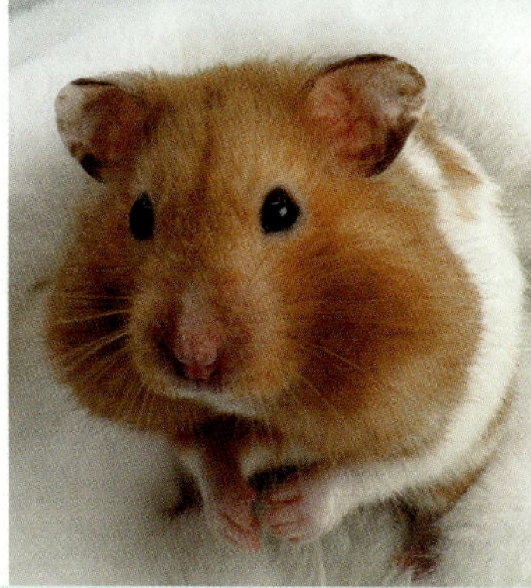

15 Having the memory of a goldfish might be a good thing! Researchers discovered the creatures could be trained to tell the difference between two musicians.

16 Horses can't breathe through their mouths—only through their nostrils. This prevents food from accidentally getting into the horse's lungs.

17 Male betta fish create a mass of tiny bubbles to build a protective nest for the female's eggs. The male places the eggs in the nest with his mouth—one egg per bubble.

18 How can you tell the difference between male and female parakeets? A male has fleshy blue skin just above its beak called a cere. A female's cere is brown.

19 Guinea pigs can poop up to 100 times a day.

20 Domesticated about 400 years ago, canaries are native to the Canary, Azores, and Madeira islands in the North Atlantic Ocean.

21 Hermit crabs don't have hard shells like other crabs. Instead, they wear seashells for protection and find bigger ones as they grow.

22 Hamsters are most active at night and will sometimes exercise for up to four hours while you're sleeping.

23 Black cats are thought to be lucky in England.

24 Horses can lock their legs in place so they can sleep standing up. (They do lie down for deep sleep!)

25 Most geckos have sticky, suction-cup-like feet to help them climb. But a leopard gecko's feet just have tiny claws. The creature rarely leaves the ground.

CHAPTER 3

MEDIA LITERACY

FACTS OR FICTION?

Media literacy—understanding and questioning information from TV, social media, newspapers, and other sources—is a hot topic right now.

Where We Get Our News

Which news source is right for you? Read on to help you decide.

LISTEN: PODCASTS

What They Are: News podcasts are prerecorded shows that can be streamed on electronic devices. They're often hosted by one or two people who provide quick highlights of the news of the day (or week) and use sound effects, guest Q&As, and quizzes to keep things fun.

What You Should Know: Often, podcast hosts "pick up" the news from other sources. This means they do not do their own reporting. Instead they read news stories from other organizations to gather information. So you don't always know the story's original source.

Cool Podcasters: Pamela Kirkland and Ryan Willard, cohosts of *The Ten News*. Kirkland has reported for CNN and *The Washington Post*, and Willard has hosted Nickelodeon's *Kids' Choice Awards Orange Carpet*. They include their sources for their stories online.

Old-School Version: News radio shows

READ: NEWS WEBSITES

What They Are: Many are versions of printed newspapers, which provide cities and towns with local news. Larger newspapers also report on national and global stories. Reporters often have "beats," or subjects they write about, such as city government, schools, or sports.

What You Should Know: Some news websites are owned by people who want others to believe their point of view and don't always write fair stories. (See page 27 to learn more.)

Cool Newspaper Reporter: Hannah Holzer, *Sacramento Bee* reporter. Holzer also wrote the TIME for Kids: *Kid Reporter Field Guide*.

Old-School Version: Print newspapers

WATCH: NEWSCASTS

What They Are: Like a podcast, newscasts feature hosts who quickly inform people about the latest current events they've watched online or on digital platforms like YouTube. A newscast also includes video footage of news-making events and interviews with people.

What You Should Know: Newscast segments are often very short and don't provide a lot of detail about each event.

Cool Newscaster: Coy Wire, host of *CNN 10* online. A former pro football player, Wire is a sports correspondent for CNN. On *CNN 10*, he helps break down the week's news, all in 10 minutes.

Old-School Version: Nightly TV news shows

READ: MAGAZINES

What It Is: A print magazine is filled with longer articles on different topics that provide thoughtful analysis about national or global current events. Reporters interview people and gather facts to write their stories, which can include photos and illustrations.

What You Should Know: News magazines usually publish once a week or monthly, so the articles are often written well before you read them.

Cool Magazine Writer: Sean Gregory, senior sports correspondent for TIME magazine. He's interviewed top athletes such as football player Saquon Barkley and basketball star Caitlin Clark.

Old-School Version: News magazines have been around since the 17th century; many now also have daily digital content, which can be more up-to-date.

Word Play

Talk like a reporter with these key definitions.

ANGLE (OR FOCUS): a story's approach or point of view

BALANCED: a story that includes the facts necessary for the readers to understand all sides of an issue

BIAS: a tendency in favor of or against an issue, an opinion, or one point of view, often in a way that seems unfair

BREAKING NEWS: a very recent or developing story that people need to know about as soon as possible

BYLINE: the name of the reporter who wrote the story

CENSORSHIP: suppressing or restricting access to materials that a person or group thinks is objectionable

COVERING (OR, TO COVER): reporting on or giving attention to a specific topic

CREDIBLE (OR RELIABLE) SOURCE: a trustworthy place to find factual information not affected by bias; credible sources can include official websites of museums, universities, government agencies, and highly reputable news organizations

DISINFORMATION: false or misleading information that's spread on purpose to deceive others

FACT: a statement that can be proven true or false

FREEDOM OF INFORMATION ACT: a US law that grants people access to public documents; reporters often file official requests under this act to get information

HEADLINE: the title of a news article that summarizes its main idea

INTERVIEW: the practice of asking a source questions to get information for a story

LIBEL: publishing false information that hurts someone's reputation

MISINFORMATION: false or inaccurate information that's spread unintentionally

PHOTOJOURNALISM: a way of documenting a story using mostly photographs or videos

PICK UP: to use information reported by another news organization

PLAGIARIZE: to pass off someone else's words or work as your own

PRIMARY SOURCE: an original document or firsthand account of an event

PUBLISHED: when a journalist's work is posted online or in a print publication, such as a newspaper or magazine

QUOTE: a word-for-word statement provided by a source; quotes are set off in quotation marks to show the words were spoken by someone else

SLANDER: speaking knowingly false information that hurts someone's reputation

TRANSCRIBE: the practice of writing down questions and answers from an interview that has been recorded

TFK Kid Reporter Shaivi Moparthi speaks with Vanessa E. Wyche, then director of NASA's Johnson Space Center.

FROM THE PAGES OF

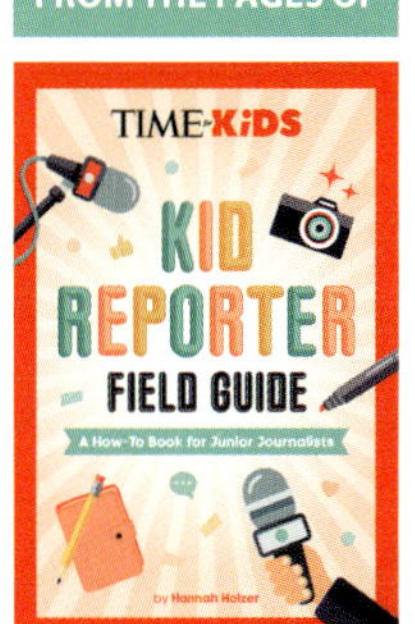

Sorting Fact from Fiction

These tips will help you tell the difference between real and untruthful news.

Khadija Qanoongo used to believe everything she read online. But after the Brooklyn, New York, student took a news literacy class, she found out that many stories on the Internet and social media are not reliable. "Now I'm very careful when I read news on the Internet," Khadija told TIME for Kids.

News literacy is the ability to sort fact from fiction and determine which sources are publishing informative and truthful news instead of news that might be biased—or just plain false. The News Literacy Project suggests these five steps to help determine whether a source of information is reliable:

Stop and Think

Why is it important for readers to find out whether a source is reliable?

1. Search your source online and see how it's described. Do legitimate, trustworthy news organizations cite this source as credible? Or do they **dispute** or **debunk** claims made by your source?

2. Does your source have an ethics code, which ensures that publications care about the truth and being honest? Reputable news organizations often show this on their website's "about" or "contact" section.

3. Is your source open about its reporting practices, the ownership of the organization, and where funding comes from? If so, are the reporting practices honest and respectable? Do the journalists have editorial control (the ability to decide what to publish), or do the owners determine what stories do or do not get covered?

4. How does your source handle errors? A credible news source owns up to its mistakes, explaining to readers how the mistakes occurred and what steps were made to correct them.

5. Use your own judgment. Does the source look, sound, and feel trustworthy? Has your source conducted original reporting, or is it using information from other websites? If something feels off, trust your gut.

If you're still unsure whether a source is credible, ask a teacher, librarian, or other trusted adult for help.

—By Hannah Holzer

POWER WORDS

debunk *verb:* to prove that a claim isn't true

dispute *verb:* to question or express doubt that a claim is accurate or valid

Why Freedom of the Press Matters

An important part of the First Amendment, a free press helps inform and protect all citizens.

Journalists question President Donald Trump at a news conference.

John Peter Zenger sat in the courtroom with lawyer Alexander Hamilton by his side. In 1735, Zenger was on trial for printing articles that criticized a colonial governor. Under an English law, Zenger was said to be guilty of "seditious libel," meaning that it was illegal to say anything bad about the government—even if it was true.

But Hamilton, who would later sign the US Constitution, argued that no one should be punished for printing what was true. The judge agreed. It was one of the first cases establishing freedom of the press in the United States.

Fifty-six years later, in 1791, the Bill of Rights was ratified, or approved. The bill included 10 amendments that laid out basic rights of US citizens. The First Amendment protected the freedom of speech, religion—and the press.

CHECKS AND BALANCES

A free press means that people can report news—even when it's bad—and not be punished by the government, police, or anyone else. The leaders who created the First Amendment believed a free press was an important part of the new country.

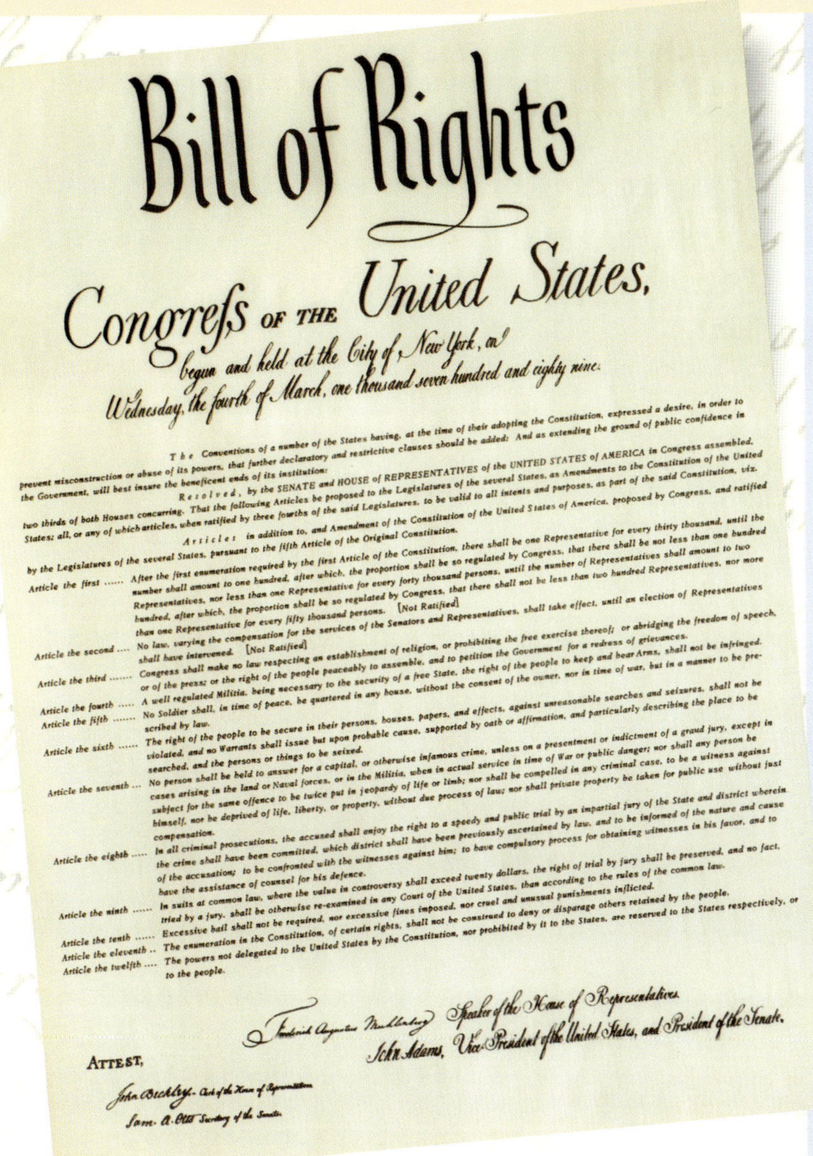

Bill of Rights

Congress OF THE United States,
begun and held at the City of New-York, on
Wednesday, the fourth of March, one thousand seven hundred and eighty nine.

The Conventions of a number of the States having, at the time of their adopting the Constitution, expressed a desire, in order to prevent misconstruction or abuse of its powers, that further declaratory and restrictive clauses should be added: And as extending the ground of public confidence in the Government, will best insure the beneficent ends of its institution:

Resolved, by the SENATE and HOUSE of REPRESENTATIVES of the UNITED STATES of AMERICA in Congress assembled, two thirds of both Houses concurring. That the following Articles be proposed to the Legislatures of the several States, as Amendments to the Constitution of the United States; all, or any of which articles, when ratified by three fourths of the said Legislatures, to be valid to all intents and purposes, as part of the said Constitution, viz.

Articles in addition to, and Amendment of the Constitution of the United States of America, proposed by Congress, and ratified by the Legislatures of the several States, pursuant to the fifth Article of the Original Constitution.

Article the first ...... After the first enumeration required by the first Article of the Constitution, there shall be one Representative for every thirty thousand, until the number shall amount to one hundred, after which, the proportion shall be so regulated by Congress, that there shall be not less than one hundred Representatives, nor less than one Representative for every forty thousand persons, until the number of Representatives shall amount to two hundred, after which, the proportion shall be so regulated by Congress, that there shall not be less than two hundred Representatives, nor more than one Representative for every fifty thousand persons. [Not Ratified]

Article the second .... No law, varying the compensation for the services of the Senators and Representatives, shall take effect, until an election of Representatives shall have intervened. [Not Ratified]

Article the third .... Congress shall make no law respecting an establishment of religion, or prohibiting the free exercise thereof; or abridging the freedom of speech, or of the press; or the right of the people peaceably to assemble, and to petition the Government for a redress of grievances.

Article the fourth ..... A well regulated Militia, being necessary to the security of a free State, the right of the people to keep and bear Arms, shall not be infringed.

Article the fifth .... No Soldier shall, in time of peace, be quartered in any house, without the consent of the owner, nor in time of war, but in a manner to be prescribed by law.

Article the sixth ...... The right of the people to be secure in their persons, houses, papers, and effects, against unreasonable searches and seizures, shall not be violated, and no Warrants shall issue but upon probable cause, supported by oath or affirmation, and particularly describing the place to be searched, and the persons or things to be seized.

Article the seventh ... No person shall be held to answer for a capital, or otherwise infamous crime, unless on a presentment or indictment of a grand jury, except in cases arising in the land or Naval forces, or in the Militia, when in actual service in time of War or public danger; nor shall any person be subject for the same offence to be twice put in jeopardy of life or limb; nor shall be compelled in any criminal case, to be a witness against himself, nor be deprived of life, liberty, or property, without due process of law; nor shall private property be taken for public use without just compensation.

Article the eighth ..... In all criminal prosecutions, the accused shall enjoy the right to a speedy and public trial by an impartial jury of the State and district wherein the crime shall have been committed, which district shall have been previously ascertained by law, and to be informed of the nature and cause of the accusation; to be confronted with the witnesses against him; to have compulsory process for obtaining witnesses in his favor, and to have the assistance of counsel for his defence.

Article the ninth ...... In suits at common law, where the value in controversy shall exceed twenty dollars, the right of trial by jury shall be preserved, and no fact, tried by a jury, shall be otherwise re-examined in any Court of the United States, than according to the rules of the common law.

Article the tenth ...... Excessive bail shall not be required, nor excessive fines imposed, nor cruel and unusual punishments inflicted.

Article the eleventh .. The enumeration in the Constitution, of certain rights, shall not be construed to deny or disparage others retained by the people.

Article the twelfth .... The powers not delegated to the United States by the Constitution, nor prohibited by it to the States, are reserved to the States respectively, or to the people.

Frederick Augustus Muhlenberg Speaker of the House of Representatives.
John Adams, Vice-President of the United States, and President of the Senate.

ATTEST,
John Beckley, Clerk of the House of Representatives.
Sam. A. Otis Secretary of the Senate.

Many laws protect the press in the United States. For instance, the government can't force a news outlet to publish information it doesn't want to publish, or tell a publication it can't publish information. The press also is protected when it accidentally prints incorrect facts.

MAKING PEOPLE SMARTER

Even with the Bill of Rights, the press still face challenges when people don't want others to have certain information. For instance, in 2023, police improperly raided a Kansas newspaper after it printed a story about the police chief. Without freedom of the press, people might not know about important events. For example, what if the government did not want people to know about a big decision it was making or a law it was enacting?

Without a free press, the government could make it illegal to report on these stories. Officials could put reporters in jail for publishing information the government did not like. Thanks to a free press, people have access to important information, and they can act on it. That's what the early leaders hoped would come from freedom of the press: that when people are informed, they can help make the country a better place.

More About Libel

Journalists can't print information that they know is false, or break laws (like robbing a house) to get facts. News outlets can also get in trouble for libel. Libel is when a news outlet publishes false information that hurts someone's reputation. But different rules apply to different people.

- If a person is a private citizen—like a teacher or a doctor—the press can be sued for libel if they should've known the facts weren't true.
- If the person is a public official—like a president or a movie star—then the false information must have been published with the intent to cause harm.

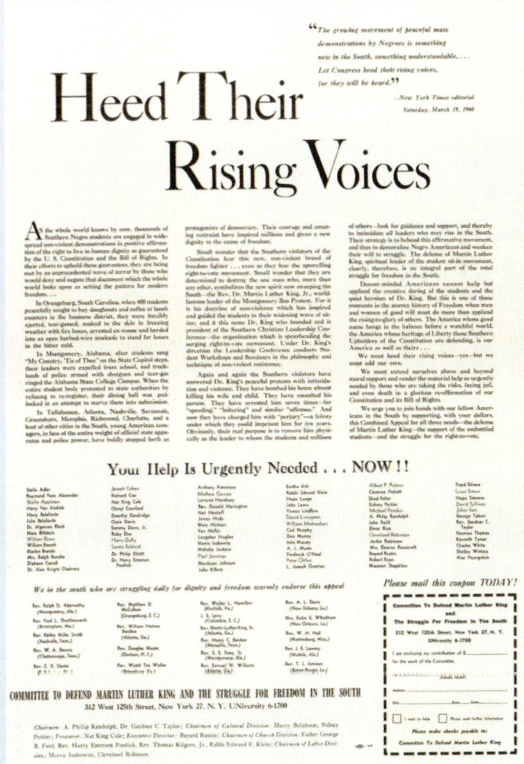

"The growing movement of peaceful mass demonstrations by Negroes is something new in the South, something understandable. . . . Let Congress heed their rising voices, for they will be heard."

—New York Times editorial
Saturday, March 19, 1960

Heed Their Rising Voices

Your Help Is Urgently Needed . . . NOW!!

We in the south who are struggling daily for dignity and freedom warmly endorse this appeal

Please mail this coupon TODAY!

Committee To Defend Martin Luther King
and
The Struggle For Freedom In The South
312 West 125th Street, New York 27, N. Y.
UNiversity 6-1700

Please make checks payable to:
Committee To Defend Martin Luther King

COMMITTEE TO DEFEND MARTIN LUTHER KING AND THE STRUGGLE FOR FREEDOM IN THE SOUTH
312 West 125th Street, New York 27, N. Y. UNiversity 6-1700

This 1960 advertisement in *The New York Times* sparked a famous libel case, *New York Times Co. v. Sullivan*. The ad protested the way civil rights activists were treated in Montgomery, Alabama. The local police supervisor, L. B. Sullivan, thought the ad criticized him and hurt his reputation, so he sued the newspaper for libel. But the US Supreme Court decided as a public official, Sullivan could be criticized by the newspaper, as long as statements weren't intentionally false.

The First Amendment

"Congress shall make no law respecting an establishment of religion, or prohibiting the free exercise thereof; or abridging the freedom of speech, or of the press; or the right of the people peaceably to assemble, and to petition the Government for a redress of grievances."

Spot the Not

See if you can tell the difference between the AI-generated photo and the real one.

You might have used AI (**artificial intelligence**) on platforms like ChatGPT to help you with research, or on Canva to create cool photos. But it's important to understand when something has been generated by AI, especially when it comes to the news. **AI-generated** content can be inaccurate, or it could even have been created just to trick you.

Play this game to see if you can spot the AI-generated images.

COOL AI HACK!

If you're not sure about a photo on the Internet, ask an adult to help you do a reverse search. You might be able to find the original source of the photo and determine if that source is credible. Another clue that the photo is AI-generated is that it won't show up as much in a search.

POWER WORDS

AI-generated *adjective:* when an AI platform has created something new based on patterns and data it's learned

artificial intelligence *noun:* a computer program that has been taught to use millions of pieces of information and images to think like a human—and then keep learning

Answers on page 200

Be the Reporter

Follow these steps to write your own news story.

Step 1: Choose your topic. For instance, is your school making any big changes right now? Are there any local businesses that have recently opened? Have any awards been given to classmates, community members, or local sports teams?

Step 2: Write down questions you have about your topic. Think about the five *W*'s and one *H*: Who, What, Why, When, Where, and How. But also come up with questions to help you tell readers why the story is important and how it will affect them.

Step 3: Conduct research on your topic at the library or online. Don't just find out what's going on now, but also investigate the history of your topic.

Step 4: Make a list of three people you want to interview for your story. For instance, if you're writing about your school, it could be your principal, teachers, and students. If you're writing about a new business, it could be the owner, customers, and a city official who approved the business.

Step 5: Schedule your interviews; they can be in person, on video, or by phone. Prepare more *W* and *H* questions to get fun details from these people. Avoid questions that can be answered with a "yes" or "no."

Step 6: Start writing! Your first paragraph, called a "lead," should tell the reader the basic who, what, why, when, where, and how of the topic.

Step 7: Keep writing, using the most important information first. Don't forget to add your quotes, which should be short and say something interesting, surprising, or funny. You should also identify who said the quote, including his or her title (sixth-grade math teacher, business owner, etc.).

Step 8: Read and reread your story. You can also ask a relative or teacher to read your story and give you advice.

CHAPTER 4

BODY AND HEALTH

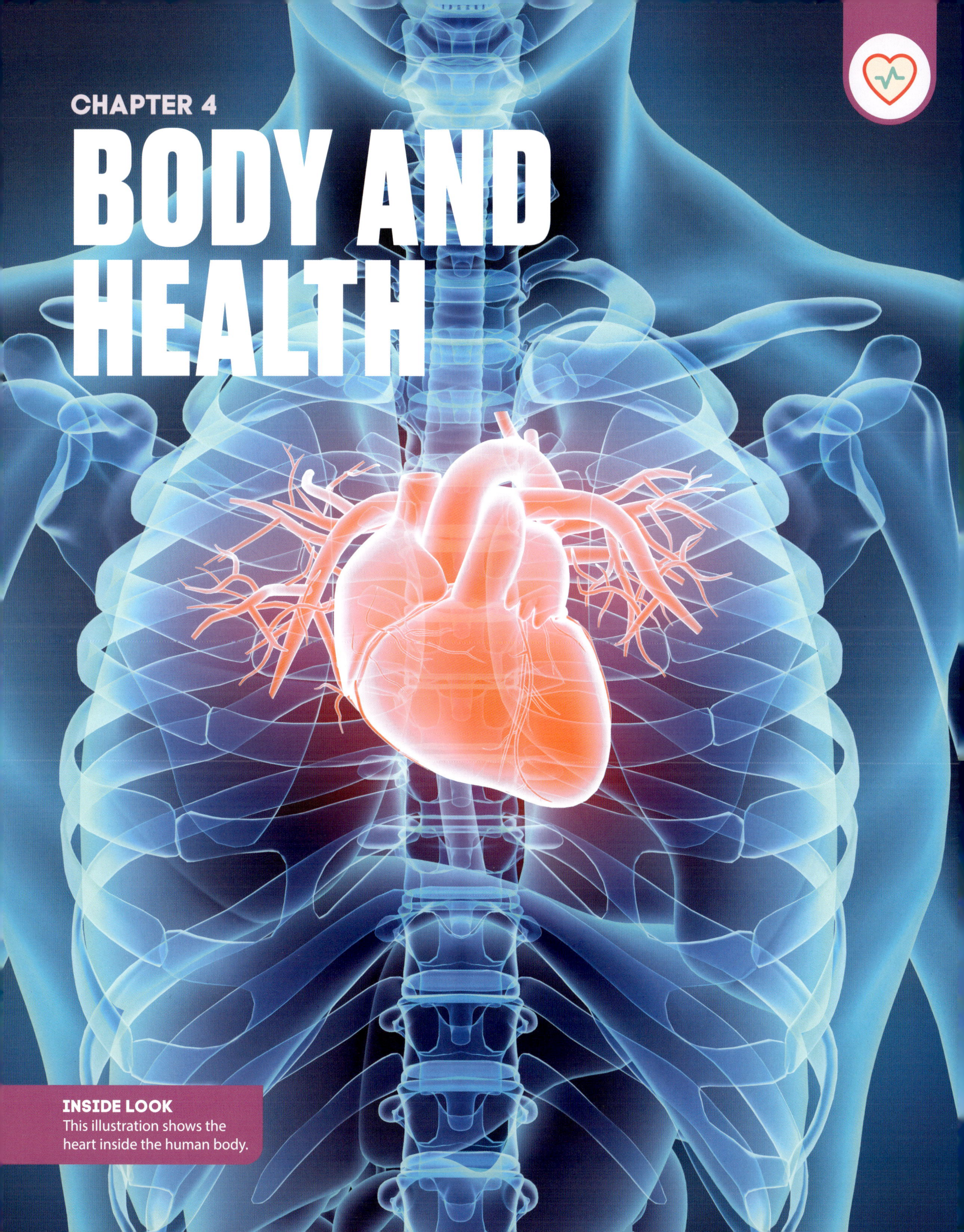

INSIDE LOOK
This illustration shows the heart inside the human body.

Your Body the Machine

The human body is like a high-performance machine, with all of its parts working together to keep you healthy. Take a look at the important organs that keep your body running.

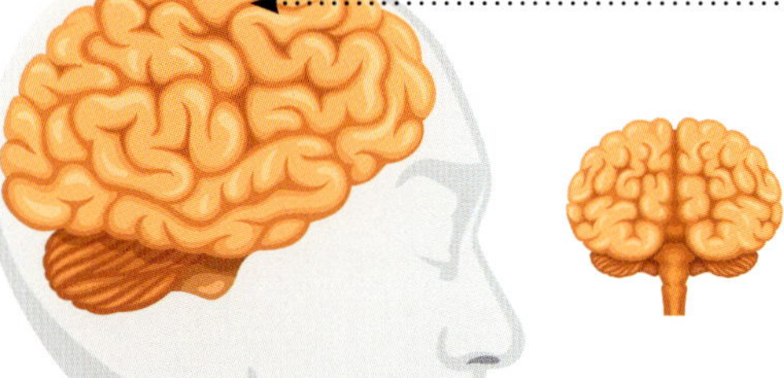

LUNGS

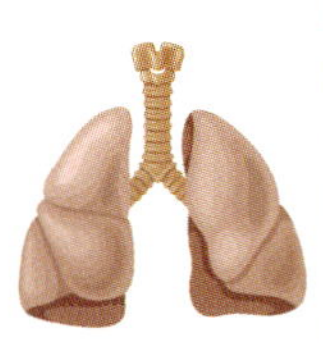

Lungs take in the air you breathe. They send life-giving oxygen to cells all over your body through tiny blood vessels called capillaries.

LIVER

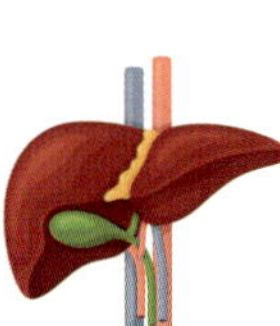

Your liver produces bile, which helps digest food that provides vitamins and minerals to your body. The liver also filters out toxins. That helps you fight disease.

STOMACH

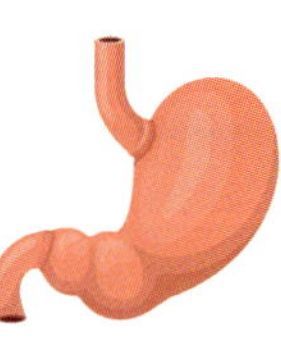

The stomach breaks down food with gastric juices, then sends it along to the small intestine as a thick liquid.

SMALL INTESTINE

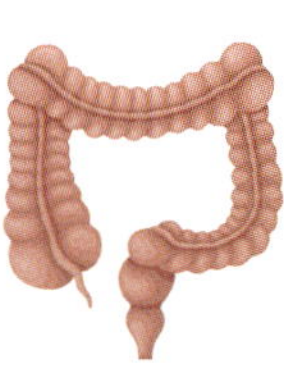

As food enters from the stomach, digestive juices seep into the small intestine to break down the food even more into stuff your body can use.

LARGE INTESTINE

If your body can't use any of the food material, the large intestine removes excess water and uses good bacteria to turn the waste into, well, your waste.

BRAIN

The brain is like the body's control center. By sending messages through cells called neurons, your brain tells your body to do everything from breathing to saying hi to your friends.

SKIN

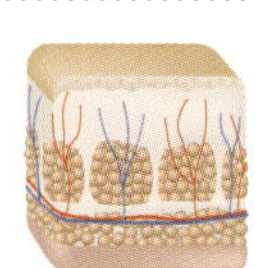

Your body's largest organ, the skin protects you from light, heat, and infection. It also helps regulate your body temperature.

HEART

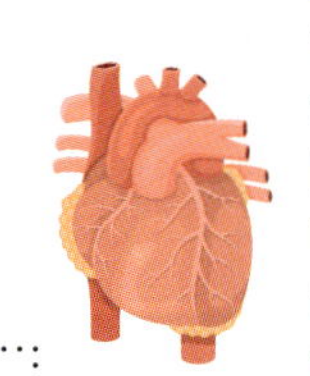

Your heart pumps blood to the lungs, where the blood picks up oxygen. Then it keeps pumping the blood cells all over the body.

PANCREAS

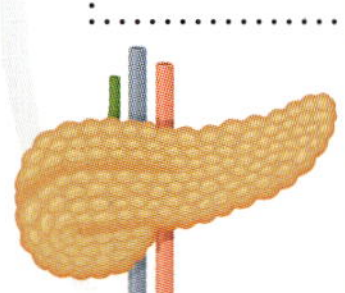

The pancreas produces enzymes that enter the small intestine to help with digestion.

KIDNEYS

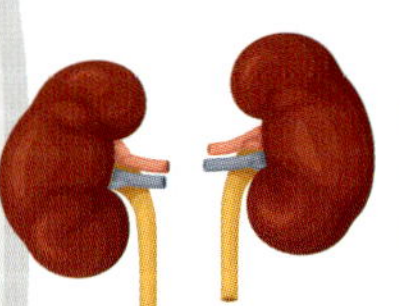

The kidneys filter waste products called urea out of the blood, then send the waste to your bladder as urine.

Brain Science

Five different parts of your brain control different functions in your body. Here's how they all work together.

THE THINKING PART

WHAT IT IS: The cerebrum

WHAT IT DOES: Controls your thinking ability, emotions, and voluntary muscles

WHY YOU NEED IT: To do things like run and swim, feel happy when you see your pet, and solve math problems

THE HOT-AND-COLD PART

WHAT IT IS: The hypothalamus

WHAT IT DOES: Regulates your body temperature

WHY YOU NEED IT: To sweat, cool down, and shiver to warm up—your body's way of getting your temperature back to normal

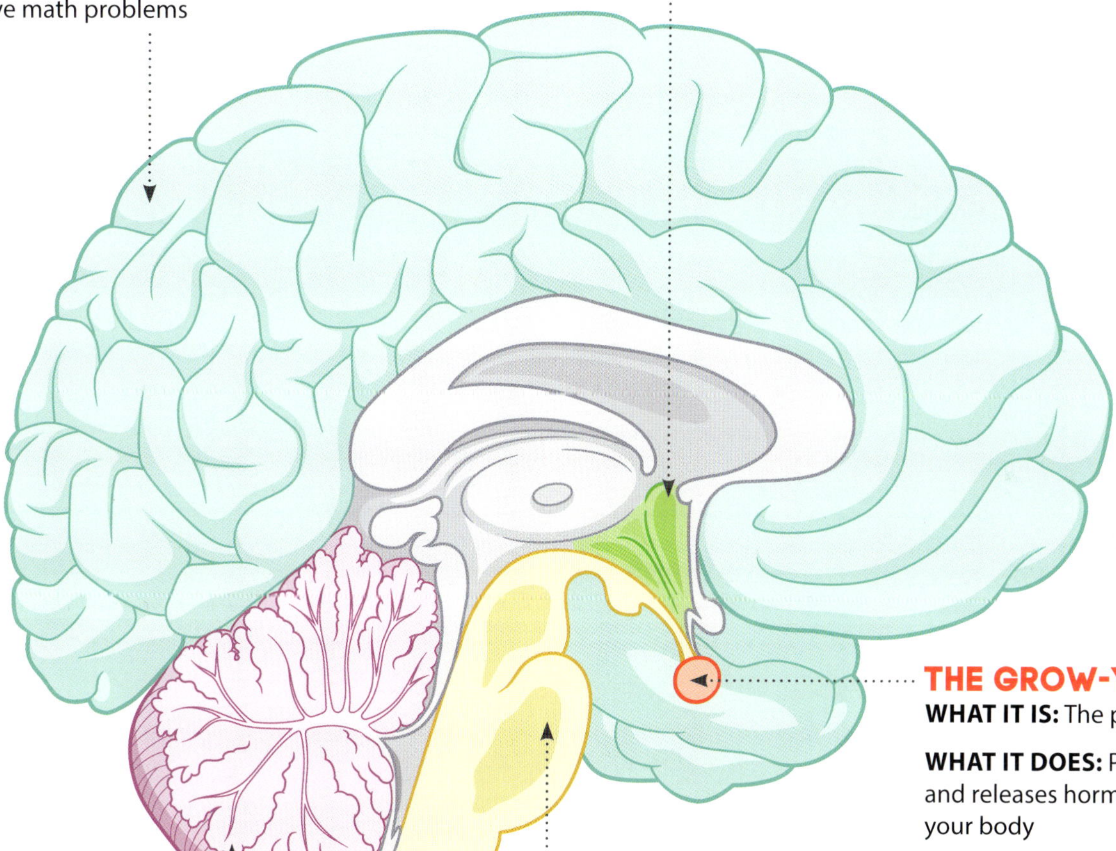

THE GROW-Y PART

WHAT IT IS: The pituitary gland

WHAT IT DOES: Produces and releases hormones into your body

WHY YOU NEED IT: To grow taller, build bones and muscle, and enter puberty

THE QUIET PART

WHAT IT IS: The brain stem

WHAT IT DOES: Controls your involuntary muscles, which work without you even knowing it

WHY YOU NEED IT: To breathe, digest food, and keep your heart beating

THE NON-KLUTZY PART

WHAT IT IS: The cerebellum

WHAT IT DOES: Controls coordination, balance, and movement

WHY YOU NEED IT: To stand upright without falling, zip around on a skateboard, and drink water while you're walking

Social Media and Mental Health

Are too many likes and comments bad for people's emotions? Read on to decide for yourself.

Feeling sad or nervous? You're not alone. Most kids feel this way from time to time, and recent studies report that nearly 1 in 7 US children ages 3 to 17 have a diagnosed mental or behavioral health condition such as **anxiety** or **depression**.

Sadness and nervousness are normal emotions. They can be caused by stress about school, gloominess over bad news, or even natural chemicals in the brain.

For most kids, these feelings don't last very long. But officials are concerned that many are finding it harder to stay mentally healthy because of one thing: social media.

SCROLL, SCROLL, SCROLL

Social media use, typically for ages 13 and up, is not always a bad thing. It can keep people connected with friends and family, provide important information, and allow for self-expression. But scrolling can also lead kids to negatively compare themselves with others, expose them to harmful comments, or make them worry that no one notices them.

That's why in 2024, Vivek H. Murthy, the US **surgeon general** at the time, recommended that social media platforms carry warning labels, much like cigarette packages do. That would require approval from Congress, but some companies are a step ahead. For instance, Zigazoo is a video-sharing app similar to TikTok for kids under 13. Users post their original videos that respond to challenges like "Teach us how to play your favorite sport," and viewers respond with emojis, stickers, or their own videos.

POWER WORDS

anxiety *noun:* ongoing feelings of uneasiness, nervousness, or fear

depression *noun:* ongoing feelings of hopelessness, loneliness, or despair

surgeon general *noun:* the chief medical doctor of the United States

WAYS TO FEEL BETTER

Murthy recommends taking frequent breaks from social media and making sure that you engage in plenty of offline activities that make you happy. Other healthy behaviors include turning off notifications so you're not tempted to constantly check in, and unfollowing people or sites that make you feel bad.

And for just getting over those every-so-often blues? TFK Kid Reporter Ronak Bhatt asked Murthy for his top tips.

Pay attention to how you feel. "A lot of times, we can go for a long time feeling sad or worried or stressed and not recognize that," Murthy says. Take a pause and check in with yourself about how you're feeling.

Connect with people you love. You don't have to discuss anything sad or serious if you don't want to. Just talking or spending time with others can improve your mood.

Talk to a trusted adult. This might be a family member, a friend, a teacher, a coach, or a school counselor or nurse.

Find sources of inspiration. Keep a list of things that make you feel good when you read, watch, or listen to them. "Poems, songs, books, speeches—whatever it might be for you," Murthy says.

Take care of your body. Eat well, stay hydrated, get good sleep, get outside, and exercise. Murthy says that physical activity lifts his mood and gets his mind off of his challenges.

Help others. "When we help other people, not only do we strengthen our [connections]," Murthy says, "we also remind ourselves that we have a lot of beauty and value and strength to add to the world."

Stop and Think

Do you think social media laws should be in place to protect kids' mental health?

Brain Busters

See how much you know about your health and the human body.

1 **Between your walk to school, marching band practice, and recess, you should have no problem getting the recommended ______________ of physical activity a day.**

A. 30 minutes
B. 60 minutes
C. 2 hours
D. I'm super healthy and don't need any physical activity.

2 **You've got a big test in the morning. ______________ should be plenty of sleep to make sure you're alert.**

A. 2 to 3 hours
B. 6 to 8 hours
C. 9 to 12 hours
D. None—I'll sleep after the test.

3 **Which foods do scientists think are key to a healthy brain?**

A. Berries
B. Sweet potatoes
C. Plums
D. All of the above

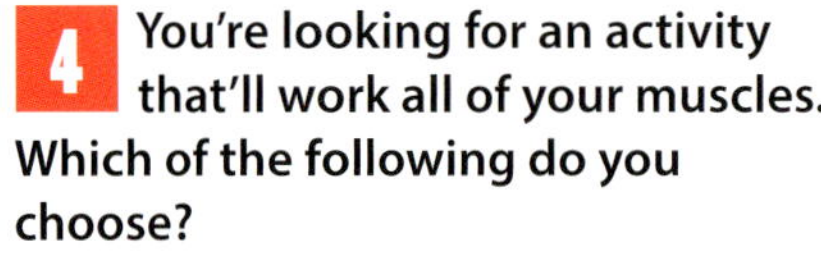

4 **You're looking for an activity that'll work all of your muscles. Which of the following do you choose?**

A. Swimming
B. Bicycling
C. Soccer
D. Texting

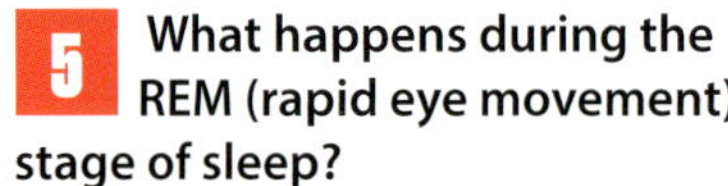

5 **What happens during the REM (rapid eye movement) stage of sleep?**

A. You start dreaming.
B. You wake up to get a drink of water.
C. Your snores go from cute to bearlike.
D. You kick the covers off the bed.

6 **How many times a day on average does a kid release gas from his or her behind (also known as a fart)?**

A. 1 to 7
B. 8 to 12
C. 13 to 21
D. 22 to 100

7 **After that 20-minute hike in the hills, you're a little parched. What should you drink?**

A. A sports drink
B. Water
C. Apple juice
D. Soda

8 **If your parents are worried about you playing video games, tell them some scientists think that ______________.**

A. playing video games might improve memory skills
B. playing video games could help hand-eye coordination
C. playing video games will guarantee you straight-A's
D. Both A and B

Answers on page 200

CHAPTER 5

CALENDARS AND HOLIDAYS

IN WITH A BANG
Fireworks mark the new year in Bangkok, Thailand.

Celebrate 2027

Year-round, people celebrate to honor religious traditions, important people, and historical events. Here are a few holidays from TimeAndDate.com.

JANUARY 1: New Year's Day

JANUARY 14: Orthodox New Year

JANUARY 18: Martin Luther King Jr. Day

FEBRUARY 1: First day of Black History Month

FEBRUARY 2: Groundhog Day

FEBRUARY 6: Lunar New Year

FEBRUARY 8: Ramadan begins+

FEBRUARY 10: Ash Wednesday

FEBRUARY 14: Valentine's Day

FEBRUARY 15: Presidents' Day

MARCH 1: First day of Women's History Month

MARCH 10: Eid al-Fitr+

MARCH 14: Daylight Saving Time starts

MARCH 17: Saint Patrick's Day

MARCH 22: Holi

MARCH 23: Purim

MARCH 26: Good Friday

MARCH 28: Easter

APRIL 22: Earth Day

APRIL 22: Passover begins*

MAY 1: First day of Asian American and Pacific Islander Heritage Month

MAY 5: Cinco de Mayo

MAY 9: Mother's Day

MAY 15: Armed Forces Day

MAY 31: Memorial Day

JUNE 6: D-Day

JUNE 14: Flag Day

JUNE 19: Juneteenth

JUNE 20: Father's Day

JULY 4: Independence Day

JULY 25: Parents' Day

SEPTEMBER 6: Labor Day

SEPTEMBER 12: National Grandparents Day

SEPTEMBER 15: First day of National Hispanic Heritage Month

SEPTEMBER 30: Navratri begins

OCTOBER 2: Rosh Hashanah begins*

OCTOBER 11: Yom Kippur*

OCTOBER 11: Columbus Day

OCTOBER 11: Indigenous Peoples' Day

OCTOBER 28: Diwali begins

OCTOBER 31: Halloween

NOVEMBER 1: First day of Native American Heritage Month

NOVEMBER 2: Election Day

NOVEMBER 7: Daylight Saving Time ends

NOVEMBER 11: Veterans Day

NOVEMBER 25: Thanksgiving

NOVEMBER 30: Giving Tuesday

DECEMBER 7: Pearl Harbor Remembrance Day

DECEMBER 25: Hanukkah begins*

DECEMBER 25: Christmas

DECEMBER 26: Kwanzaa begins

DECEMBER 31: New Year's Eve

+Muslim holidays can change depending on the lunar calendar.
**Jewish holidays begin at sundown the evening before and can change depending on the Hebrew and lunar calendars.*

Your Year in Review

Find the year you were born below, then read about a few notable events that happened then.

BIRTH YEAR: 2014

FEBRUARY 11: Women's ski jumping makes its Olympic debut at the Winter Games in Sochi, Russia.

OCTOBER 27: Taylor Swift's album *1989* quickly climbs the charts.

NOVEMBER 16: After a 10-year journey, robotic lander *Philae* touches down on a comet named Agilkia, marking the first time a spacecraft landed on a comet.

BIRTH YEAR: 2015

APRIL 24: The very first Apple Watch (Series 0) is released.

MAY 2: Princess Charlotte, daughter of Prince William and Kate Middleton of the United Kingdom, is born.

JULY 14: After traveling through space for more than seven years, *New Horizons* becomes the first spacecraft to explore the dwarf planet Pluto and its moons up close.

BIRTH YEAR: 2016

AUGUST 30: Dav Pilkey publishes the first Dog Man book.

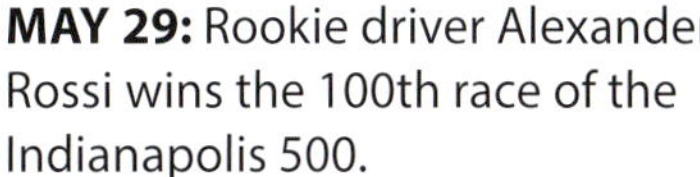

MAY 29: Rookie driver Alexander Rossi wins the 100th race of the Indianapolis 500.

OCTOBER: A data firm announces that for the first time globally, more people are accessing the Internet on mobile devices than on desktops.

BIRTH YEAR: 2017

AUGUST 21: A solar eclipse passes over North America, with its path of totality (when the moon completely covers the sun) stretching from Oregon to South Carolina.

AUGUST AND SEPTEMBER: Hurricanes batter the United States. Harvey hits Texas and Louisiana, Irma lashes Florida and Puerto Rico, and Maria continues to devastate Puerto Rico as well as other Caribbean islands.

SEPTEMBER 26: ByteDance launches TikTok globally.

DECEMBER 15: *Star Wars: Episode VIII—The Last Jedi* releases nationwide and quickly becomes the year's top-grossing movie.

BIRTH YEAR: 2018

APRIL 22: *Harry Potter and the Cursed Child* premieres on Broadway in New York City. The play, which debuted in London in 2016, takes place 19 years after the events of *The Deathly Hollows.*

JULY 10: Twelve boys and their soccer coach are rescued from a flooded cave in Thailand after being trapped for 18 days.

NOVEMBER 18: Mickey Mouse turns 90; he made his big-screen debut in *Steamboat Willie* in 1928.

BIRTH YEAR: 2019

APRIL 10: The Event Horizon Telescope captures the first-ever image of a black hole.

JULY 7: For the second time in a row, the US women's soccer team wins the FIFA Women's World Cup, defeating Netherlands in the final match.

NOVEMBER: SARS-CoV-2, otherwise known as COVID-19, is discovered. Four months later, the World Health Organization declared the disease a pandemic, or an outbreak that affects a large portion of the global population.

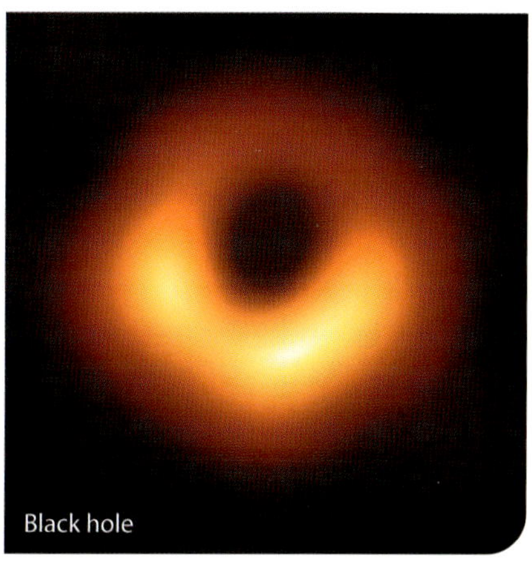

Black hole

Birthstone Bling

Dig into these facts about each month's gemstone.

JANUARY

THE GEM: Garnet

WHERE THEY'RE FOUND: All over the world

COLOR CODED: Garnets are often red but can be purplish, green, yellow, and orange.

LEGENDARY POWERS: Protection and love

BLING BASICS: Some sandy beaches contain red-colored grains that are actually tiny garnets.

STONE STARS: Oprah Winfrey, business leader; Catherine, princess of Wales (Kate Middleton)

FEBRUARY

THE GEM: Amethyst

WHERE THEY'RE FOUND: Brazil, United States, Uruguay

COLOR CODED: Amethysts are always purple but can range from pale to vibrant.

LEGENDARY POWERS: Clear-headedness and healing ability

BLING BASICS: Heating an amethyst takes away its color or turns it yellow.

STONE STARS: Saquon Barkley, football player; Shakira, singer

MARCH

THE GEM: Aquamarine

WHERE THEY'RE FOUND: Brazil, India, Madagascar, Russia, Sri Lanka, United States

COLOR CODED: Aquamarine can also appear bluish green.

LEGENDARY POWERS: Happiness and supersmarts

BLING BASICS: "Aquamarine" comes from the Latin word for "seawater" and was once thought to protect sailors.

STONE STARS: Katie Ledecky, Olympic swimmer; Amancio Ortega, Zara founder

APRIL

THE GEM: Diamond

WHERE THEY'RE FOUND: Brazil; Canada; Australia; Namibia, South Africa, and other African countries; Russia; United States

COLOR CODED: People have found red, blue, yellow, and even black diamonds.

LEGENDARY POWERS: Strength and eternal love

BLING BASICS: The hardest naturally occurring substance, diamonds can take millions of years to form.

STONE STARS: Alyssa Naeher, soccer player; Jackie Chan, actor

MAY

THE GEM: Emerald

WHERE THEY'RE FOUND: Australia, Austria, Colombia, Egypt, Norway, Russia, United States

COLOR CODED: Some emeralds have blue undertones.

LEGENDARY POWERS: Intelligence and fair-mindedness

BLING BASICS: One of the oldest emerald mines was owned by Cleopatra.

STONE STARS: Mark Zuckerberg, cofounder and CEO of Meta / Facebook; Dwayne Johnson, actor

JUNE

THE GEM: Pearl

WHERE THEY'RE FOUND: Anywhere mollusks are! Mollusks grow in fresh and salt water all over the world.

COLOR CODED: If the pearls are created by humans on farms, colors can be black, green, gold, silver, or various pastels.

LEGENDARY POWERS: Wisdom and leadership

BLING BASICS: In ancient Greece, some believed that pearls were tears from gods; in China, many thought they were tears from dragons.

STONE STARS: Ariana Grande, singer and actor; Rick Riordan, author

The idea of associating stones that bring good luck and health with certain months might go back thousands of years. But some gem experts believe that the modern idea of wearing bling associated with one's birth month dates to 16th-century Poland. Polish immigrants later made the practice popular in the United States.

Over the years, jewelers have added more gemstones to the original list, so many months have more than one. We highlight some below. Find your month to learn more—including what "powers" people once believed these stones held.

◂ Uncut emerald cluster

JULY

THE GEM: Ruby

WHERE THEY'RE FOUND: Myanmar, Sri Lanka, Thailand

COLOR CODED: Some rubies have pink or orange undertones.

LEGENDARY POWERS: Strength and calmness

BLING BASICS: "Rubies" found in Australia and Arizona are actually garnets.

STONE STARS: Tui T. Sutherland, author; Shohei Ohtani, baseball player

AUGUST

THE GEM: Peridot

WHERE THEY'RE FOUND: Egypt, Myanmar, United States

COLOR CODED: A peridot's yellowish undertone makes it look different from the deeper-green emerald.

LEGENDARY POWERS: Protection from night ghoulies

BLING BASICS: Peridots are found in meteorites that fall to Earth's surface.

STONE STARS: Breanna Stewart, basketball player; Steve Chen, cofounder of YouTube.

SEPTEMBER

THE GEM: Sapphire

WHERE THEY'RE FOUND: Australia, India, Madagascar, Myanmar, Sri Lanka, Russia, South Africa, United States

COLOR CODED: Sapphires come in almost every color—from yellow to purple to green—except red.

LEGENDARY POWERS: Protection from harm and envy

BLING BASICS: Alexandrite sapphires appear blue in daylight and red or violet under artificial light.

STONE STARS: Serena Williams, tennis player; Beyoncé Knowles, singer and entrepreneur

OCTOBER

THE GEM: Opal

WHERE THEY'RE FOUND: Australia, Honduras, India, Japan, Mexico, New Zealand, United States

COLOR CODED: Opals are the only gemstones that can sparkle with color when moved. But not all opals can do this.

LEGENDARY POWERS: Healing (mostly of the eyes) and luck

BLING BASICS: An opal's shimmer is caused by light bouncing off the mineral silica, the stone's main ingredient.

STONE STARS: "Weird Al" Yankovic, singer and comedian; Anil Menon, astronaut

NOVEMBER

THE GEM: Topaz

WHERE THEY'RE FOUND: Afghanistan, Australia, Brazil, Germany, Italy, Japan, Mexico, Nigeria, Pakistan, Russia, Sri Lanka, United States

COLOR CODED: Topaz can also be yellow, brown, blue, and red.

LEGENDARY POWERS: Strength, clear thinking, and protection against poison

BLING BASICS: Pure topaz is clear and often mistaken for diamonds.

STONE STARS: DJ Khaled, music producer; Scarlett Johansson, actress

DECEMBER

THE GEM: Turquoise

WHERE THEY'RE FOUND: China, Iran, Russia, United States

COLOR CODED: Turquoise can be blue, green, and yellowish gray.

LEGENDARY POWERS: Love and success

BLING BASICS: Turquoise represents the sky and water and is sacred to many Native American communities in the southwestern United States.

STONE STARS: Kristin Kish, chef and TV host; Jason Reynolds, author

It's the Year of the Goat!

Cool traditions are a big part of Lunar New Year.

A long, colorful dragon dances through a street in China, its movements controlled by long poles held by people wearing red and gold. Drummers keep time for the dragon's wavelike moves while children run around carrying red lanterns. This is the Lantern Festival, a celebration on the last night of Lunar New Year.

All over the world, people celebrate Lunar New Year to mark the arrival of spring. It's a time to reconnect with family, eat amazing food, and usher in good luck for the rest of the year. And if it's your zodiac year, it could be an especially lucky 12 months for you.

Lunar New Year is based on the moon's cycles, so it can start on different days in different countries. (It usually starts in January or February.) And though many who celebrate have similar traditions no matter where they live—such as cleaning houses to sweep out bad luck and giving kids money in lucky red envelopes—different Asian cultures have their own way of bringing in the new year.

VIETNAM

Lunar New Year in Vietnam is called Tết, a time when families go to temple to pray for good luck and health. They also eat treats like sticky rice cakes and avoid throwing anything away on New Year's Day. This is meant to avoid tossing out any good luck.

WHAT'S YOUR ZODIAC YEAR?

Years in the Chinese calendar are represented by 12 animals called zodiac signs. One legend says that an emperor selected these animals as guards based on their traits, and that people born under these signs might have similar traits. Find your year, then decide if you agree with this legend.

GOAT

MOST RECENT BIRTH YEARS: 1979, 1991, 2003, 2015, 2027

TRAITS: Kindness, happiness

SNAKE

MOST RECENT BIRTH YEARS: 1977, 1989, 2001, 2013, 2025

TRAITS: Leadership, joyfulness

RABBIT

MOST RECENT BIRTH YEARS: 1975, 1987, 1999, 2011, 2023

TRAITS: Attentiveness, wittiness

HORSE

MOST RECENT BIRTH YEARS: 1978, 1990, 2002, 2014, 2026

TRAITS: Faithfulness, skillfulness

DRAGON

MOST RECENT BIRTH YEARS: 1976, 1988, 2000, 2012, 2024

TRAITS: Excellence, honorableness

TIGER

MOST RECENT BIRTH YEARS: 1974, 1986, 1998, 2010, 2022

TRAITS: Bravery, powerfulness

SINGAPORE

About 75 percent of people in Singapore are of Chinese descent, so Lunar New Year is hugely popular in this country. Pineapple tarts are a favorite treat. (Pineapples are thought to bring good luck.) People also look forward to the giant floats and dancing lions and dragons of the Chingay Parade.

SOUTH KOREA

Lasting three days, Lunar New Year in South Korea celebrates ancestors and elders. Dressed in traditional Korean clothing called *hanbok*, many children bow to their grandparents in exchange for good-luck money. One fun activity is kite-flying.

CHINA

Called the Spring Festival in China, Lunar New Year is the most important holiday in this country and lasts for 15 days. People wear new clothes, often in the lucky colors of red and gold, and might cook a whole fish that represents wealth. Sometimes lucky coins are hidden inside for kids to find as they eat!

OX

MOST RECENT BIRTH YEARS: 1973, 1985, 1997, 2009, 2021

TRAITS: Kindness, selflessness

PIG

MOST RECENT BIRTH YEARS: 1971, 1983, 1995, 2007, 2019

TRAITS: Fearlessness, calmness

ROOSTER

MOST RECENT BIRTH YEARS: 1969, 1981, 1993, 2005, 2017

TRAITS: Honesty, determination

RAT

MOST RECENT BIRTH YEARS: 1972, 1984, 1996, 2008, 2020

TRAITS: Intelligence, strength

DOG

MOST RECENT BIRTH YEARS: 1970, 1982, 1994, 2006, 2018

TRAITS: Helpfulness, luckiness

MONKEY

MOST RECENT BIRTH YEARS: 1968, 1980, 1992, 2004, 2016

TRAITS: Cleverness, protectiveness

Holidays Around the World

Travel these pages to check out some important celebrations.

JUNETEENTH

Celebrated on June 19 in the United States, Juneteenth marks the day in 1865 when enslaved people in Galveston, Texas, learned that slavery had been abolished. Over the years, the celebration, also called Emancipation Day or Freedom Day, spread. Today, Black people celebrate with parades, family reunions, and feasts featuring red dishes—such as barbecue and strawberry drinks—thought to represent power and sacrifice.

DIWALI

Also called the Festival of Lights, Diwali is a five-day holiday in India, usually in October or November, to celebrate good overcoming evil. People light clay lamps and create patterned artwork called *rangoli* made from colored powder or sand. The last night is filled with parties and fireworks.

A Diwali festival in Maharashtra, India

MIDSUMMER

Celebrated around the summer solstice in June, Midsummer in Sweden dates back some 800 years. Back then, people believed that plants gained magical healing powers during this time of year. Today, people wear crowns of flowers and dance around a maypole to celebrate the longest day of the year and the coming warm weather.

DÍA DE LOS MUERTOS

Mexican legend says that on November 1 and 2, spirits of the dead return home to spend time with relatives. People in Mexico build altars and decorate cemeteries to welcome back their ancestors. Día de los Muertos (Day of the Dead) is a happy two-day celebration filled with candied skulls, skeleton puppets, and lots of music and food.

RAMADAN

Muslims around the world celebrate Ramadan. A period of reflection and prayer, this holy month (which occurs at different times every year) requires healthy adults to fast, or not eat or drink, from dawn to dusk. Kids may take part, too. After sunset, friends and family gather for meals; on the last night, Muslims celebrate Eid al-Fitr, or the "Feast of Fast-Breaking."

Festival Fun

See if you can match the celebration with its location.

BUÑOL, SPAIN

SHETLAND ISLANDS, SCOTLAND

INDIA

1 Junkanoo (December 26) is a giant parade filled with colorful costumes, lively dances, and music with cowbells and drums that celebrates this island-nation's culture.

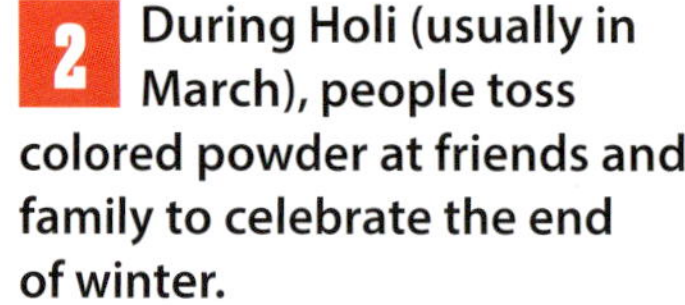
2 During Holi (usually in March), people toss colored powder at friends and family to celebrate the end of winter.

3 Usually in February or March, Carnival in this location is a festival in which attendees dress in elaborate masks and costumes styled from the Middle Ages.

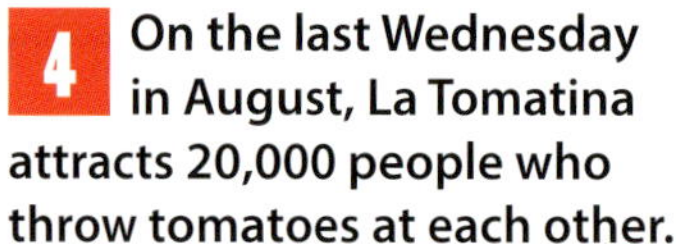
4 On the last Wednesday in August, La Tomatina attracts 20,000 people who throw tomatoes at each other.

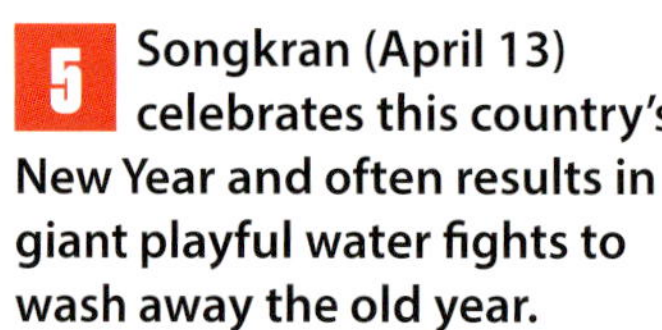
5 Songkran (April 13) celebrates this country's New Year and often results in giant playful water fights to wash away the old year.

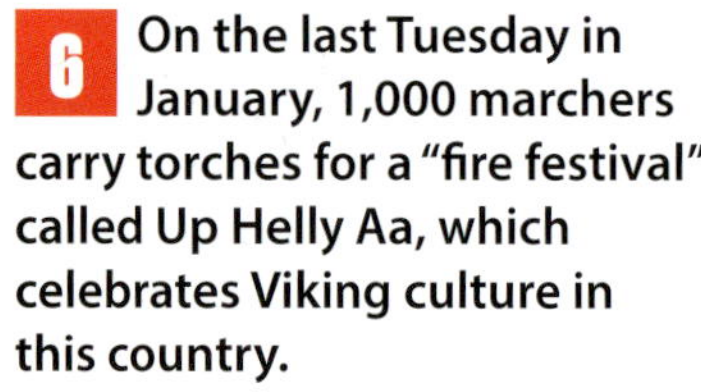
6 On the last Tuesday in January, 1,000 marchers carry torches for a "fire festival" called Up Helly Aa, which celebrates Viking culture in this country.

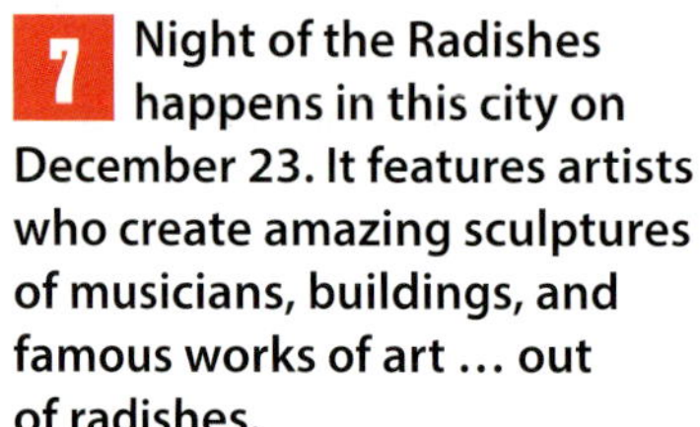
7 Night of the Radishes happens in this city on December 23. It features artists who create amazing sculptures of musicians, buildings, and famous works of art … out of radishes.

Answers on page 200

THAILAND

OAXACA, MEXICO

THE BAHAMAS

VENICE, ITALY

CHAPTER 6

TECHNOLOGY AND INVENTIONS

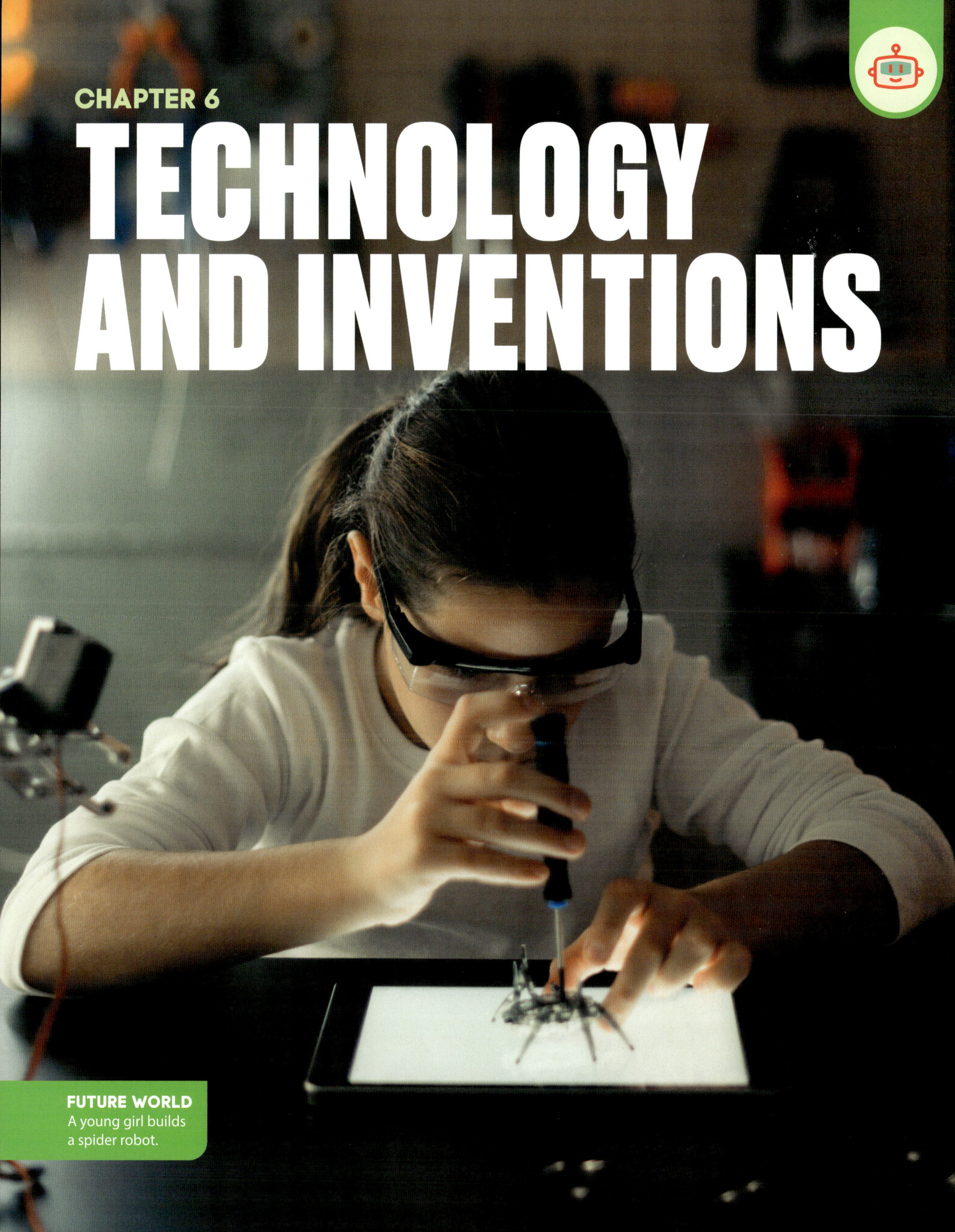

FUTURE WORLD
A young girl builds a spider robot.

Tech: Then and Now

See how much technology has changed since your parents were kids.

CAR DASHBOARDS

Then: Listening to music in cars used to mean planning ahead. Vehicles like the 1997 Toyota Camry allowed you to pop in one audio cassette or CD at a time, or turn dials and punch buttons to find a good radio station. And if the driver didn't want to listen to whatever you did … too bad for you!

Now: Most car entertainment systems are connected to your mobile devices via Bluetooth. So the endless playlists on your phone or tablet are available to you—hands-free—in the car. And if the driver wants to listen to something different for four hours, no problem—just use your headphones and zone out to whatever's on your device.

MOBILE PHONES

Then: In 1996, the Motorola StarTAC was the iPhone of its day. The world's first flip phone, the device gave you up to four hours of talking time (no texts!), storage for 100 phone numbers, an antenna for better reception, and two batteries.

FAST FACT

According to the World Factbook, China has the most mobile phone subscribers—1.8 billion. India has the second most, and the United States comes in third.

Now: Most mobile phones do it all: They send and receive calls like the StarTAC, but they also allow you to text with friends, scroll the Internet, watch movies, listen to music, ask questions, play games, and so much more.

THE INTERNET

Then: Going online in 1996 meant connecting your computer to a telephone (so no phone calls at the same time) and waiting 30 seconds for each page to load. You could check email—but only if your friends were on the same platform—and maybe look at a couple of news sites. That's it! YouTube and Google didn't exist, and Amazon sold only books. Internet users spent about 30 minutes a month online.

Now: We're online about six and a half hours *a day*. Wireless connections make it easy to search the Internet anytime, anyplace, for just about anything you want.

FROM THE PAGES OF

Dreaming of a Cure

Heman Bekele has been recognized by TIME magazine for inventing a bar of soap that could change how people treat skin cancer.

When Heman Bekele was six, he got a chemistry set. He used it to mix "potions." Only his parents paid attention. By the time Heman was 15 and a 10th grader at Woodson High, in Fairfax, Virginia, a lot more people were watching his work.

In October 2023, 3M and Discovery Education named Heman the winner of their Young Scientist Challenge. His prize: $25,000. His accomplishment: inventing a soap that could one day treat and prevent some forms of skin cancer.

It could be years before the soap is available to buy. But Heman is determined. That summer, he spent most days in a lab at the Johns Hopkins Bloomberg School of Public Health in Baltimore, Maryland. When he went back to school, he was at the lab less often. But he'll keep working to make his dream come true.

"I'm really passionate about skin-cancer research," he told TIME. "One day, my bar of soap will be able to make a direct impact on somebody else's life."

That passion and the desire to help others earned Heman the title of TIME's Kid of the Year.

BRIGHT IDEA

Heman moved to the United States when he was four. But he was born in Addis Ababa, the capital of Ethiopia, in Africa. Heman remembers seeing people there out in the sun without protection for their skin. They were **vulnerable** to skin cancer. It's a disease that can be caused by too much exposure to the sun.

Heman's parents told him about the dangers of spending too much time outdoors without sunscreen or proper clothing. "I realized what a big problem the sun [is] when you're exposed to it for a long time," he says.

Skin-cancer treatments can cost about $40,000. Heman wondered if there was a more affordable way for people to begin to treat the disease. He thought of adding a skin-cancer medicine to "something that everyone can use," Heman says. "Everyone uses soap and water for cleaning. So soap would probably be the best option."

NEXT LEVEL

Heman needed help to bring his idea to life. He came across the 3M challenge. He submitted a video explaining what he had in mind. Soon, he received an invitation to speak in front of a panel of judges. That day, he was named the winner.

Since then, Heman has been hard at work. Experts are guiding him. One is Deborah Isabelle, a **mentor** from 3M. Isabelle describes Heman as a "very inspiring young man."

Heman encourages kids to dream big. "Just keep inventing," he says. "Keep thinking of new ways to improve our world."

—By Jeffrey Kluger for TIME

POWER WORDS

mentor *noun:* someone who shares knowledge

vulnerable *adjective:* open to attack, harm, or damage

FROM THE PAGES OF
TIME for KIDS

World's Best Inventions

TIME magazine recognizes the world's best new inventions. Some of these address global problems. Others make life more fun. Here are TIME for Kids' recent favorites. Which one is yours?

GROW AND GLOW

Why stop and smell the roses when you can stop and smell the glowing petunias? By day, FIREFLY PETUNIAS look like normal white flowers. When it gets dark, they glow like the moon. They might look magical. But their glow is a matter of science. The company Light Bio spliced petunia DNA with that of **bioluminescent** mushrooms. The result is glow-in-the-dark flowers you can grow at home.

—*By Jeff Wilser*

POWER WORD

bioluminescent *adjective:* describes the light that emits from a living organism due to a chemical reaction in its body

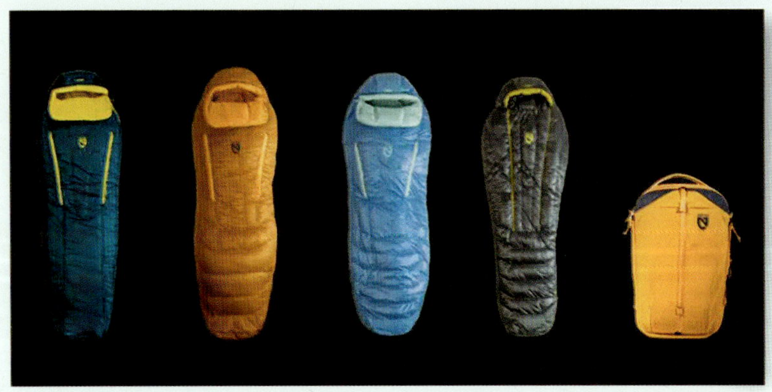

ECO-FRIENDLY CAMPING

Outdoor enthusiasts care about the environment. But camping equipment isn't always eco-friendly. That's why NEMO Equipment created its ENDLESS PROMISE camping equipment. The backpacks and sleeping bags are made from polyester, a recyclable material. And Nemo promises to repair, recycle, or resell the equipment. The company will take it back when customers are ready for something new.

—*By Jeff Wilser*

GAMING ON THE GO

All video games need a screen, right? Not the TECNO POCKET GO gaming system. It has two parts. It has a controller. And it has a pair of augmented-reality glasses. The glasses show a huge display of the game you're playing. You don't need a TV or computer to use it! The headset tracks your head movements. It simulates vibrations. These provide a better experience. Users can even sync the glasses to their phone and other devices.

—By Ashley Mateo

MINI MOTOR

Ready to go fast? BIMOTAL ELEVATE is a palm-size motor. It turns a standard pedal bike into an electric bike, or e-bike. The motor clips onto the wheel of a regular bike. It powers the bike as you pedal. It can get your bike up to 20 miles an hour (32 km/h). And it's not just for fun. Search-and-rescue teams are using it. They're motorizing gurneys. These are wheeled boards that carry injured people. A faster gurney means faster medical care.

—By Chris Stokel-Walker

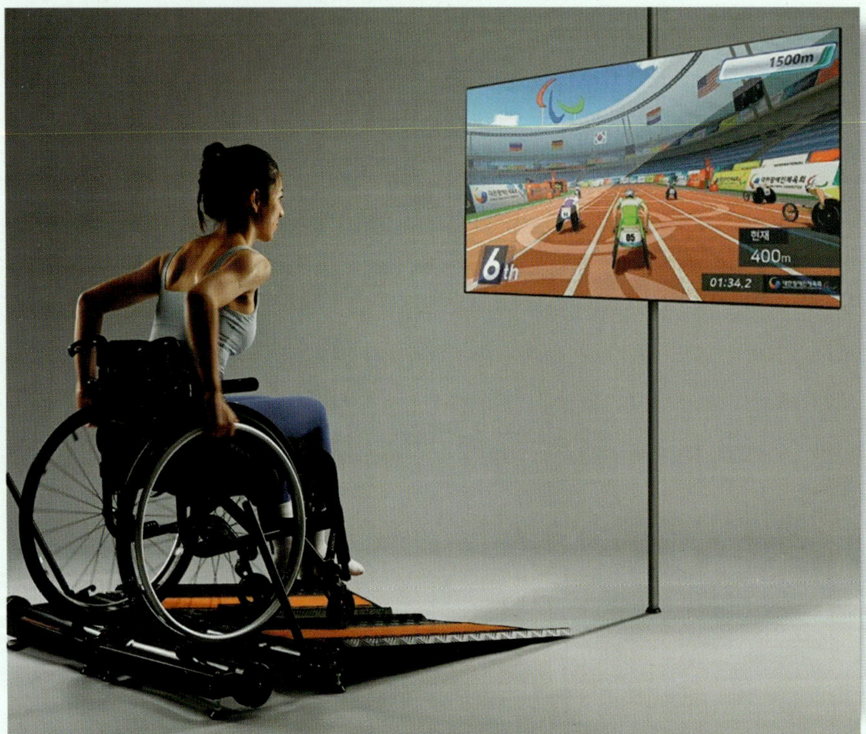

INCLUSIVE EXERCISE

Standard treadmills are designed for people to walk or jog in place. But people who use wheelchairs need exercise equipment, too. WHEELY-X is a treadmill designed for wheelchair users. It pairs with fitness apps. It offers workout games. Wheely-X was created by Kangsters. The company focuses on technology for users with disabilities. Kangsters is selling the product to private users, gyms, hospitals, and rehab centers.

—By Jamie Ducharme

BOTS ON THE JOB

Imagine having a robot as your coworker. Some employers are making this a reality. That's partly thanks to DIGIT, a humanoid bot created by Agility Robotics. Digit can be trained by AI to do a variety of tasks. In 2023, Amazon announced that it would train the bots to help with basic tasks in warehouses. Digit bots work separately from humans for safety purposes. But the bots may someday work with people.

—By Chris Stokel-Walker

READ IN COLOR

It used to be hard to read a graphic novel on an electronic reading device, or e-reader. That's no longer the case. Rakuten Kobo's KOBO LIBRA COLOUR is the first mainstream e-reader with a color e-ink screen that gets illustrations just right. The device is small. But its colors pop. Users can enjoy their favorite comics and graphic novels without compromising the quality of the artwork. Kobo also sells a stylus. It pairs with the Libra Colour. You can use it to highlight text in color.

—By Raymond Wong

DAZZLING DISC

Frisbees have been flung around parks, beaches, and yards for decades. But the TOSY company wants to reinvent the game. The FLYING DISC has 36 red, green, and blue LED lights. They're activated as it's thrown. The lights produce more than 16 million color variations. A rechargeable battery doesn't just keep the lights on. It activates a "lost mode" that helps you find the disc if it goes astray.

—By Chris Stokel-Walker

Future Tech

What will the world look like 30 years from now? Who knows? But here are a few fun predictions from futuristic thinkers—including TIME for Kids reporters.

Moon bases will be fully operational and open for vacations—for a hefty price.

Microscopic robots called nanobots will patrol inside your body to protect your physical and mental health.

Countries will connect to electrical "supergrids" that allow them to share green sources of power, as well as provide resources to underdeveloped areas.

Most cars will be self-driving and either hybrid or all-electric.

Energy will come mostly from solar and wind sources. Your house or school might have special windows or paint that collects sunlight.

You'll have two brains—your physical brain and your computer brain—and they'll be connected to each other.

The latest hypersonic jet engines will help you fly anywhere in the world in about two and a half hours.

Many people will be able to experience spaceflight—not just the super wealthy.

Powerful 3D printers will create everything from bedroom furniture to customized family cars.

Artificial intelligence highway networks will control traffic flow, which means you'll get places faster and safer.

Plants will cover buildings to help absorb carbon dioxide, which contributes to global warming, from the air.

Smart buildings will produce their own food from farms on the top floors, which also trap rain and mist for irrigation.

Solar power stations on the moon will beam energy back to Earth.

Airplane walls and ceilings will be transparent, so you'll feel like you're floating through the clouds.

Artificial general intelligence (AGI), in which computer programs match or exceed human thinking or reasoning, will become common.

That means robots and machines will make decisions based on common sense, display emotions, move like you do, and speak in natural language. Some predict we'll consider this technology "human."

OVERHEARD

DISHA RAI

13, Illinois

Households will have devices that let people project holograms of loved ones right in front of them. We'll be able to interact with people as if they were in the same room, even if they're thousands of miles away!

MILO BHUSHAN

10, South Carolina

Robots will do everything for us, but I think people might get bored with that. So we'll start being more independent again. Except for chores. No one will be inspired to rediscover chores. Robots will be stuck doing that forever.

DYLAN LANDAW

10, New York

Computers will read your mind and do what you want without you typing keyboard commands. And we'll all have personal robots that fly around with you, helping you with tasks and answering your questions.

EVELYN PENG

12, New York

Robots might flip crepes at a creperie, drive flying cars, or even put out fires.

About 3.7 million people will be 100 years old or older—compared to just 95,000 in 1990.

25 Fast Facts

Scan through these incredible "bytes" of information about technology.

1 Your brain has over 19,000 times more memory than a high-speed home computer.

2 Ada Lovelace became the first computer programmer after she identified a language of symbols used in a calculating machine in 1843.

3 The first modern computer was 50 feet (15 m) long. That's as long as a basketball court is wide.

4 The Statue of Liberty could fit inside Nevada's Las Vegas Sphere, which contains 160,000 square feet (14,864 sq m) of screens designed to make you feel as if you're inside the concert you're watching.

5 There are more mobile phones in the world than people.

6 Pazzi the robot can make 80 pizzas in an hour. Its robotic arms can roll the dough, pour on sauce, sprinkle toppings, pop the pie in the oven, slice it up, and deliver it to the customer—all in about five minutes.

7 The very first video uploaded to YouTube, on April 23, 2005, was called "Me at the zoo" and featured a guy standing in front of elephants at California's San Diego Zoo.

8 Connections between the human brain and machines—called brain-computer interfaces—are allowing paralyzed people to turn thoughts into email.

9 Why aren't keyboard letters in alphabetical order? Some people believe that it was to slow down fast typers so the original typewriter keys wouldn't get stuck.

10 The Firefox search engine is named for the red panda, which is sometimes called a firefox in its Southeast Asian habitat.

11 Ping-pong-like "dragon eggs" dropped from drones can create small, controlled fires that burn vegetation and prevent larger wildfires from spreading.

12 Technology inspired by nature—called biomimicry—has resulted in water repellents based on bird feathers, tape that mimics gecko feet, and glue inspired by snail mucus.

13 Scientists think they're close to translating whale language so that humans can have conversations with sea mammals.

14 *Roblox* holds the Guinness World Record for the largest user-generated content platform, with more than 71.5 million daily active users and more than 4 million active games.

15 Conservationists hide GPS tracking technology inside 3D-printed sea turtle eggs to find poachers stealing the precious cargo.

16 Virtual reality isn't just for gaming—it can also help doctors practice surgeries.

17 Apple cofounder Steve Jobs was diagnosed with a reading disorder called dyslexia.

18 Japan is testing a new superspeed train that uses high-powered magnets to hover above the tracks and reach speeds of 375 miles an hour (603 km/h).

19 The 2024 Summer Olympics in Paris, France, featured miniature robo-cars that used cameras and sensors to drive javelins, shotputs, discuses, and rugby balls off the field.

20 Netflix was once a mail-order business that sent out DVDs for people to watch and return, sort of like a rental library.

21 One car can change its colors based on the driver's mood.

22 Experts estimate that, worldwide, more than 23 billion texts are sent every day.

23 One full day in Minecraft is just 20 minutes in real time.

24 Kids watch or use screens about four to six hours a day.

25 The latest space suits are designed with moon landings in mind: Helmet headlights light up the dark surface, flexible boots walk on rough terrain, and suit materials protect astronauts from lunar dust.

CHAPTER 7

COUNTRIES OF THE WORLD

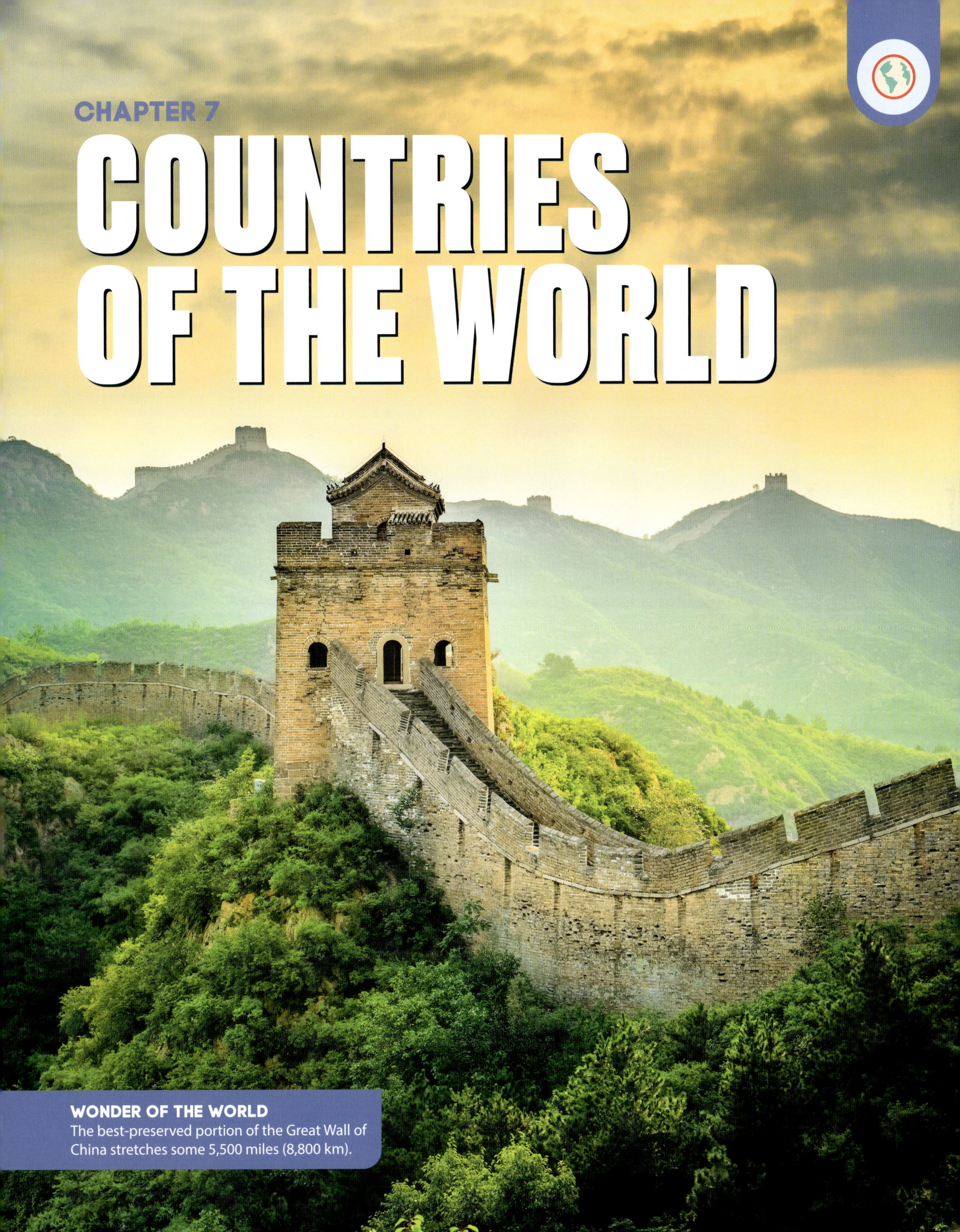

WONDER OF THE WORLD
The best-preserved portion of the Great Wall of China stretches some 5,500 miles (8,800 km).

Political Map of the World

180° 150° W 120° W 90° W 60° W 30° W

Greenland (DENMARK)
ARCTIC
RUSSIA
Alaska (US)
60° N
ICELAND
UNITED KINGDOM
IRELAND
CANADA
NORTH PACIFIC OCEAN
UNITED STATES
NORTH ATLANTIC OCEAN
PORTUGAL
SPAIN
30° N
MOROCCO
MEXICO
Tropic of Cancer (23°26′ N)
THE BAHAMAS
CUBA
DOMINICAN REPUBLIC
JAMAICA
ST. KITTS AND NEVIS
ANTIGUA AND BARBUDA
BELIZE
HAITI
DOMINICA
HONDURAS
ST. LUCIA
ST. VINCENT AND THE GRENADINES
BARBADOS
GUATEMALA
GRENADA
EL SALVADOR
NICARAGUA
TRINIDAD AND TOBAGO
COSTA RICA
VENEZUELA
GUYANA
PANAMA
SURINAME
French Guiana (FRANCE)
COLOMBIA
CABO VERDE
MAURITANIA
MALI
SENEGAL
THE GAMBIA
BURKINA FASO
GUINEA-BISSAU
GUINEA
SIERRA LEONE
CÔTE D'IVOIRE
GHANA
LIBERIA
0°
Equator (0°)
ECUADOR
SOUTH ATLANTIC OCEAN
BRAZIL
PERU
SAMOA
BOLIVIA
TONGA
Tropic of Capricorn (23°26′ S)
PARAGUAY
ARGENTINA
30° S
CHILE
URUGUAY
SOUTH PACIFIC OCEAN
60° S
SOUTHERN

180° 150° W 120° W 90° W 60° W 30° W

0° 30° E 60° E 90° E 120° E 150° E 180°

1 NETHERLANDS
2 BELGIUM
3 LIECHTENSTEIN
4 LUXEMBOURG
5 SWITZERLAND
6 MONACO
7 SAN MARINO
8 VATICAN CITY
9 ALBANIA
10 MONTENEGRO
11 BOSNIA & HERZEGOVINA
12 CROATIA
13 SLOVENIA
14 AUSTRIA
15 CZECHIA
16 SLOVAKIA
17 HUNGARY
18 SERBIA
19 KOSOVO
20 N. MACEDONIA
21 MOLDOVA

OCEAN
Arctic Circle (66°34′ N)
60° N
RUSSIA
NORWAY
SWEDEN
FINLAND
ESTONIA
LATVIA
LITHUANIA
DENMARK
GERMANY
POLAND
BELARUS
UKRAINE
FRANCE
ROMANIA
ITALY
BULGARIA
ANDORRA
GREECE
KAZAKHSTAN
MONGOLIA
GEORGIA
AZERBAIJAN
ARMENIA
TURKEY
UZBEKISTAN
TURKMENISTAN
KYRGYZSTAN
TAJIKISTAN
NORTH KOREA
SOUTH KOREA
JAPAN
NORTH PACIFIC OCEAN
30° N
CHINA
MALTA
TUNISIA
CYPRUS
LEBANON
ISRAEL
SYRIA
IRAQ
JORDAN
IRAN
AFGHANISTAN
KUWAIT
BAHRAIN
QATAR
PAKISTAN
NEPAL
BHUTAN
ALGERIA
LIBYA
EGYPT
SAUDI ARABIA
UNITED ARAB EMIRATES
OMAN
INDIA
BANGLADESH
MYANMAR (BURMA)
LAOS
NIGER
CHAD
SUDAN
ERITREA
YEMEN
DJIBOUTI
THAILAND
VIETNAM
CAMBODIA
PHILIPPINES
BENIN
TOGO
NIGERIA
CAMEROON
CENTRAL AFRICAN REPUBLIC
SOUTH SUDAN
ETHIOPIA
SOMALIA
SRI LANKA
MALDIVES
BRUNEI
MALAYSIA
PALAU
FEDERATED STATES OF MICRONESIA
MARSHALL ISLANDS
EQ. GUINEA
GABON
SÃO TOMÉ AND PRÍNCIPE
REP. OF THE CONGO
DEMOCRATIC REPUBLIC OF THE CONGO
UGANDA
KENYA
RWANDA
BURUNDI
SINGAPORE
Equator (0°)
0°
KIRIBATI
NAURU
INDONESIA
PAPUA NEW GUINEA
SOLOMON ISLANDS
TANZANIA
SEYCHELLES
COMOROS
TIMOR-LESTE
TUVALU
ANGOLA
ZAMBIA
MALAWI
INDIAN OCEAN
VANUATU
FIJI
MOZAMBIQUE
ZIMBABWE
MADAGASCAR
MAURITIUS
NAMIBIA
BOTSWANA
AUSTRALIA
SOUTH PACIFIC OCEAN
30° S
ESWATINI
SOUTH AFRICA
LESOTHO
NEW ZEALAND
OCEAN
60° S
Antarctic Circle (66°34′ S)

0° 30° E 60° E 90° E 120° E 150° E 180°

Physical Map of the World

180° 150° W 120° W 90° W 60° W 30° W

GREENLAND
Arctic
Arctic Circle (66°34' N)
Yukon
60° N
Bering Sea
Gulf of Alaska
ALEUTIAN ISLANDS
Hudson Bay
ROCKY MOUNTAINS
GREAT PLAINS
NORTH AMERICA
Great Lakes
APPALACHIAN MTS
Colorado
Mississippi
Rio Grande
North Atlantic Ocean
North Pacific Ocean
30° N
HAWAIIAN ISLANDS
Atlas
Gulf of Mexico
Tropic of Cancer (23°26' N)
Caribbean Sea
CENTRAL AMERICA
0°
AMAZON BASIN
Amazon
Equator (0°)
SOUTH AMERICA
ANDES MOUNTAINS
Brazilian Highlands
South Pacific Ocean
South Atlantic Ocean
30° S
Patagonia
60° S
Antarctic Circle (66°34' S)
Southern

180° 150° W 120° W 90° W 60° W 30° W

0° 30° E 60° E 90° E 120° E 150° E 180°

SCANDINAVIA
EUROPE
Rhine
ALPS
Danube
Volga
Ural Mtns.
Black Sea
Caucasus Mtns.
Caspian Sea
Mediterranean Sea
S I B E R I A
Lake Baikal
A S I A
GOBI DESERT
Sea of Okhotsk
Bering Sea
Sea of Japan
TIBETAN PLATEAU
HIMALAYAS
Ganges
Yangtze
East China Sea
North Pacific Ocean
SAHARA
Nile
Red Sea
Persian Gulf
ARABIAN PENINSULA
DECCAN PLATEAU
Arabian Sea
Bay of Bengal
Mekong
South China Sea
Philippine Sea
AFRICA
Great Rift Valley
CONGO BASIN
Congo
MICRONESIA
SUNDA ISLANDS
Indian Ocean
MADAGASCAR
KALAHARI DESERT
Tropic of Capricorn (23°26′ S)
Great Barrier Reef
Coral Sea
Great Sandy Desert
AUSTRALIA
Great Victoria Desert
Great Dividing Range
South Pacific Ocean
Tasman Sea
ANTARCTICA
60° N 30° N 0° 30° S 60° S

AFGHANISTAN

LOCATION: Asia

CAPITAL: Kabul

AREA: 252,072 square miles (652,867 sq km)

POPULATION ESTIMATE (MID-YEAR 2024): 48,001,842

GOVERNMENT: Theocracy

LANGUAGES: Afghan Persian / Dari, Pashto (both official)

MONEY: Afghan Afghani

FUN FACT: The world's first oil paintings were created in the Afghan caves of Bamiyan around 650 B.C.

ALBANIA

LOCATION: Europe

CAPITAL: Tirana

AREA: 11,082 square miles (28,703 sq km)

POPULATION ESTIMATE (MID-YEAR 2024): 2,579,534

GOVERNMENT: Parliamentary republic

LANGUAGES: Albanian (official), Greek

MONEY: Lek

FUN FACT: In some places, people nod their head to say "no" and shake it side to side to say "yes."

ALGERIA

LOCATION: Africa

CAPITAL: Algiers

AREA: 919,590 square miles (2,381,741 sq km)

POPULATION ESTIMATE (MID-YEAR 2024): 47,022,473

GOVERNMENT: Presidential republic

LANGUAGES: Arabic, Tamazight (both official); French dialect

MONEY: Algerian dinar

FUN FACT: The world's tallest minaret (a tower atop a mosque) is in Algeria. It's 867 feet (264.3 m) tall.

ANDORRA

LOCATION: Europe

CAPITAL: Andorra la Vella

AREA: 181 square miles (468 sq km)

POPULATION ESTIMATE (MID-YEAR 2024): 85,370

GOVERNMENT: Parliamentary democracy

LANGUAGES: Catalan (official), Castilian, Portuguese, French

MONEY: Euro

FUN FACT: Andorra has never had an army or a defense department.

ANGOLA

LOCATION: Africa

CAPITAL: Luanda

AREA: 481,351 square miles (1,246,700 sq km)

POPULATION ESTIMATE (MID-YEAR 2024): 37,709,928

GOVERNMENT: Presidential republic

LANGUAGES: Portuguese (official), Umbundu, Kikongo, other African languages

MONEY: Kwanza

FUN FACT: *Catatos* is a crunchy Angolan dish made with fried caterpillars. Some say it tastes like prawns.

ANTIGUA AND BARBUDA

LOCATION: Caribbean

CAPITAL: Saint John's

AREA: 171 square miles (442 sq km)

POPULATION ESTIMATE (MID-YEAR 2024): 102,634

GOVERNMENT: Parliamentary democracy under a constitutional monarchy

LANGUAGES: English (official), Antiguan Creole

MONEY: East Caribbean dollar

FUN FACT: The highest point on the island of Antigua (1,330 feet, 405 m) was officially renamed Mount Obama in 2009 after the US president.

ARGENTINA

LOCATION: South America

CAPITAL: Buenos Aires

AREA: 1,044,319 square miles (2,704,789 sq km)

POPULATION ESTIMATE (MID-YEAR 2024): 45,306,215

GOVERNMENT: Presidential republic

LANGUAGES: Spanish (official), Italian, English, German, French, Native languages

MONEY: Argentine peso

FUN FACT: Gauchos are like cowboys—they herd cattle and horses and are a part of the country's culture.

ARMENIA

LOCATION: Asia

CAPITAL: Yerevan

AREA: 11,484 square miles (29,743 sq km)

POPULATION ESTIMATE (MID-YEAR 2024): 2,976,765

GOVERNMENT: Parliamentary democracy

LANGUAGES: Armenian (official)

MONEY: Dram

FUN FACT: Chess is a mandatory school subject for second, third, and fourth graders.

AUSTRALIA

LOCATION: Continent of Australia

CAPITAL: Canberra

AREA: 2,968,385 square miles (7,688,126 sq km)

POPULATION ESTIMATE (MID-YEAR 2024): 26,768,598

GOVERNMENT: Federal parliamentary democracy under a constitutional monarchy

LANGUAGES: English

MONEY: Australian dollar

FUN FACT: Australia is both a country and a continent!

AUSTRIA

LOCATION: Europe

CAPITAL: Vienna

AREA: 32,388 square miles (83,884 sq km)

POPULATION ESTIMATE (MID-YEAR 2024): 9,147,000

GOVERNMENT: Federal parliamentary republic

LANGUAGES: German (official nationwide); Croatian, Hungarian (both official in Burgenland); Slovene (official in southern Carinthia)

MONEY: Euro

FUN FACT: The home of the region's 18th- and 19th-century emperors, Schönbrunn Palace boasts 1,441 rooms—but tourists can view only 45.

AZERBAIJAN

LOCATION: Asia

CAPITAL: Baku

AREA: 33,166 square miles (85,900 sq km)

POPULATION ESTIMATE (MID-YEAR 2024): 10,650,239

GOVERNMENT: Presidential republic

LANGUAGES: Azerbaijani / Azeri (official)

MONEY: Azerbaijani manat

FUN FACT: *Chovqan* is an ancient Azerbaijani game: Teams use wooden mallets to hit a ball while riding horses.

THE BAHAMAS

LOCATION: Caribbean

CAPITAL: Nassau

AREA: 5,382 square miles (13,939 sq km)

POPULATION ESTIMATE (MID-YEAR 2024): 410,862

GOVERNMENT: Constitutional parliamentary democracy under a constitutional monarchy

LANGUAGES: English (official), Creole

MONEY: Bahamian dollar

FUN FACT: The Royal Bahamas Police Force's marching band appears on the $1 note.

BAHRAIN

LOCATION: Middle East

CAPITAL: Manama

AREA: 304 square miles (787 sq km)

POPULATION ESTIMATE (MID-YEAR 2024): 1,566,888

GOVERNMENT: Constitutional monarchy

LANGUAGES: Arabic (official), English, Farsi, Urdu

MONEY: Bahraini dinar

FUN FACT: This island-nation is connected to Saudi Arabia on the mainland by 15 miles (24 km) of bridges.

BANGLADESH

LOCATION: Asia

CAPITAL: Dhaka

AREA: 56,977 square miles (147,570 sq km)

POPULATION ESTIMATE (MID-YEAR 2024): 168,697,184

GOVERNMENT: Parliamentary republic

LANGUAGES: Bangla / Bengali (official)

MONEY: Taka

FUN FACT: Bangladesh has six seasons: summer, monsoon, autumn, late autumn, winter, and spring.

BARBADOS

LOCATION: Caribbean

CAPITAL: Bridgetown

AREA: 167 square miles (432 sq km)

POPULATION ESTIMATE (MID-YEAR 2024): 304,139

GOVERNMENT: Parliamentary republic

LANGUAGES: English (official), Bajan (English-based Creole)

MONEY: Barbadian or Bajan dollar

FUN FACT: Imported to Barbados from India, mongooses are considered good luck if one crosses your path.

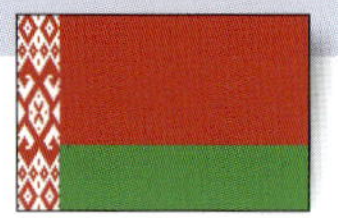

BELARUS

LOCATION: Europe

CAPITAL: Minsk

AREA: 80,166 square miles (207,629 sq km)

POPULATION ESTIMATE (MID-YEAR 2024): 9,501,451

GOVERNMENT: Presidential republic

LANGUAGES: Russian, Belarusian (both official)

MONEY: Belarusian ruble

FUN FACT: Shared with Poland, the Białowieża Forest is Europe's oldest nature preserve.

BELGIUM

LOCATION: Europe

CAPITAL: Brussels

AREA: 11,849 square miles (30,689 sq km)

POPULATION ESTIMATE (MID-YEAR 2024): 11,903,530

GOVERNMENT: Federal parliamentary democracy under a constitutional monarchy

LANGUAGES: Dutch, French, German (all official)

MONEY: Euro

FUN FACT: The Comic Strip Trail in Brussels features more than 80 outdoor murals by Belgian artists.

BELIZE

LOCATION: Central America

CAPITAL: Belmopan

AREA: 8,867 square miles (22,965 sq km)

POPULATION ESTIMATE (MID-YEAR 2024): 415,789

GOVERNMENT: Parliamentary democracy under a constitutional monarchy

LANGUAGES: English (official), Spanish, Creole, Maya

MONEY: Belizean dollar

FUN FACT: Part of Belize Barrier Reef, the Great Blue Hole is a giant sinkhole that plunges more than 400 feet (122 m).

BENIN

LOCATION: Africa

CAPITAL: Porto-Novo

AREA: 44,310 square miles (114,763 sq km)

POPULATION ESTIMATE (MID-YEAR 2024): 14,697,052

GOVERNMENT: Presidential republic

LANGUAGES: French (official), Indigenous languages such as Fon, Yom, and Yoruba

MONEY: CFA franc

FUN FACT: The Temple of Pythons is a shrine to a Vodun serpent god, and about 60 pythons slither the grounds.

BHUTAN

LOCATION: Asia

CAPITAL: Thimphu

AREA: 14,824 square miles (38,394 sq km)

POPULATION ESTIMATE (MID-YEAR 2024): 884,546

GOVERNMENT: Constitutional monarchy

LANGUAGES: Dzongkha (official), Sharchopkha, Lhotshamkha

MONEY: Ngultrum

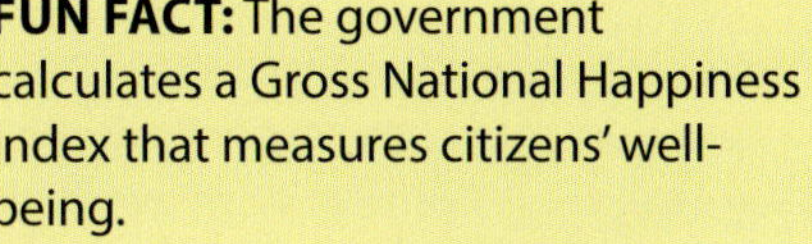

FUN FACT: The government calculates a Gross National Happiness Index that measures citizens' well-being.

BOLIVIA

LOCATION: South America

CAPITAL: La Paz (executive, legislative), Sucre (judicial)

AREA: 424,162 square miles (1,098,581 sq km)

POPULATION ESTIMATE (MID-YEAR 2024): 12,311,974

GOVERNMENT: Presidential republic

LANGUAGES: Spanish, Quechua, Aymara, Guarani (all official)

MONEY: Boliviano

FUN FACT: During the wet season, water on the Uyuni salt flat in southwest Bolivia reflects sunlight. It looks like a big mirror.

BOSNIA AND HERZEGOVINA

LOCATION: Europe

CAPITAL: Sarajevo

AREA: 19,772 square miles (51,209 sq km)

POPULATION ESTIMATE (MID-YEAR 2024): 3,677,149

GOVERNMENT: Parliamentary republic

LANGUAGES: Bosnian, Serbian, Croatian (all official)

MONEY: Convertible mark

FUN FACT: The Sahat-Kula clock tower in Sarajevo is a lunar clock, set by the day's sunset.

BOTSWANA

LOCATION: Africa

CAPITAL: Gaborone

AREA: 224,606 square miles (581,730 sq km)

POPULATION ESTIMATE (MID-YEAR 2024): 2,450,668

GOVERNMENT: Parliamentary republic

LANGUAGES: English (official), Setswana, Sekalanga, Shekgalagadi

MONEY: Pula

FUN FACT: The Kalahari Desert covers about 70 percent of Botswana.

BRAZIL

LOCATION: South America

CAPITAL: Brasília

AREA: 3,285,872 square miles (8,510,418 sq km)

POPULATION ESTIMATE (MID-YEAR 2024): 220,051,512

GOVERNMENT: Federal presidential republic

LANGUAGES: Portuguese (official), Spanish, German, English, Amerindian languages

MONEY: Real

FUN FACT: About 91,500 insect species live in Brazil—about 9 percent of the world's known species.

BRUNEI

LOCATION: Asia

CAPITAL: Bandar Seri Begawan

AREA: 2,226 square miles (5,765 sq km)

POPULATION ESTIMATE (MID-YEAR 2024): 491,900

GOVERNMENT: Constitutional sultanate

LANGUAGES: Malay (official), English, Chinese dialects

MONEY: Bruneian dollar

FUN FACT: More than 30,000 people live in Kampong Ayer, a 600-year-old city built on stilts above a river.

BULGARIA

LOCATION: Europe

CAPITAL: Sofia

AREA: 42,614 square miles (110,372 sq km)

POPULATION ESTIMATE (MID-YEAR 2024): 6,782,659

GOVERNMENT: Parliamentary republic

LANGUAGES: Bulgarian (official), Turkish, Romani

MONEY: Lev

FUN FACT: The Rock-Hewn Churches of Ivanovo are a series of 12th-century chapels and churches dug into caves.

BURKINA FASO

LOCATION: Africa

CAPITAL: Ouagadougou

AREA: 104,542 square miles (270,764 sq km)

POPULATION ESTIMATE (MID-YEAR 2024): 22,930,371

GOVERNMENT: Transitional presidential republic

LANGUAGES: French (official), Mossi, Fula, Gourmantche, Dyula

MONEY: CFA franc

FUN FACT: About 90 percent of people here are farmers or raise livestock.

BURUNDI

LOCATION: Africa

CAPITAL: Gitega (political capital), Bujumbara (economic capital)

AREA: 10,747 square miles (27,834 sq km)

POPULATION ESTIMATE (MID-YEAR 2024): 13,590,102

GOVERNMENT: Presidential republic

LANGUAGES: Kirundi, French, English (all official); Swahili

MONEY: Burundian franc

FUN FACT: A symbol of Burundi is a drum called the *karyenda*, which often is played alongside traditional dances.

CABO VERDE

LOCATION: Africa

CAPITAL: Praia

AREA: 1,557 square miles (4,033 sq km)

POPULATION ESTIMATE (MID-YEAR 2024): 611,014

GOVERNMENT: Parliamentary republic

LANGUAGES: Portuguese (official), Crioulo

MONEY: Cape Verdean escudo

FUN FACT: A traditional art form in Cabo Verde is *morna*, a blend of music, poetry, and dance.

CAMBODIA

LOCATION: Asia

CAPITAL: Phnom Penh

AREA: 69,898 square miles (181,035 sq km)

POPULATION ESTIMATE (MID-YEAR 2024): 17,063,669

GOVERNMENT: Parliamentary constitutional monarchy

LANGUAGES: Khmer (official)

MONEY: Cambodian riel

FUN FACT: Using radar that could "see" through the jungle, scientists rediscovered an ancient city in this country.

CAMEROON

LOCATION: Africa

CAPITAL: Yaoundé

AREA: 179,942 square miles (466,050 sq km)

POPULATION ESTIMATE (MID-YEAR 2024): 30,966,105

GOVERNMENT: Presidential republic

LANGUAGES: English, French (both official); various Indigenous languages

MONEY: CFA franc

FUN FACT: Pipes installed in Lake Nyos help prevent rising poisonous gas from a collapsed volcano.

CANADA

LOCATION: North America

CAPITAL: Ottawa

AREA: 3,855,081 square miles (9,984,670 sq km)

POPULATION ESTIMATE (MID-YEAR 2024): 38,904,514

GOVERNMENT: Federal parliamentary democracy under a constitutional monarchy

LANGUAGES: English, French (both official); Chinese

MONEY: Canadian dollar

FUN FACT: Canada has more lakes than the rest of the world combined.

CENTRAL AFRICAN REPUBLIC

LOCATION: Africa

CAPITAL: Bangui

AREA: 240,323 square miles (622,436 sq km)

POPULATION ESTIMATE (MID-YEAR 2024): 5,650,957

GOVERNMENT: Presidential republic

LANGUAGES: French (official), Sangho (national language), tribal languages

MONEY: CFA franc

FUN FACT: Both savannas and forests are found in Manovo-Gounda Saint Floris National Park.

CHAD

LOCATION: Africa

CAPITAL: N'Djamena

AREA: 495,753 square miles (1,284,000 sq km)

POPULATION ESTIMATE (MID-YEAR 2024): 19,093,595

GOVERNMENT: Presidential republic

LANGUAGES: French, Arabic (both official); Sara

MONEY: CFA franc

FUN FACT: A small group of specially adapted crocodiles lives in Ennedi Massif, a region in the Sahara.

CHILE

LOCATION: South America

CAPITAL: Santiago

AREA: 291,929 square miles (756,096 sq km)

POPULATION ESTIMATE (MID-YEAR 2024): 18,998,355

GOVERNMENT: Presidential republic

LANGUAGES: Spanish (official), English, Indigenous languages

MONEY: Chilean peso

FUN FACT: Giant stone figures called *moai* dot Chile's Easter Island (Rapa Nui in the Indigenous language).

CHINA

LOCATION: Asia

CAPITAL: Beijing

AREA: 3,696,097 square miles (9,572,900 sq km)

POPULATION ESTIMATE (MID-YEAR 2024): 1,407,929,929

GOVERNMENT: Communist state

LANGUAGES: Chinese Mandarin (official), Yue (Cantonese), Wu (Shanghainese), local dialects

MONEY: Chinese yuan

FUN FACT: In part of the Great Wall of China, workers bound bricks with a sticky substance made from rice.

COLOMBIA

LOCATION: South America

CAPITAL: Bogotá

AREA: 440,829 square miles (1,141,748 sq km)

POPULATION ESTIMATE (MID-YEAR 2024): 49,588,357

GOVERNMENT: Presidential republic

LANGUAGES: Spanish (official), Indigenous languages

MONEY: Colombian peso

FUN FACT: The rivers and lakes in Chingaza National Park supply about 70 percent of Bogotá's drinking water.

COMOROS

LOCATION: Africa

CAPITAL: Moroni

AREA: 719 square miles (1,861 sq km)

POPULATION ESTIMATE (MID-YEAR 2024): 900,141

GOVERNMENT: Federal presidential republic

LANGUAGES: Arabic, French, Shikomoro (all official); Comorian

MONEY: Comorian franc

FUN FACT: The island of Mayotte is still a French territory, unlike the other islands of this country.

CONGO, DEMOCRATIC REPUBLIC OF THE

LOCATION: Africa

CAPITAL: Kinshasa

AREA: 905,405 square miles (2,345,000 sq km)

POPULATION ESTIMATE (MID-YEAR 2024): 115,403,027

GOVERNMENT: Semi-presidential republic

LANGUAGES: French (official), Lingala, Kingwana, Kikongo, Tshiluba

MONEY: Congolese franc

FUN FACT: The Ituri Forest is the only place where you can see wild okapi, a close relative of the giraffe.

CONGO, REPUBLIC OF THE

LOCATION: Africa

CAPITAL: Brazzaville

AREA: 132,046 square miles (342,000 sq km)

POPULATION ESTIMATE (MID-YEAR 2024): 6,097,665

GOVERNMENT: Presidential republic

LANGUAGES: French (official), French Lingala, Monokutuba, local languages

MONEY: CFA franc

FUN FACT: Chimpanzees live in the jungles around Diosso Gorge, a canyon with colorful rock formations.

COSTA RICA

LOCATION: Central America

CAPITAL: San José

AREA: 19,730 square miles (51,100 sq km)

POPULATION ESTIMATE (MID-YEAR 2024): 5,265,575

GOVERNMENT: Presidential republic

LANGUAGES: Spanish (official), English

MONEY: Costa Rican colón

FUN FACT: Scientists monitor at least 10 volcanoes here for signs of eruption.

CÔTE D'IVOIRE

LOCATION: Africa

CAPITAL: Yamoussoukro

AREA: 124,503 square miles (322,462 sq km)

POPULATION ESTIMATE (MID-YEAR 2024): 31,113,762

GOVERNMENT: Presidential republic

LANGUAGES: French (official), Dioula and other Native dialects

MONEY: CFA franc

FUN FACT: Chimpanzees in Taï National Park have been observed using stone and wooden tools to crack nuts.

CROATIA

LOCATION: Europe

CAPITAL: Zagreb

AREA: 21,851 square miles (56,594 sq km)

POPULATION ESTIMATE (MID-YEAR 2024): 4,090,839

GOVERNMENT: Parliamentary republic

LANGUAGES: Croatian (official), Serbian

MONEY: Euro

FUN FACT: Croatia has more than 1,100 islands, islets, and reefs.

CUBA

LOCATION: Caribbean

CAPITAL: Havana

AREA: 42,426 square miles (109,884 sq km)

POPULATION ESTIMATE (MID-YEAR 2024): 10,163,370

GOVERNMENT: Communist state

LANGUAGES: Spanish (official)

MONEY: Cuban peso

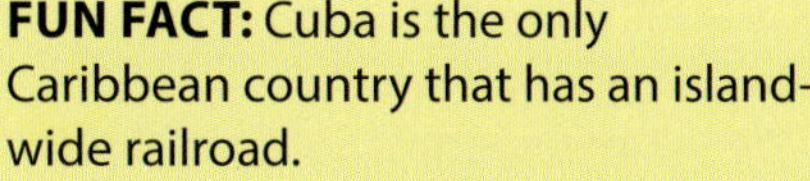

FUN FACT: Cuba is the only Caribbean country that has an island-wide railroad.

CYPRUS

LOCATION: Middle East

CAPITAL: Nicosia

AREA: 3,572 square miles (9,251 sq km)

POPULATION ESTIMATE (MID-YEAR 2024): 1,320,525

GOVERNMENT: Presidential republic

LANGUAGES: Greek, Turkish (both official); English

MONEY: Euro

FUN FACT: Legend says that Aphrodite, the Greek goddess of love, was born on this island.

CZECH REPUBLIC (CZECHIA)

LOCATION: Europe

CAPITAL: Prague

AREA: 30,452 square miles (78,870 sq km)

POPULATION ESTIMATE (MID-YEAR 2024): 10,837,890

GOVERNMENT: Parliamentary republic

LANGUAGES: Czech (official), Slovak

MONEY: Koruna

FUN FACT: Nearly a half mile (721 m) long, Sky Bridge 721 is the longest pedestrian suspension bridge.

DENMARK

LOCATION: Europe

CAPITAL: Copenhagen

AREA: 16,585 square miles (42,954 sq km)

POPULATION ESTIMATE (MID-YEAR 2024): 6,009,711

GOVERNMENT: Parliamentary constitutional monarchy

LANGUAGES: Danish (official), English, Faroese, Greenlandic (an Inuit dialect)

MONEY: Danish krone

FUN FACT: Nine out of 10 Danes own a bike. About 50 percent of people who live in Copenhagen bike to work.

DJIBOUTI

LOCATION: Africa

CAPITAL: Djibouti

AREA: 8,880 square miles (23,000 sq km)

POPULATION ESTIMATE (MID-YEAR 2024): 994,974

GOVERNMENT: Presidential republic

LANGUAGES: French, Arabic (both official); Somali, Afar

MONEY: Djiboutian franc

FUN FACT: *Skoudehkaris* is a traditional dish made in one pot with lamb, rice, spices, and tomato sauce.

DOMINICA

LOCATION: Caribbean

CAPITAL: Roseau

AREA: 290 square miles (751 sq km)

POPULATION ESTIMATE (MID-YEAR 2024): 74,661

GOVERNMENT: Parliamentary republic

LANGUAGES: English (official), French patois

MONEY: East Caribbean dollar

FUN FACT: The sisserou parrot on the flag is a critically endangered species that lives only on this island.

DOMINICAN REPUBLIC

LOCATION: Caribbean

CAPITAL: Santo Domingo

AREA: 18,619 square miles (48,223 sq km)

POPULATION ESTIMATE (MID-YEAR 2024): 10,815,857

GOVERNMENT: Presidential republic

LANGUAGES: Spanish (official)

MONEY: Dominican peso

FUN FACT: In 2020, scientists found a new species of snake in the Dominican Republic, the three-foot-long (1-m) Hispaniolan vine boa.

EAST TIMOR (TIMOR-LESTE)

LOCATION: Asia

CAPITAL: Dili

AREA: 5,772 square miles (14,950 sq km)

POPULATION ESTIMATE (MID-YEAR 2024): 1,386,442

GOVERNMENT: Semi-presidential republic

LANGUAGES: Tetun, Portuguese (both official); Indonesian, English, Indigenous languages

MONEY: US dollar

FUN FACT: Ataúro Island turned the Timorese practice of *tara bandu*—a code of conservation—into law.

ECUADOR

LOCATION: South America

CAPITAL: Quito

AREA: 99,170 square miles (256,850 sq km)

POPULATION ESTIMATE (MID-YEAR 2024): 18,309,984

GOVERNMENT: Presidential republic

LANGUAGES: Castilian Spanish (official), Quechua, other Indigenous languages

MONEY: US dollar

FUN FACT: The giant tortoises that live on Ecuador's Galápagos Islands can live to be more than 150 years old.

EGYPT

LOCATION: Africa

CAPITAL: Cairo

AREA: 384,788 square miles (996,603 sq km)

POPULATION ESTIMATE (MID-YEAR 2024): 111,247,248

GOVERNMENT: Presidential republic

LANGUAGES: Arabic (official), English, French

MONEY: Egyptian pound

FUN FACT: Carved about 4,500 years ago, the Great Sphinx of Giza is thought by many to represent Pharaoh Khafre.

EL SALVADOR

LOCATION: Central America

CAPITAL: San Salvador

AREA: 8,124 square miles (21,041 sq km)

POPULATION ESTIMATE (MID-YEAR 2024): 6,788,544

GOVERNMENT: Presidential republic

LANGUAGES: Spanish (official), Nawat

MONEY: US dollar

FUN FACT: Surfers flock to Punta Roca beach, where waves can reach eight feet (3 m) high.

EQUATORIAL GUINEA

LOCATION: Africa

CAPITAL: Malabo

AREA: 10,831 square miles (28,052 sq km)

POPULATION ESTIMATE (MID-YEAR 2024): 1,795,834

GOVERNMENT: Presidential republic

LANGUAGES: Spanish, Portuguese, French (all official); Fang, Bubi

MONEY: CFA franc

FUN FACT: The 155-mile-long (248-km) Mbini River is navigable for only about 12 miles (20 km).

ERITREA

LOCATION: Africa

CAPITAL: Asmara

AREA: 46,757 square miles (121,100 sq km)

POPULATION ESTIMATE (MID-YEAR 2024): 6,343,956

GOVERNMENT: Presidential republic

LANGUAGES: Tigrinya, Arabic, English (all official); Tigre, Kunama, Afar

MONEY: Nakfa

FUN FACT: *Asmara* means "they [women] made them unite" in the Tigrinya language.

ESTONIA

LOCATION: Europe

CAPITAL: Tallinn

AREA: 17,505 square miles (45,339 sq km)

POPULATION ESTIMATE (MID-YEAR 2024): 1,342,910

GOVERNMENT: Parliamentary republic

LANGUAGES: Estonian (official), Russian

MONEY: Euro

FUN FACT: *Kiiking* is an Estonian sport in which athletes stand on a giant swing and rotate all the way around.

ESWATINI

LOCATION: Africa

CAPITAL: Mbabane (executive, judicial), Lombamba (legislative)

AREA: 6,704 square miles (17,364 sq km)

POPULATION ESTIMATE (MID-YEAR 2024): 1,138,089

GOVERNMENT: Monarchy

LANGUAGES: English, siSwati (both official)

MONEY: Lilangeni

FUN FACT: Eswatini ferns and flowering plants total more than 2,600 species.

ETHIOPIA

LOCATION: Africa

CAPITAL: Addis Ababa

AREA: 432,432 square miles (1,120,000 sq km)

POPULATION ESTIMATE (MID-YEAR 2024): 118,550,298

GOVERNMENT: Federal parliamentary republic

LANGUAGES: Amharic (official), Oromo, Somali, Tigrigna / Tigrinya, Afar (all official regional languages), other local languages

MONEY: Birr

FUN FACT: The Ethiopian calendar has 13 months, with the month of Pagume having only 5 or 6 days.

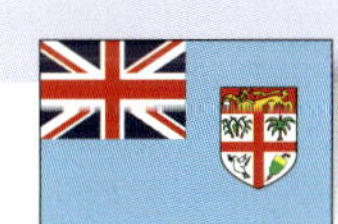

FIJI

LOCATION: Oceania

CAPITAL: Suva

AREA: 7,055 square miles (18,272 sq km)

POPULATION ESTIMATE (MID-YEAR 2024): 951,611

GOVERNMENT: Parliamentary republic

LANGUAGES: English, iTaukei, Fiji Hindi (all official)

MONEY: Fijian dollar

FUN FACT: Sri Siva Subramaniya is the largest Hindu temple in the Pacific.

FINLAND

LOCATION: Europe

CAPITAL: Helsinki

AREA: 130,689 square miles (338,485 sq km)

POPULATION ESTIMATE (MID-YEAR 2024): 5,548,944

GOVERNMENT: Parliamentary republic

LANGUAGES: Finnish, Swedish (both official)

MONEY: Euro

FUN FACT: Taking a sauna—hanging out in a steam-filled room to sweat—is a daily ritual for many Finns.

FRANCE

LOCATION: Europe

CAPITAL: Paris

AREA: 210,016 square miles (543,941 sq km)

POPULATION ESTIMATE (MID-YEAR 2024): 68,374,591

GOVERNMENT: Semi-presidential republic

LANGUAGES: French (official)

MONEY: Euro

FUN FACT: After a 2019 fire, workers used a digital map of the nearly 900-year-old Notre-Dame to restore it.

GABON

LOCATION: Africa

CAPITAL: Libreville

AREA: 103,346 square miles (267,667 sq km)

POPULATION ESTIMATE (MID-YEAR 2024): 2,455,105

GOVERNMENT: Presidential republic

LANGUAGES: French (official), Fang, Myene, Nzebi, Bapounou / Eschira, Bandjabi

MONEY: CFA franc

FUN FACT: In coastal Loango National Park, hippos "surf" ocean waves and elephants wander the beach.

THE GAMBIA

LOCATION: Africa

CAPITAL: Banjul

AREA: 4,127 square miles (10,689 sq km)

POPULATION ESTIMATE (MID-YEAR 2024): 2,523,327

GOVERNMENT: Presidential republic

LANGUAGES: English (official), Mandinka, Wolof, Fula, other local languages

MONEY: Dalasi

FUN FACT: The Gambia is the smallest country in mainland Africa in size.

GEORGIA

LOCATION: Asia

CAPITAL: Tbilisi

AREA: 26,911 square miles (69,700 sq km)

POPULATION ESTIMATE (MID-YEAR 2024): 4,900,961

GOVERNMENT: Semi-presidential republic

LANGUAGES: Georgian (official), Azeri, Armenian, Abkhaz (official regional)

MONEY: Lari

FUN FACT: More than a third of this country is forested. Animals such as brown bears and lynx roam the land.

GERMANY

LOCATION: Europe

CAPITAL: Berlin

AREA: 138,068 square miles (357,596 sq km)

POPULATION ESTIMATE (MID-YEAR 2024): 84,119,100

GOVERNMENT: Federal parliamentary republic

LANGUAGES: German (official); Danish, Frisian, Sorbian, Romani (official minority languages)

MONEY: Euro

FUN FACT: Neuschwanstein Castle, the inspiration for Sleeping Beauty Castle at Disneyland, began construction in 1868.

GHANA

LOCATION: Africa

CAPITAL: Accra

AREA: 92,098 square miles (238,533 sq km)

POPULATION ESTIMATE (MID-YEAR 2024): 34,589,092

GOVERNMENT: Presidential republic

LANGUAGES: English (official), Asante, Ewe, Fante, Boron / Brong, Dagomba, other Indigenous languages

MONEY: Cedi

FUN FACT: Many Ghanaian parents give their children names based on the day of the week they were born.

GREECE

LOCATION: Europe

CAPITAL: Athens

AREA: 50,984 square miles (132,049 sq km)

POPULATION ESTIMATE (MID-YEAR 2024): 10,461,091

GOVERNMENT: Parliamentary republic

LANGUAGES: Greek (official), English, French

MONEY: Euro

FUN FACT: Although 80 percent of Greece is mountainous, a beach is never more than 85 miles (137 km) away.

GRENADA

LOCATION: Caribbean

CAPITAL: Saint George's

AREA: 133 square miles (344 sq km)

POPULATION ESTIMATE (MID-YEAR 2024): 114,621

GOVERNMENT: Parliamentary democracy under a constitutional monarchy

LANGUAGES: English (official), French patois

MONEY: East Caribbean dollar

FUN FACT: The Molinere Bay Underwater Sculpture Park features 75 works of art for swimmers to explore.

GUATEMALA

LOCATION: Central America

CAPITAL: Guatemala City

AREA: 42,042 square miles (108,889 sq km)

POPULATION ESTIMATE (MID-YEAR 2024): 18,255,216

GOVERNMENT: Presidential republic

LANGUAGES: Spanish (official), Maya languages

MONEY: Quetzal

FUN FACT: People descended from the ancient Maya make up about 51 percent of the Guatemalan population.

GUINEA

LOCATION: Africa

CAPITAL: Conakry

AREA: 94,925 square miles (245,857 sq km)

POPULATION ESTIMATE (MID-YEAR 2024): 13,986,179

GOVERNMENT: Presidential republic

LANGUAGES: French (official), Pular, Maninka, Susu, other Indigenous languages

MONEY: Guinean franc

FUN FACT: *Talbotiella cheekii*, a tree discovered in Guinea in 2015, sprouts fruit in exploding pods.

GUINEA-BISSAU

LOCATION: Africa

CAPITAL: Bissau

AREA: 13,948 square miles (36,125 sq km)

POPULATION ESTIMATE (MID-YEAR 2024): 2,132,325

GOVERNMENT: Semi-presidential republic

LANGUAGES: Portuguese (official), Portuguese-based Creole, Pular, Mandingo

MONEY: CFA franc

FUN FACT: About 44,000 green sea turtle hatchlings scurry to the ocean from the uninhabited Poilão Island.

GUYANA

LOCATION: South America

CAPITAL: Georgetown

AREA: 83,011 square miles (214,999 sq km)

POPULATION ESTIMATE (MID-YEAR 2024): 794,099

GOVERNMENT: Republic

LANGUAGES: English (official), Guyanese Creole, other Indigenous languages

MONEY: Guyanese dollar

FUN FACT: At 741 feet (226 m), Kaieteur Falls in Kaieteur National Park is the largest single-drop waterfall.

HAITI

LOCATION: Caribbean

CAPITAL: Port-au-Prince

AREA: 10,450 square miles (27,065 sq km)

POPULATION ESTIMATE (MID-YEAR 2024): 11,753,943

GOVERNMENT: Semi-presidential republic

LANGUAGES: French, Creole (both official)

MONEY: Gourde

FUN FACT: Haiti takes up the western third of the island of Hispaniola; the Dominican Republic sits on the rest.

HONDURAS

LOCATION: Central America

CAPITAL: Tegucigalpa

AREA: 43,433 square miles (112,492 sq km)

POPULATION ESTIMATE (MID-YEAR 2024): 9,529,188

GOVERNMENT: Presidential republic

LANGUAGES: Spanish (official), Amerindian dialects

MONEY: Lempira

FUN FACT: The Mosquito Coast in Honduras was named for the Indigenous Mistiko people—not the insect.

HUNGARY

LOCATION: Europe

CAPITAL: Budapest

AREA: 35,916 square miles (93,023 sq km)

POPULATION ESTIMATE (MID-YEAR 2024): 9,855,745

GOVERNMENT: Parliamentary republic

LANGUAGES: Hungarian (official), English, German, Russian

MONEY: Forint

FUN FACT: The seven-mile (11-km) Children's Railway is operated by kids who take tickets and manage arrivals and departures.

ICELAND

LOCATION: Europe

CAPITAL: Reykjavík

AREA: 39,768 square miles (103,000 sq km)

POPULATION ESTIMATE (MID-YEAR 2024): 364,036

GOVERNMENT: Unitary parliamentary republic

LANGUAGES: Icelandic (official), English, Polish, Nordic languages, German

MONEY: Icelandic krona

FUN FACT: The flag celebrates nature: red for volcanoes, white for glaciers, and blue for the sea.

INDIA

LOCATION: Asia

CAPITAL: New Delhi

AREA: 1,269,292 square miles (3,287,469 sq km)

POPULATION ESTIMATE (MID-YEAR 2024): 1,409,128,296

GOVERNMENT: Federal parliamentary republic

LANGUAGES: Hindi, English (both official); Bengali, Marathi, Telugu, Tamil, Gujarati, Urdu, other local languages

MONEY: Indian rupee

FUN FACT: In 2023, India overtook China as the most populous country in the world.

INDONESIA

LOCATION: Asia

CAPITAL: Jakarta

AREA: 730,660 square miles (1,892,410 sq km)

POPULATION ESTIMATE (MID-YEAR 2024): 281,562,465

GOVERNMENT: Presidential republic

LANGUAGES: Bahasa Indonesia (official), English, Dutch, local dialects

MONEY: Rupiah

FUN FACT: The world's largest lizard, the Komodo dragon, lives only on Komodo Island (and a few others nearby).

IRAN

LOCATION: Middle East

CAPITAL: Tehran

AREA: 629,670 square miles (1,630,848 sq km)

POPULATION ESTIMATE (MID-YEAR 2024): 88,386,937

GOVERNMENT: Theocratic republic

LANGUAGES: Persian Farsi (official), Turkic dialects, Kurdish

MONEY: Iranian rial

FUN FACT: Called Persia for thousands of years, Iran is one of the oldest civilizations in the world.

IRAQ

LOCATION: Middle East

CAPITAL: Baghdad

AREA: 167,974 square miles (435,052 sq km)

POPULATION ESTIMATE (MID-YEAR 2024): 42,083,436

GOVERNMENT: Federal parliamentary republic

LANGUAGES: Arabic, Kurdish (both official); Turkmen, Syriac

MONEY: Iraqi dinar

FUN FACT: Famous for textiles, Baghdad was an important stop on the Silk Road.

IRELAND

LOCATION: Europe

CAPITAL: Dublin

AREA: 27,458 square miles (71,118 sq km)

POPULATION ESTIMATE (MID-YEAR 2024): 5,233,461

GOVERNMENT: Parliamentary republic

LANGUAGES: English, Irish / Gaelic (both official)

MONEY: Euro

FUN FACT: Newgrange is an ancient stone burial mound that's older than the Great Pyramid of Giza.

ISRAEL

LOCATION: Middle East

CAPITAL: Jerusalem

AREA: 8,522 square miles (22,072 sq km)

POPULATION ESTIMATE (MID-YEAR 2024): 9,402,617

GOVERNMENT: Parliamentary democracy

LANGUAGES: Hebrew (official), Arabic, English

MONEY: New Israeli shekels

FUN FACT: Jerusalem contains sacred monuments for Jewish, Muslim, and Christian people.

ITALY

LOCATION: Europe

CAPITAL: Rome

AREA: 116,629 square miles (302,069 sq km)

POPULATION ESTIMATE (MID-YEAR 2024): 60,964,931

GOVERNMENT: Parliamentary republic

LANGUAGES: Italian (official), German, French, Slovene

MONEY: Euro

FUN FACT: About $1.52 million worth of coins were tossed into Rome's Trevi Fountain in 2022.

JAMAICA

LOCATION: Caribbean

CAPITAL: Kingston

AREA: 4,244 square miles (10,991 sq km)

POPULATION ESTIMATE (MID-YEAR 2024): 2,823,713

GOVERNMENT: Parliamentary democracy under a constitutional monarchy

LANGUAGES: English (official), Jamaican patois

MONEY: Jamaican dollar

FUN FACT: Dominoes is a popular game in Jamaica but has special "Jamaican-style" rules.

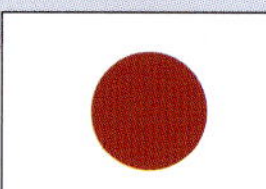

JAPAN

LOCATION: Asia

CAPITAL: Tokyo

AREA: 145,934 square miles (377,969 sq km)

POPULATION ESTIMATE (MID-YEAR 2024): 123,201,945

GOVERNMENT: Parliamentary constitutional monarchy

LANGUAGES: Japanese

MONEY: Yen

FUN FACT: About 1,660 Buddhist temples and more than 400 Shinto shrines are in Kyoto.

JORDAN

LOCATION: Middle East

CAPITAL: Amman

AREA: 34,283 square miles (88,794 sq km)

POPULATION ESTIMATE (MID-YEAR 2024): 11,174,024

GOVERNMENT: Parliamentary constitutional monarchy

LANGUAGES: Arabic (official), English

MONEY: Jordanian dinar

FUN FACT: The Jordan Trail is a 420-mile (675-km) hiking path that takes travelers the length of the country.

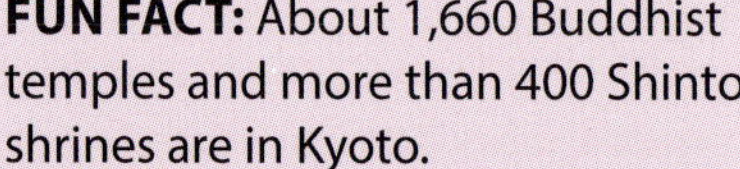

KAZAKHSTAN

LOCATION: Asia

CAPITAL: Astana

AREA: 1,052,084 square miles (2,724,900 sq km)

POPULATION ESTIMATE (MID-YEAR 2024): 20,260,006

GOVERNMENT: Presidential republic

LANGUAGES: Kazakh, Russian (both official); English

MONEY: Tenge

FUN FACT: Most farm-grown apples descend from an ancient species that still grows wild in Kazakhstan.

KENYA

LOCATION: Africa

CAPITAL: Nairobi

AREA: 224,960 square miles (582,646 sq km)

POPULATION ESTIMATE (MID-YEAR 2024): 54,571,282

GOVERNMENT: Presidential republic

LANGUAGES: English, Kiswahili (both official); Indigenous languages

MONEY: Kenyan shilling

FUN FACT: Millions of lesser flamingos flock to salty Bogoria and Naivasha lakes in Kenya to breed.

KIRIBATI

LOCATION: Oceania

CAPITAL: Tarawa

AREA: 313 square miles (811 sq km)

POPULATION ESTIMATE (MID-YEAR 2024): 116,545

GOVERNMENT: Presidential republic

LANGUAGES: English (official), Gilbertese

MONEY: Australian dollar

FUN FACT: Kiribati is the first country to celebrate the New Year every year.

KOREA, NORTH

LOCATION: Asia

CAPITAL: Pyongyang

AREA: 47,573 square miles (123,214 sq km)

POPULATION ESTIMATE (MID-YEAR 2024): 26,298,666

GOVERNMENT: Communist state with one-man dictatorship

LANGUAGES: Korean (official)

MONEY: North Korean won

FUN FACT: North Korea has been ruled by the same family since 1948.

KOREA, SOUTH

LOCATION: Asia

CAPITAL: Seoul

AREA: 38,696 square miles (100,222 sq km)

POPULATION ESTIMATE (MID-YEAR 2024): 51,530,947

GOVERNMENT: Presidential republic

LANGUAGES: Korean (official), English

MONEY: South Korean won

FUN FACT: The sport of taekwondo originated in South Korea.

KOSOVO

LOCATION: Europe

CAPITAL: Pristina

AREA: 4,210 square miles (10,905 sq km)

POPULATION ESTIMATE (MID-YEAR 2024): 1,977,093

GOVERNMENT: Parliamentary republic

LANGUAGES: Albanian, Serbian (both official); Bosnian, Turkish

MONEY: Euro

FUN FACT: Kosovo didn't participate in any Olympics until 2016.

KUWAIT

LOCATION: Middle East

CAPITAL: Kuwait City

AREA: 6,880 square miles (17,818 sq km)

POPULATION ESTIMATE (MID-YEAR 2024): 3,138,355

GOVERNMENT: Constitutional emirate

LANGUAGES: Arabic (official), English

MONEY: Kuwaiti dinar

FUN FACT: Camel racing is popular in Kuwait; the camels are ridden by remote-controlled robo-jockeys.

KYRGYZSTAN

LOCATION: Asia

CAPITAL: Bishkek

AREA: 77,199 square miles (199,945 sq km)

POPULATION ESTIMATE (MID-YEAR 2024): 6,172,101

GOVERNMENT: Parliamentary republic

LANGUAGES: Kyrgyz, Russian (both official); Uzbek

MONEY: Kyrgyzstani som

FUN FACT: Archery is an event at the World Nomad Games, which celebrate the traditional nomadic lifestyle.

LAOS

LOCATION: Asia

CAPITAL: Vientiane

AREA: 91,428 square miles (236,800 sq km)

POPULATION ESTIMATE (MID-YEAR 2024): 7,953,556

GOVERNMENT: Communist state

LANGUAGES: Lao (official), French, English

MONEY: Kip

FUN FACT: The Plain of Jars is an archaeological outdoor site containing more than 2,000 tube-shaped stone jars.

LATVIA

LOCATION: Europe

CAPITAL: Riga

AREA: 24,940 square miles (64,594 sq km)

POPULATION ESTIMATE (MID-YEAR 2024): 1,907,341

GOVERNMENT: Parliamentary republic

LANGUAGES: Latvian (official), Russian

MONEY: Euro

FUN FACT: At the Latvian Song and Dance Festival, about 6,000 people are onstage singing at the same time.

LEBANON

LOCATION: Middle East

CAPITAL: Beirut

AREA: 4,036 square miles (10,452 sq km)

POPULATION ESTIMATE (MID-YEAR 2024): 5,756,974

GOVERNMENT: Parliamentary democratic republic

LANGUAGES: Arabic (official), French, English, Armenian

MONEY: Lebanese pound

FUN FACT: People from the ancient city of Tyre were called purple people because of the dye they produced.

LESOTHO

LOCATION: Africa

CAPITAL: Maseru

AREA: 11,720 square miles (30,355 sq km)

POPULATION ESTIMATE (MID-YEAR 2024): 2,227,548

GOVERNMENT: Parliamentary constitutional monarchy

LANGUAGES: Sesotho, English (both official); Phuthi, Xhosa, Zulu

MONEY: Loti

FUN FACT: A plateau in Lesotho is the source of South Africa's two largest rivers—the Tugela and the Orange.

LIBERIA

LOCATION: Africa

CAPITAL: Monrovia

AREA: 37,466 square miles (97,036 sq km)

POPULATION ESTIMATE (MID-YEAR 2024): 5,437,249

GOVERNMENT: Presidential republic

LANGUAGES: English (official), Indigenous languages

MONEY: Liberian dollar

FUN FACT: Liberia was created as a country for freed Black people who were once enslaved in the United States.

LIBYA

LOCATION: Africa

CAPITAL: Tripoli

AREA: 647,180 square miles (1,676,198 sq km)

POPULATION ESTIMATE (MID-YEAR 2024): 7,361,263

GOVERNMENT: Transitional

LANGUAGES: Arabic (official), Italian, English, Tamazight

MONEY: Libyan dinar

FUN FACT: Two giant sand dunes in the Sahara—known as the Ubari and Murzuq sand seas—can be seen from space.

LIECHTENSTEIN

LOCATION: Europe

CAPITAL: Vaduz

AREA: 62 square miles (160 sq km)

POPULATION ESTIMATE (MID-YEAR 2024): 40,272

GOVERNMENT: Constitutional monarchy

LANGUAGES: German (official, Alemannic dialect)

MONEY: Swiss franc

FUN FACT: The prince of Liechtenstein lives in a castle that was built as a fort in the early 1200s.

LITHUANIA

LOCATION: Europe

CAPITAL: Vilnius

AREA: 25,207 square miles (65,286 sq km)

POPULATION ESTIMATE (MID-YEAR 2024): 2,835,340

GOVERNMENT: Semi-presidential republic

LANGUAGES: Lithuanian (official), Russian, Polish

MONEY: Euro

FUN FACT: More than 100,000 crosses and other religious icons cover the Hill of Crosses.

LUXEMBOURG

LOCATION: Europe

CAPITAL: Luxembourg

AREA: 998 square miles (2,586 sq km)

POPULATION ESTIMATE (MID-YEAR 2024): 682,815

GOVERNMENT: Constitutional monarchy

LANGUAGES: Luxembourgish, French, German (all official); Portuguese

MONEY: Euro

FUN FACT: The Bock Casemates are underground tunnels that were once used for defense and hiding places.

MADAGASCAR

LOCATION: Africa

CAPITAL: Antananarivo

AREA: 228,531 square miles (591,896 sq km)

POPULATION ESTIMATE (MID-YEAR 2024): 29,452,714

GOVERNMENT: Semi-presidential republic

LANGUAGES: Malagasy, French (both official); English

MONEY: Malagasy ariary

FUN FACT: Most animals here—including about 100 species of lemurs—live nowhere else but Madagascar.

MALAWI

LOCATION: Africa

CAPITAL: Lilongwe

AREA: 45,853 square miles (118,760 sq km)

POPULATION ESTIMATE (MID-YEAR 2024): 21,763,309

GOVERNMENT: Presidential republic

LANGUAGES: English (official), Chewa, other Indigenous languages

MONEY: Malawian kwacha

FUN FACT: An area of Malawi called Chongoni contains the most rock art in Central Africa.

MALAYSIA

LOCATION: Asia

CAPITAL: Kuala Lumpur

AREA: 127,752 square miles (330,877 sq km)

POPULATION ESTIMATE (MID-YEAR 2024): 34,564,810

GOVERNMENT: Constitutional monarchy

LANGUAGES: Bahasa Malaysia (official), English, Chinese, Tamil

MONEY: Ringgit

FUN FACT: Malaysia's *Rafflesia* is often called the corpse flower because of its stench.

MALDIVES

LOCATION: Asia

CAPITAL: Malé

AREA: 114 square miles (298 sq km)

POPULATION ESTIMATE (MID-YEAR 2024): 388,858

GOVERNMENT: Presidential republic

LANGUAGES: Dhivehi (official), English

MONEY: Rufiyaa

FUN FACT: The plankton-filled waters of the Maldives attract hundreds of whale sharks every year.

MALI

LOCATION: Africa

CAPITAL: Bamako

AREA: 479,242 square miles (1,241,238 sq km)

POPULATION ESTIMATE (MID-YEAR 2024): 21,990,607

GOVERNMENT: Semi-presidential republic

LANGUAGES: Bambara, Bobo, Bozo, and 10 other official languages; French

MONEY: CFA franc

FUN FACT: Mansa Musa, who ruled Mali in the 14th century, is thought to be the richest person ever.

MALTA

LOCATION: Europe

CAPITAL: Valletta

AREA: 122 square miles (315 sq km)

POPULATION ESTIMATE (MID-YEAR 2024): 518,231

GOVERNMENT: Parliamentary republic

LANGUAGES: Maltese, English (both official)

MONEY: Euro

FUN FACT: Traditionally, Malta fishers worked in boats painted red, yellow, and blue called *luzzijiet*.

MARSHALL ISLANDS

LOCATION: Oceania

CAPITAL: Majuro

AREA: 70 square miles (181 sq km)

POPULATION ESTIMATE (MID-YEAR 2024): 82,011

GOVERNMENT: Mixed presidential-parliamentary system (free association with the US)

LANGUAGES: Marshallese (official)

MONEY: US dollar

FUN FACT: The capital city of Majuro is an atoll of 64 islets. (An atoll is a coral island made from a reef surrounding a lagoon.)

MAURITANIA

LOCATION: Africa

CAPITAL: Nouakchott

AREA: 397,953 square miles (1,030,700 sq km)

POPULATION ESTIMATE (MID-YEAR 2024): 5,053,386

GOVERNMENT: Presidential republic

LANGUAGES: Arabic (official), Pular, Soninke, Wolof, French

MONEY: Ouguiya

FUN FACT: Though Mauritania is mostly desert, it has a savanna region with gazelles, ostriches, and hyenas.

MAURITIUS

LOCATION: Africa

CAPITAL: Port Louis

AREA: 775 square miles (2,007 sq km)

POPULATION ESTIMATE (MID-YEAR 2024): 1,310,504

GOVERNMENT: Parliamentary republic

LANGUAGES: English (official), Creole, Bhojpuri, French

MONEY: Mauritian rupee

FUN FACT: Mauritius is the only African country in which Hinduism is the dominant religion.

MEXICO

LOCATION: North America

CAPITAL: Mexico City

AREA: 758,445 square miles (1,964,375 sq km)

POPULATION ESTIMATE (MID-YEAR 2024): 130,739,927

GOVERNMENT: Federal presidential republic

LANGUAGES: Spanish (official), Indigenous languages

MONEY: Mexican peso

FUN FACT: The jaguar was sacred to ancient people living in what is now Mexico.

MICRONESIA, FEDERATED STATES OF

LOCATION: Oceania

CAPITAL: Palikir

AREA: 271 square miles (701 sq km)

POPULATION ESTIMATE (MID-YEAR 2024): 99,603

GOVERNMENT: Federal republic (free association with the US)

LANGUAGES: English (official), Chuukese, Kosrean, Pohnpeian, Yapese

MONEY: US dollar

FUN FACT: Found on Micronesia, the coconut crab can crush a coconut with its large, superstrong pincers.

MOLDOVA

LOCATION: Europe

CAPITAL: Chișinău

AREA: 13,067 square miles (33,843 sq km)

POPULATION ESTIMATE (MID-YEAR 2024): 3,599,528

GOVERNMENT: Parliamentary republic

LANGUAGES: Romanian (official), Moldovan, Russian

MONEY: Moldovan leu

FUN FACT: The horned animal on the country's flag is an aurochs, an extinct native ox.

MONACO

LOCATION: Europe

CAPITAL: Monaco

AREA: 0.8 square mile (2.1 sq km)

POPULATION ESTIMATE (MID-YEAR 2024): 31,813

GOVERNMENT: Constitutional monarchy

LANGUAGES: French (official), English, Italian, Monegasque

MONEY: Euro

FUN FACT: At the Monaco Grand Prix, race cars zoom through streets at up to 180 miles an hour (290 km/h).

MONGOLIA

LOCATION: Asia

CAPITAL: Ulaanbaatar

AREA: 603,953 square miles (1,564,241 sq km)

POPULATION ESTIMATE (MID-YEAR 2024): 3,504,207

GOVERNMENT: Semi-presidential republic

LANGUAGES: Mongolian (official), Turkic, Russian

MONEY: Togrog / tugrik

FUN FACT: The Kazakh people of Mongolia hunt foxes and other small animals with the help of golden eagles.

MONTENEGRO

LOCATION: Europe

CAPITAL: Podgorica

AREA: 5,360 square miles (13,883 sq km)

POPULATION ESTIMATE (MID-YEAR 2024): 599,849

GOVERNMENT: Parliamentary republic

LANGUAGES: Montenegrin (official), Serbian, Bosnian, Albanian

MONEY: Euro

FUN FACT: Montenegro means "black mountain" in Italian.

MOROCCO

LOCATION: Africa

CAPITAL: Rabat

AREA: 161,004 square miles (417,000 sq km)

POPULATION ESTIMATE (MID-YEAR 2024): 37,387,585

GOVERNMENT: Parliamentary constitutional monarchy

LANGUAGES: Arabic, Tamazight (both official); French

MONEY: Moroccan dirham

FUN FACT: Many people live in the historical center of Fès—but no cars are allowed.

MOZAMBIQUE

LOCATION: Africa

CAPITAL: Maputo

AREA: 308,641 square miles (799,380 sq km)

POPULATION ESTIMATE (MID-YEAR 2024): 33,350,954

GOVERNMENT: Presidential republic

LANGUAGES: Portuguese (official), Makhuwa, Tsonga, other Mozambican languages

MONEY: Metical

FUN FACT: Lake Nyasa (the portion of Lake Malawi that's in Mozambique) has hundreds of species of fish.

MYANMAR (BURMA)

LOCATION: Asia

CAPITAL: Nay Pyi Taw

AREA: 261,217 square miles (676,553 sq km)

POPULATION ESTIMATE (MID-YEAR 2024): 57,527,139

GOVERNMENT: Military government

LANGUAGES: Burmese (official), minority languages

MONEY: Kyat

FUN FACT: Pwe is a popular art form in Myanmar and features outdoor human or puppet shows about the Buddha.

NAMIBIA

LOCATION: Africa

CAPITAL: Windhoek

AREA: 318,259 square miles (824,292 sq km)

POPULATION ESTIMATE (MID-YEAR 2024): 2,803,660

GOVERNMENT: Presidential republic

LANGUAGES: English (official), Oshiwambo languages, Nama / Damara, Kavango languages, Afrikaans

MONEY: Namibian dollar

FUN FACT: Only about 7,500 to 10,000 cheetahs are left in the wild, and 2,500 of them live in Namibia.

NAURU

LOCATION: Oceania

CAPITAL: Yaren District (unofficial)

AREA: 8 square miles (21 sq km)

POPULATION ESTIMATE (MID-YEAR 2024): 9,892

GOVERNMENT: Parliamentary republic

LANGUAGES: Nauruan (official), English

MONEY: Australian dollar

FUN FACT: This island has no rivers or streams. Water is shipped in, and people collect rain from their roofs.

NEPAL

LOCATION: Asia

CAPITAL: Kathmandu

AREA: 56,827 square miles (147,181 sq km)

POPULATION ESTIMATE (MID-YEAR 2024): 31,122,387

GOVERNMENT: Federal parliamentary republic

LANGUAGES: Nepali (official), Maithali, Bhojpuri, Tharu, Tamang

MONEY: Nepalese rupee

FUN FACT: Nepal has the greatest altitude change of any country in the world, from sea level to the peak of Mount Everest.

NETHERLANDS

LOCATION: Europe

CAPITAL: Amsterdam

AREA: 14,030 square miles (36,337 sq km)

POPULATION ESTIMATE (MID-YEAR 2024): 17,772,378

GOVERNMENT: Parliamentary constitutional monarchy

LANGUAGES: Dutch (official), Frisian (official in Fryslan)

MONEY: Euro

FUN FACT: The Dutch produce 4.2 billion tulips every year, the most in the world.

NEW ZEALAND

LOCATION: Oceania

CAPITAL: Wellington

AREA: 102,587 square miles (265,700 sq km)

POPULATION ESTIMATE (MID-YEAR 2024): 5,161,211

GOVERNMENT: Parliamentary democracy under a constitutional monarchy

LANGUAGES: English, Maori, New Zealand Sign Language (all official)

MONEY: New Zealand dollar

FUN FACT: New Zealand has no snakes on land. But beachgoers have spotted sea snakes near the shores.

NICARAGUA

LOCATION: Central America

CAPITAL: Managua

AREA: 50,337 square miles (130,373 sq km)

POPULATION ESTIMATE (MID-YEAR 2024): 6,676,948

GOVERNMENT: Presidential republic

LANGUAGES: Spanish (official), Indigenous languages

MONEY: Córdoba

FUN FACT: Lake Nicaragua is fresh water, but ocean creatures like sharks live in its waters.

NIGER

LOCATION: Africa

CAPITAL: Niamey

AREA: 489,189 square miles (1,267,000 sq km)

POPULATION ESTIMATE (MID-YEAR 2024): 26,342,784

GOVERNMENT: Transitional military government

LANGUAGES: French (official), Hausa, Zarma, other Indigenous languages

MONEY: CFA franc

FUN FACT: Agadez Mosque has an 88-foot (27-m) minaret made entirely out of mud bricks.

NIGERIA

LOCATION: Africa

CAPITAL: Abuja

AREA: 356,667 square miles (923,768 sq km)

POPULATION ESTIMATE (MID-YEAR 2024): 236,747,130

GOVERNMENT: Federal presidential republic

LANGUAGES: English (official), Hausa, Yoruba, Igbo, Fulani, 500+ other Indigenous languages

MONEY: Naira

FUN FACT: Nigeria's film industry is called "Nollywood" and produces about 2,500 movies every year.

NORTH MACEDONIA

LOCATION: Europe

CAPITAL: Skopje

AREA: 9,821 square miles (25,436 sq km)

POPULATION ESTIMATE (MID-YEAR 2024): 2,135,622

GOVERNMENT: Parliamentary republic

LANGUAGES: Macedonian, Albanian (both official); Turkish, Romani

MONEY: Macedonian denar

FUN FACT: Bordering North Macedonia, Lake Ohrid is the deepest lake in the Balkans region.

NORWAY

LOCATION: Europe

CAPITAL: Oslo

AREA: 148,499 square miles (384,482 sq km)

POPULATION ESTIMATE (MID-YEAR 2024): 5,509,733

GOVERNMENT: Parliamentary constitutional monarchy

LANGUAGES: Bokmal Norwegian, Nynorsk Norwegian (both official); Sami (locally official)

MONEY: Norwegian krone

FUN FACT: Archaeologists found 1,200-year-old "god house" remains, built to worship Norse gods such as Thor.

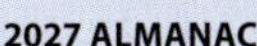

OMAN

LOCATION: Middle East

CAPITAL: Muscat

AREA: 119,498 square miles (309,500 sq km)

POPULATION ESTIMATE (MID-YEAR 2024): 3,901,992

GOVERNMENT: Monarchy

LANGUAGES: Arabic (official), English, Baluchi, Swahili, Urdu, Indian dialects

MONEY: Omani rial

FUN FACT: The weekend in Oman is Friday and Saturday instead of Saturday and Sunday.

PAKISTAN

LOCATION: Asia

CAPITAL: Islamabad

AREA: 307,373 square miles (796,096 sq km)

POPULATION ESTIMATE (MID-YEAR 2024): 252,363,571

GOVERNMENT: Federal parliamentary republic

LANGUAGES: English, Urdu (both official); Punjabi, Pashto, Sindhi

MONEY: Pakistani rupee

FUN FACT: Pakistan produces 70 percent of the world's soccer balls, called footballs in most of the world.

PALAU

LOCATION: Oceania

CAPITAL: Melekeok

AREA: 188 square miles (488 sq km)

POPULATION ESTIMATE (MID-YEAR 2024): 21,864

GOVERNMENT: Presidential republic in free association with the US

LANGUAGES: English (official), Palauan (official on most islands), Filipino

MONEY: US dollar

FUN FACT: Visitors must sign the "Palau Pledge" to promise they'll respect the nation's nature and culture.

PANAMA

LOCATION: Central America

CAPITAL: Panama City

AREA: 29,081 square miles (75,320 sq km)

POPULATION ESTIMATE (MID-YEAR 2024): 4,470,241

GOVERNMENT: Presidential republic

LANGUAGES: Spanish (official), Indigenous languages

MONEY: Balboa

FUN FACT: Coiba Island National Park is a former prison colony where divers can spot hammerheads and whales.

PAPUA NEW GUINEA

LOCATION: Oceania

CAPITAL: Port Moresby

AREA: 178,354 square miles (461,937 sq km)

POPULATION ESTIMATE (MID-YEAR 2024): 10,046,233

GOVERNMENT: Parliamentary democracy under a constitutional monarchy

LANGUAGES: Tok Pisin, English, Hiri Motu (all official); some 839 Indigenous languages

MONEY: Kina

FUN FACT: The number of Indigenous languages spoken here make up about 12 percent of the world's languages.

PARAGUAY

LOCATION: South America

CAPITAL: Asunción

AREA: 157,047 square miles (406,752 sq km)

POPULATION ESTIMATE (MID-YEAR 2024): 7,522,549

GOVERNMENT: Presidential republic

LANGUAGES: Spanish, Guarani (both official)

MONEY: Guarani

FUN FACT: Paraguay doesn't border an ocean—but it still has a navy that protects the country's riverways.

PERU

LOCATION: South America

CAPITAL: Lima

AREA: 496,171 square miles (1,285,082 sq km)

POPULATION ESTIMATE (MID-YEAR 2024): 32,600,249

GOVERNMENT: Presidential republic

LANGUAGES: Spanish, Quechua, Aymara (all official); other Indigenous languages

MONEY: Nuevo sol

FUN FACT: Some believe that Machu Picchu, an ancient structure in the Andes mountains, served as a vacation home for the Inca royal family.

PHILIPPINES

LOCATION: Asia

CAPITAL: Manila

AREA: 115,830 square miles (300,000 sq km)

POPULATION ESTIMATE (MID-YEAR 2024): 118,277,063

GOVERNMENT: Presidential republic

LANGUAGES: Filipino (based on Tagalog), English (both official); many regional languages and dialects

MONEY: Philippine peso

FUN FACT: Taal Volcano is known as a "decade volcano" because of its huge potential for destruction.

POLAND

LOCATION: Europe

CAPITAL: Warsaw

AREA: 120,423 square miles (311,895 sq km)

POPULATION ESTIMATE (MID-YEAR 2024): 38,746,310

GOVERNMENT: Parliamentary republic

LANGUAGES: Polish (official), many minority languages

MONEY: Zloty

FUN FACT: Warsaw's historic center was rebuilt after being destroyed during World War II.

PORTUGAL

LOCATION: Europe

CAPITAL: Lisbon

AREA: 35,608 square miles (92,225 sq km)

POPULATION ESTIMATE (MID-YEAR 2024): 10,207,177

GOVERNMENT: Semi-presidential republic

LANGUAGES: Portuguese, Mirandese (both official)

MONEY: Euro

FUN FACT: At midnight on New Year's Eve, many people here make 12 wishes with 12 raisins, one for each month.

QATAR

LOCATION: Middle East

CAPITAL: Doha

AREA: 4,493 square miles (11,637 sq km)

POPULATION ESTIMATE (MID-YEAR 2024): 2,552,088

GOVERNMENT: Constitutional monarchy

LANGUAGES: Arabic (official), English

MONEY: Qatari riyal

FUN FACT: The second Tuesday in February is National Sport Day in Qatar to encourage people to stay healthy.

ROMANIA

LOCATION: Europe

CAPITAL: Bucharest

AREA: 92,045 square miles (238,397 sq km)

POPULATION ESTIMATE (MID-YEAR 2024): 18,148,155

GOVERNMENT: Semi-presidential republic

LANGUAGES: Romanian (official), Hungarian, Romani

MONEY: Romanian leu

FUN FACT: A 131-foot-tall (40-m) stone face of a 2,000-year-old king looms over the Danube River in Romania.

RUSSIA

LOCATION: Europe and Asia

CAPITAL: Moscow

AREA: 6,592,812 square miles (17,075,400 sq km)

POPULATION ESTIMATE (MID-YEAR 2024): 140,820,810

GOVERNMENT: Semi-presidential federation

LANGUAGES: Russian (official), Tatar, Chechen

MONEY: Russian ruble

FUN FACT: Russia is just 55 miles (89 km) from Alaska across the Bering Strait.

RWANDA

LOCATION: Africa

CAPITAL: Kigali

AREA: 10,169 square miles (26,338 sq km)

POPULATION ESTIMATE (MID-YEAR 2024): 13,623,302

GOVERNMENT: Presidential republic

LANGUAGES: Kinyarwanda, French, English, Swahili (all official)

MONEY: Rwandan franc

FUN FACT: More than half of the world's endangered mountain gorillas live in the Virunga Mountains bordering Rwanda.

SAINT KITTS AND NEVIS

LOCATION: Caribbean

CAPITAL: Basseterre

AREA: 102 square miles (263 sq km)

POPULATION ESTIMATE (MID-YEAR 2024): 55,133

GOVERNMENT: Federal parliamentary democracy under a constitutional monarchy

LANGUAGES: English (official)

MONEY: Eastern Caribbean dollar

FUN FACT: If you live on Saint Kitts, you're a "Kittian." If you live on Nevis, you're a "Nevisian."

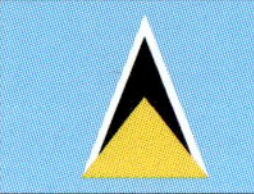

SAINT LUCIA

LOCATION: Caribbean

CAPITAL: Castries

AREA: 238 square miles (616 sq km)

POPULATION ESTIMATE (MID-YEAR 2024): 168,038

GOVERNMENT: Parliamentary democracy under a constitutional monarchy

LANGUAGES: English (official), Saint Lucian Creole

MONEY: Eastern Caribbean dollar

FUN FACT: Some think Edward Teach—also known as the pirate Blackbeard—stashed his treasure here.

SAINT VINCENT AND THE GRENADINES

LOCATION: Caribbean

CAPITAL: Kingstown

AREA: 150 square miles (388 sq km)

POPULATION ESTIMATE (MID-YEAR 2024): 100,647

GOVERNMENT: Parliamentary democracy under a constitutional monarchy

LANGUAGES: English (official), Vincentian Creole English, French patois

MONEY: Eastern Caribbean dollar

FUN FACT: Brought here to feed enslaved people, the breadfruit is now a symbol of the formerly enslaved people's history and freedom.

SAMOA

LOCATION: Oceania

CAPITAL: Apia

AREA: 1,093 square miles (2,830 sq km)

POPULATION ESTIMATE (MID-YEAR 2024): 208,853

GOVERNMENT: Parliamentary republic

LANGUAGES: Samoan (Polynesian), English (both official)

MONEY: Tala

FUN FACT: Many Samoans get a traditional leg tattoo, or *tatau*, to show that one is becoming an adult.

SAN MARINO

LOCATION: Europe

CAPITAL: San Marino

AREA: 24 square miles (61 sq km)

POPULATION ESTIMATE (MID-YEAR 2024): 35,095

GOVERNMENT: Parliamentary republic

LANGUAGES: Italian (official)

MONEY: Euro

FUN FACT: San Marino sits on the slopes of Mount Titano, which protected the country from invaders.

SÃO TOMÉ AND PRÍNCIPE

LOCATION: Africa

CAPITAL: São Tomé

AREA: 386 square miles (1,001 sq km)

POPULATION ESTIMATE (MID-YEAR 2024): 223,561

GOVERNMENT: Semi-presidential republic

LANGUAGES: Portuguese (official), Forro, Cabo Verdian, French, Angolar, English

MONEY: Dobra

FUN FACT: The Great Canine is a half-mile-tall (663-m) tower of hardened magma from an extinct volcano.

SAUDI ARABIA

LOCATION: Middle East

CAPITAL: Riyadh

AREA: 829,995 square miles (2,149,690 sq km)

POPULATION ESTIMATE (MID-YEAR 2024): 36,544,431

GOVERNMENT: Monarchy

LANGUAGES: Arabic (official)

MONEY: Saudi riyal

FUN FACT: Every year, over two million Muslims perform the hajj, a pilgrimage to the sacred city of Mecca.

SENEGAL

LOCATION: Africa

CAPITAL: Dakar

AREA: 75,951 square miles (196,712 sq km)

POPULATION ESTIMATE (MID-YEAR 2024): 18,847,519

GOVERNMENT: Presidential republic

LANGUAGES: French (official), Wolof, Pulaar, Jola, Mandinka

MONEY: CFA franc

FUN FACT: Taxi drivers often attach long clumps of horse hair to their cars to bring them good fortune.

SERBIA

LOCATION: Europe

CAPITAL: Belgrade

AREA: 29,957 square miles (77,589 sq km)

POPULATION ESTIMATE (MID-YEAR 2024): 6,652,212

GOVERNMENT: Parliamentary republic

LANGUAGES: Serbian (official), Hungarian, Bosnian

MONEY: Serbian dinar

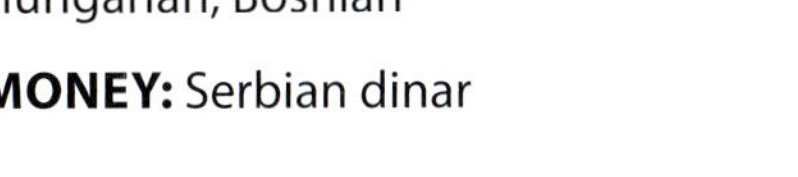

FUN FACT: Pule is a Serbian cheese made from donkey and goat milk. A pound usually costs about $575.

SEYCHELLES

LOCATION: Africa

CAPITAL: Victoria

AREA: 172 square miles (446 sq km)

POPULATION ESTIMATE (MID-YEAR 2024): 98,187

GOVERNMENT: Presidential republic

LANGUAGES: Seychellois Creole, English, French (all official)

MONEY: Seychelles rupee

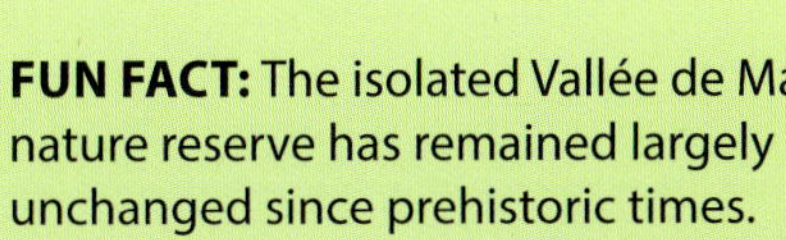

FUN FACT: The isolated Vallée de Mai nature reserve has remained largely unchanged since prehistoric times.

SIERRA LEONE

LOCATION: Africa

CAPITAL: Freetown

AREA: 28,158 square miles (72,929 sq km)

POPULATION ESTIMATE (MID-YEAR 2024): 9,121,049

GOVERNMENT: Presidential republic

LANGUAGES: English (official), Mende, Temne, Krio

MONEY: Leone

FUN FACT: Freetown was founded as a refuge for formerly enslaved people from British colonies and other empires.

SINGAPORE

LOCATION: Asia

CAPITAL: Singapore

AREA: 284 square miles (735 sq km)

POPULATION ESTIMATE (MID-YEAR 2024): 6,028,459

GOVERNMENT: Parliamentary republic

LANGUAGES: English, Chinese (Mandarin and other dialects), Malay, Tamil (all official)

MONEY: Singapore dollar

FUN FACT: Throughout the capital, clusters of tiny outdoor stands cook and sell cheap and fast food like minced pork noodles.

SLOVAKIA

LOCATION: Europe

CAPITAL: Bratislava

AREA: 18,932 square miles (49,034 sq km)

POPULATION ESTIMATE (MID-YEAR 2024): 5,563,649

GOVERNMENT: Parliamentary republic

LANGUAGES: Slovak (official), Hungarian, Roma

MONEY: Euro

FUN FACT: The *fujara* is a six-foot-long (2-m) flutelike instrument traditionally played by Slovak shepherds.

SLOVENIA

LOCATION: Europe

CAPITAL: Ljubljana

AREA: 7,827 square miles (20,271 sq km)

POPULATION ESTIMATE (MID-YEAR 2024): 2,158,404

GOVERNMENT: Parliamentary republic

LANGUAGES: Slovene (official), Croatian, Serbo-Croatian, Bosnian, Serbian

MONEY: Euro

FUN FACT: Slovenia's Škocjan Caves has an underground canyon river with plunging waterfalls.

SOLOMON ISLANDS

LOCATION: Oceania

CAPITAL: Honiara

AREA: 11,740 square miles (30,407 sq km)

POPULATION ESTIMATE (MID-YEAR 2024): 726,799

GOVERNMENT: Parliamentary democracy under a constitutional monarchy

LANGUAGES: English (official), Melanesian pidgin, some 120 Indigenous languages

MONEY: Solomon Islands dollar

FUN FACT: About 335 bird species have been observed on the Solomon Islands.

SOMALIA

LOCATION: Africa

CAPITAL: Mogadishu

AREA: 246,199 square miles (637,657 sq km)

POPULATION ESTIMATE (MID-YEAR 2024): 19,654,460

GOVERNMENT: Federal parliamentary republic

LANGUAGES: Somali, Arabic (both official); Italian, English

MONEY: Somali shilling

FUN FACT: Somalia has the longest coastline in Africa, stretching about 2,000 miles (3,330 km).

SOUTH AFRICA

LOCATION: Africa

CAPITAL: Pretoria (executive), Cape Town (legislative), Bloemfontein (judicial)

AREA: 471,356 square miles (1,220,813 sq km)

POPULATION ESTIMATE (MID-YEAR 2024): 60,442,647

GOVERNMENT: Parliamentary republic

LANGUAGES: Zulu, Xhosa, Afrikaans, Sepedi, Setswana, English, Sesotho, Tsonga, Swati, Tshivenda, Ndebele, South African sign language (all official)

MONEY: Rand

FUN FACT: South Africa is not snowy, but African penguins live along its coast and build nests in the sand.

SPAIN

LOCATION: Europe

CAPITAL: Madrid

AREA: 195,360 square miles (505,983 sq km)

POPULATION ESTIMATE (MID-YEAR 2024): 47,280,433

GOVERNMENT: Parliamentary constitutional monarchy

LANGUAGES: Castilian Spanish (official), Catalan, Galician, Basque, Aranese

MONEY: Euro

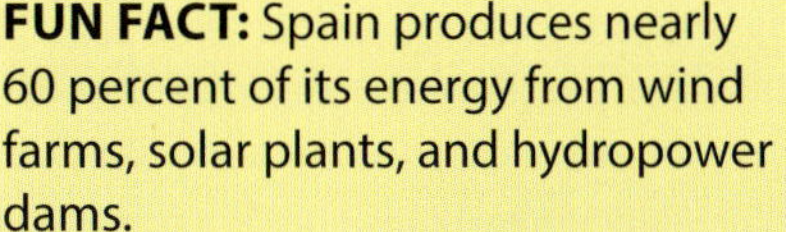

FUN FACT: Spain produces nearly 60 percent of its energy from wind farms, solar plants, and hydropower dams.

SRI LANKA

LOCATION: Asia

CAPITAL: Colombo (executive, judicial), Sri Jayewardenepura Kotte (legislative)

AREA: 25,332 square miles (65,610 sq km)

POPULATION ESTIMATE (MID-YEAR 2024): 21,982,608

GOVERNMENT: Presidential republic

LANGUAGES: Sinhala, Tamil (both official); English

MONEY: Sri Lankan rupee

FUN FACT: About 7,000 Sri Lankan elephants live in the island's forests.

SUDAN

LOCATION: Africa

CAPITAL: Khartoum

AREA: 710,689 square miles (1,840,687 sq km)

POPULATION ESTIMATE (MID-YEAR 2024): 50,467,278

GOVERNMENT: Presidential republic

LANGUAGES: Arabic, English (both official); Nubian, Ta Bedawie, Fur

MONEY: Sudanese pound

FUN FACT: Sudan has more than twice as many pyramids as Egypt.

SOUTH SUDAN

LOCATION: Africa

CAPITAL: Juba

AREA: 248,775 square miles (644,329 sq km)

POPULATION ESTIMATE (MID-YEAR 2024): 12,703,714

GOVERNMENT: Presidential republic

LANGUAGES: English (official), Arabic, other Indigenous languages

MONEY: South Sudan pound

FUN FACT: Nearly six million antelope migrate through South Sudan's Boma and Badingilo National Parks.

SURINAME

LOCATION: South America

CAPITAL: Paramaribo

AREA: 63,251 square miles (163,820 sq km)

POPULATION ESTIMATE (MID-YEAR 2024): 646,758

GOVERNMENT: Presidential republic

LANGUAGES: Dutch (official), English, Surinamese, Caribbean Hindustani, Javanese

MONEY: Surinamese dollar

FUN FACT: Working with Indigenous people, scientists discovered 60 new species in a remote forest in 2013.

SWEDEN

LOCATION: Europe

CAPITAL: Stockholm

AREA: 172,751 square miles (447,425 sq km)

POPULATION ESTIMATE (MID-YEAR 2024): 10,589,835

GOVERNMENT: Parliamentary constitutional monarchy

LANGUAGES: Swedish, Finnish, Sami, Romani, Yiddish, Meankieli (all official)

MONEY: Swedish krona

FUN FACT: In some parts of northern Sweden, the sun never sets for about four to six weeks.

SWITZERLAND

LOCATION: Europe

CAPITAL: Bern

AREA: 15,942 square miles (41,291 sq km)

POPULATION ESTIMATE (MID-YEAR 2024): 8,860,574

GOVERNMENT: Federal republic

LANGUAGES: German / Swiss German, French, Italian, Romansh (all official); English

MONEY: Swiss franc

FUN FACT: Cows, dogs, and other domestic animals are protected by law in Switzerland.

SYRIA

LOCATION: Middle East

CAPITAL: Damascus

AREA: 71,480 square miles (185,180 sq km)

POPULATION ESTIMATE (MID-YEAR 2024): 23,865,423

GOVERNMENT: Transitional government

LANGUAGES: Arabic (official), Kurdish, Armenian, Aramaic, Circassian, French, English

MONEY: Syrian pound

FUN FACT: The world's first-known library was found in the 5,000-year-old city of Ebla.

TAJIKISTAN

LOCATION: Asia

CAPITAL: Dushanbe

AREA: 54,595 square miles (141,400 sq km)

POPULATION ESTIMATE (MID-YEAR 2024): 10,394,063

GOVERNMENT: Presidential republic

LANGUAGES: Tajik (official), Uzbek, Kyrgyz, Russian

MONEY: Somoni

FUN FACT: Lake Iskanderkul is Turkish for Lake Alexander the Great, named after the historic ruler.

TANZANIA

LOCATION: Africa

CAPITAL: Dodoma

AREA: 365,058 square miles (945,500 sq km)

POPULATION ESTIMATE (MID-YEAR 2024): 67,189,599

GOVERNMENT: Presidential republic

LANGUAGES: Swahili, English (both official); Arabic, many local languages

MONEY: Tanzanian shilling

FUN FACT: Made up of three inactive volcanoes, Mount Kilimanjaro is Africa's tallest mountain.

THAILAND

LOCATION: Asia

CAPITAL: Bangkok

AREA: 198,123 square miles (513,140 sq km)

POPULATION ESTIMATE (MID-YEAR 2024): 69,920,998

GOVERNMENT: Constitutional monarchy

LANGUAGES: Thai (official), English

MONEY: Baht

FUN FACT: The formal name of Bangkok, Thailand's capital, has 168 letters.

TOGO

LOCATION: Africa

CAPITAL: Lomé

AREA: 21,853 square miles (56,600 sq km)

POPULATION ESTIMATE (MID-YEAR 2024): 8,917,994

GOVERNMENT: Presidential republic

LANGUAGES: French (official), Ewe, Mina, Kabye, Dagomba

MONEY: CFA franc

FUN FACT: Teen boys who are members of the Kabyè people compete in wrestling matches to show strength and courage.

TONGA

LOCATION: Oceania

CAPITAL: Nuku'alofa

AREA: 251 square miles (650 sq km)

POPULATION ESTIMATE (MID-YEAR 2024): 104,889

GOVERNMENT: Constitutional monarchy

LANGUAGES: Tongan, English (both official)

MONEY: Pa'anga

FUN FACT: Nearly 100-foot-tall (30-m) sprays of water shoot out at the Mapu'a 'a Vaea Blowholes.

TRINIDAD AND TOBAGO

LOCATION: Caribbean

CAPITAL: Port of Spain

AREA: 1,980 square miles (5,128 sq km)

POPULATION ESTIMATE (MID-YEAR 2024): 1,408,966

GOVERNMENT: Parliamentary republic

LANGUAGES: English (official), Creole English, Caribbean Hindustani, Creole French, Spanish, Chinese

MONEY: Trinidad and Tobago dollar

FUN FACT: The largest-known single brain coral—a giant coral with brain-like ridges—is found in the waters off Trinidad and Tobago.

TUNISIA

LOCATION: Africa

CAPITAL: Tunis

AREA: 63,170 square miles (163,610 sq km)

POPULATION ESTIMATE (MID-YEAR 2024): 12,048,847

GOVERNMENT: Parliamentary republic

LANGUAGES: Arabic (official), French, Tamazight

MONEY: Tunisian dinar

FUN FACT: Tunisia boasts the biggest Roman colosseum in Africa. It could hold 35,000 spectators.

TURKEY (TÜRKIYE)

LOCATION: Europe and Asia

CAPITAL: Ankara

AREA: 297,144 square miles (769,604 sq km)

POPULATION ESTIMATE (MID-YEAR 2024): 84,119,531

GOVERNMENT: Presidential republic

LANGUAGES: Turkish (official), Kurdish

MONEY: Turkish lira

FUN FACT: Nearly all of Turkey is on the continent of Asia, but a sliver of it is in Europe.

TURKMENISTAN

LOCATION: Asia

CAPITAL: Ashgabat

AREA: 189,656 square miles (491,210 sq km)

POPULATION ESTIMATE (MID-YEAR 2024): 5,744,151

GOVERNMENT: Presidential republic

LANGUAGES: Turkmen (official), Russian, Uzbek

MONEY: Turkmenistani manat

FUN FACT: Local farmers have been cultivating melons in Turkmenistan's valleys for hundreds of years.

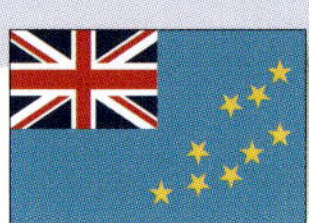

TUVALU

LOCATION: Oceania

CAPITAL: Funafuti

AREA: 10 square miles (26 sq km)

POPULATION ESTIMATE (MID-YEAR 2024): 11,733

GOVERNMENT: Parliamentary democracy under a constitutional monarchy

LANGUAGES: Tuvaluan, English (both official); Samoan, Kiribati

MONEY: Tuvaluan dollar or Australian dollar

FUN FACT: The yellow stars on Tuvalu's flag represent the country's atolls and islands.

UGANDA

LOCATION: Africa

CAPITAL: Kampala

AREA: 93,264 square miles (241,553 sq km)

POPULATION ESTIMATE (MID-YEAR 2024): 49,283,041

GOVERNMENT: Presidential republic

LANGUAGES: English, Swahili (both official); Luganda, other Niger-Congo languages, Nilo-Saharan languages, Arabic

MONEY: Ugandan shilling

FUN FACT: Lake Victoria, also known as Victoria Nyanza and other Indigenous names, is Africa's biggest lake.

UKRAINE

LOCATION: Europe

CAPITAL: Kyiv

AREA: 233,030 square miles (603,549 sq km)

POPULATION ESTIMATE (MID-YEAR 2024): 35,661,826

GOVERNMENT: Semi-presidential republic

LANGUAGES: Ukrainian (official), Russian

MONEY: Hryvnia

FUN FACT: Easter eggs in Ukraine are called *pysanky* and are often decorated with complex geometric designs.

UNITED ARAB EMIRATES

LOCATION: Middle East

CAPITAL: Abu Dhabi

AREA: 27,422 square miles (71,024 sq km)

POPULATION ESTIMATE (MID-YEAR 2024): 10,032,213

GOVERNMENT: Federation of monarchies

LANGUAGES: Arabic (official), English, Hindi, Malayalam, Urdu

MONEY: Emirati dirhams

FUN FACT: Palm Jumeirah is a series of human-made islands that look like a giant palm tree from the air.

UNITED KINGDOM

LOCATION: Europe

CAPITAL: London

AREA: 93,629 square miles (242,500 sq km)

POPULATION ESTIMATE (MID-YEAR 2024): 68,459,055

GOVERNMENT: Parliamentary constitutional monarchy

LANGUAGES: English (official), Scots Gaelic (official in Scotland), Welsh (official in Wales), Scots, Irish, Cornish

MONEY: British pound

FUN FACT: Some believe the giant, circular Stonehenge was a calendar to track the sun's movements.

UNITED STATES

LOCATION: North America

CAPITAL: Washington, DC

AREA: 3,796,742 square miles (9,833,517 sq km)

POPULATION ESTIMATE (MID-YEAR 2024): 336,482,168

GOVERNMENT: Constitutional federal republic

LANGUAGES: English, Spanish, Chinese

MONEY: US dollar

FUN FACT: The world's first national park was Yellowstone, established in 1872 by President Ulysses S. Grant.

URUGUAY

LOCATION: South America

CAPITAL: Montevideo

AREA: 74,655 square miles (193,356 sq km)

POPULATION ESTIMATE (MID-YEAR 2024): 3,451,805

GOVERNMENT: Presidential republic

LANGUAGES: Spanish (official)

MONEY: Uruguayan peso

FUN FACT: Uruguay provides every student ages 6 to 15 with a laptop and wireless Internet connections at their schools.

UZBEKISTAN

LOCATION: Asia

CAPITAL: Tashkent

AREA: 173,348 square miles (448,971 sq km)

POPULATION ESTIMATE (MID-YEAR 2024): 36,520,593

GOVERNMENT: Presidential republic

LANGUAGES: Uzbek (official), Russian, Tajik

MONEY: Uzbekistani som

FUN FACT: Made with lamb or beef, *plov* is the country's national dish.

VANUATU

LOCATION: Oceania

CAPITAL: Port-Vila

AREA: 4,742 square miles (12,281 sq km)

POPULATION ESTIMATE (MID-YEAR 2024): 318,007

GOVERNMENT: Parliamentary republic

LANGUAGES: Bislama, English, French (all official); over 100 Indigenous languages

MONEY: Vatu

FUN FACT: Bungee jumping is thought to have been inspired by the Vanuatuan sport of land diving.

VATICAN CITY (HOLY SEE)

LOCATION: Europe

CAPITAL: Vatican City

AREA: 0.17 square mile (0.44 sq km)

POPULATION ESTIMATE (MID-YEAR 2024): 1,000 (2022 est)

GOVERNMENT: Ecclesiastical

LANGUAGES: Italian, Latin, French

MONEY: Euro

FUN FACT: The world's smallest country, Vatican City is entirely inside Rome, the capital of Italy.

VENEZUELA

LOCATION: South America

CAPITAL: Caracas

AREA: 353,839 square miles (916,445 sq km)

POPULATION ESTIMATE (MID-YEAR 2024): 31,250,306

GOVERNMENT: Federal presidential republic

LANGUAGES: Spanish (official), Indigenous languages

MONEY: Bolivar

FUN FACT: Right after dusk about 300 days a year, Catatumbo lightning strikes up to 28 times a minute for about 9 hours a day.

VIETNAM

LOCATION: Asia

CAPITAL: Hanoi

AREA: 127,932 square miles (331,345 sq km)

POPULATION ESTIMATE (MID-YEAR 2024): 105,758,975

GOVERNMENT: Communist state

LANGUAGES: Vietnamese (official), English, French, Chinese, Khmer

MONEY: Dong

FUN FACT: A cave called Hang Son Doong is so big that you could fly a jet plane through some of its passages.

YEMEN

LOCATION: Middle East

CAPITAL: Sanaa

AREA: 175,676 square miles (455,000 sq km)

POPULATION ESTIMATE (MID-YEAR 2024): 33,737,887

GOVERNMENT: Transitional

LANGUAGES: Arabic (official)

MONEY: Yemeni rial

FUN FACT: The unique dragon's blood tree grows only on a Yemeni island.

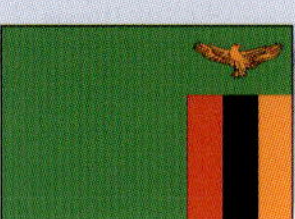

ZAMBIA

LOCATION: Africa

CAPITAL: Lusaka

AREA: 290,583 square miles (752,612 sq km)

POPULATION ESTIMATE (MID-YEAR 2024): 20,799,116

GOVERNMENT: Presidential republic

LANGUAGES: English (official), Bemba, Nyanja, Tonga

MONEY: Zambian kwacha

FUN FACT: People can swim to the edge of Victoria Falls (or Mosi-oa-Tunya in one Indigenous language).

ZIMBABWE

LOCATION: Africa

CAPITAL: Harare

AREA: 150,871 square miles (390,757 sq km)

POPULATION ESTIMATE (MID-YEAR 2024): 17,150,352

GOVERNMENT: Presidential republic

LANGUAGES: Shona, Ndebele, English, 13 minority languages (all official)

MONEY: Zimbabwe gold

FUN FACT: Victoria Falls straddles the border between Zimbabwe and Zambia.

Physical globes and maps use colors and textures to show natural features. These three globes (from left: North and South America, Europe and Africa, and Asia) represent grassy areas in green, deserts in brown, mountainous areas in brown, rocky textures, and oceans in blue. (Darker blue signals deeper waters.)

25 Fast Facts

Gobble up these tidbits about food around the world.

1 Venezuelan families gather during Christmas to make *hallacas*, a type of tamale whose recipe is passed down through generations.

2 The red tomatoes, white mozzarella cheese, and green basil in Italy's traditional margherita pizza reminds many people of the colors in that country's flag.

3 Many people in Japan celebrate the winter solstice, called Toji, by eating pumpkin for good luck.

4 Grown in countries like Indonesia and Malaysia, durian is a fruit that's so stinky, it's banned on some trains and buses in Singapore.

5 People in the United States often eat turkey on Thanksgiving, but the Native Americans and Puritans who dined together in 1621 likely ate deer and shellfish.

7 In Jamaica, people often eat curried chicken stew in coconut milk for breakfast.

8 *Räksmörgås* is a classic open-faced sandwich in Sweden that has peeled shrimp topped with mayonnaise and egg.

9 The Canadian comfort dish of french fries and cheese curds in gravy is called poutine, which is slang for "mess" in the local French language that many speak.

10 Injera is a flat, spongy bread common in Ethiopia that's used as both a plate that food is topped on, and a utensil to pick up the food.

11 People from Finland and Netherlands drink more coffee than anyone else in the world.

12 South Korean moviegoers might snack on dried cuttlefish; in China, it's salted dried plums.

6 Friends and family in countries like Lebanon share *mezze*, a collection of small dishes like hummus, stuffed grape leaves (often called dolmas), and an eggplant dip called baba ghanoush.

13 Pineapples, which are indigenous to South America, don't grow on trees—they grow in stalky shrublike plants close to the ground.

14 Fried grasshoppers called *chapulines* can be a popcorn-like snack or a taco topping in Mexico.

15 Smoothies in India are called lassi; a popular kind is made by blending mango, yogurt, milk, and ice.

16 When people in Afghanistan and Iran started growing carrots more than 1,000 years ago, the veggies were likely purple and yellow, not orange.

17 Dough stuffed with different fillings is a staple all over the world. They include *jiaozi* in China, pierogi in Poland, *varenyky* in Ukraine, *manti* in Turkey, and dumplings in the United States.

18 Many dishes from Thailand blend sour, sweet, salty, bitter, and spicy flavors to bring harmony to the food.

19 Loudly slurping ramen (noodles) in Japan is not considered rude. Some believe it makes the dish taste better, and others are just in a hurry!

20 Cotton candy is called fairy floss in Australia.

21 Fried tarantula is a popular street food in Cambodia. (It's said to taste like crab!)

22 Originally grown in Southeast Asia, bananas are scientifically classified as berries.

23 People in Morocco often simmer chicken, beef, and fish stews in a tagine, a round, flat cooking vessel with a lid that looks like a tall, pointy hat. Tagine is also what the stew is called.

24 Many people in Spain don't eat dinner until 9 p.m. or later.

25 Made from lamb, pork, and beef, a hot dog in Iceland is called *pylsur*. It's often served with *remolaði*, a mayo-based sauce with pickles, vinegar, and onions.

Hot Spots

Test your geography smarts about places around the world with this fun quiz.

1 Which country is the biggest by land area?

A. United States
B. Canada
C. Russia
D. China

2 How many countries does the world's longest mountain range, the South American Andes, stretch through?

A. Five
B. Six
C. Seven
D. Eight

3 If you were driving in a straight line to the peak of Nepal's Mount Everest, the world's tallest mountain, how far would you drive?

A. 1.8 miles (2.9 km)
B. 5.5 miles (8.8 km)
C. 10 miles (16 km)
D. 23.3 miles (37.5 km)

4 Flowing from Peru to Brazil, the Amazon River is the _______________.

A. largest river in the world
B. widest river in the world
C. deepest river in the world
D. calmest river in the world

5 More people live in which city than any other in the world?

A. Mexico City, Mexico
B. New York City, USA
C. New Delhi, India
D. Tokyo, Japan

6 With its maze of twisting tunnels, Mammoth Cave in the US state of _______________ is the longest cave system in the world.

A. Texas
B. Utah
C. Kentucky
D. Washington

7 Which country has the largest population of wild tigers in the world?

A. China
B. India
C. Russia
D. Vietnam

8 Which are the only three countries to be completely surrounded by one other country?

A. Portugal, Kenya, El Salvador
B. Laos, Luxembourg, Uruguay
C. Malawi, Belize, Iran
D. Lesotho, San Marino, Vatican City

9 **With a median age of 15 years old, _______________ has the youngest population in the world.**

A. Canada
B. Yemen
C. Argentina
D. Niger

10 **Which country has the most national parks?**

A. United States
B. Australia
C. Thailand
D. Israel

11 **What kind of tree is Hyperion, the world's tallest?**

A. Coast redwood, found in California's Redwood National Park
B. Mountain ash, found in Nevada's Ash Meadows National Refuge
C. Grand fir, found in Wyoming's Grand Teton National Park
D. Himalayan cypress, found in Florida's Big Cypress National Preserve

12 **Canada and the United States share what?**

A. Lake Superior, the world's biggest freshwater lake
B. The longest land border
C. Horse-riding police officers called Mounties
D. A and B

13 **The country of _______________ has 59 volcanoes that have been active since 1950, the most in the world.**

A. Indonesia
B. Chile
C. Japan
D. Papua New Guinea

14 **Which of the seven continents is the largest?**

A. Asia
B. Africa
C. Antarctica
D. North America

15 **Which is the world's largest desert, a region that gets very little precipitation?**

A. Sahara
B. Mohave
C. Antarctica
D. Gobi

16 **Which country is the only place in the world where sifakas, or lemurs, live in the wild?**

A. Vietnam
B. Madagascar
C. Japan
D. Greece

The "It" Lists

Popular names, greetings, and languages around the world

POPULAR BABY NAMES

COUNTRY	GIRLS	BOYS
France	Elea	Alois
India	Saanvi	Adhvik
Israel	Tamar	Ori
Japan	Honoka	Haruta
Mexico	Valentina	Santiago
Russia	Sofia	Artyom
Saudi Arabia	Sara	Mohammad
South Africa	Melokuhle	Lethabo
Turkey/Türkiye	Zeynep	Yusuf
United States	Olivia	Liam

MOST SPOKEN LANGUAGES

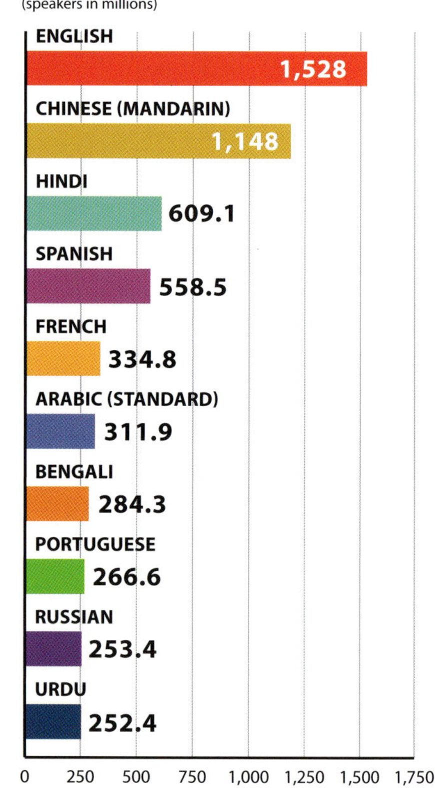

HOW TO SAY HELLO

COUNTRY	LANGUAGE	WORD	PRONUNCIATION
China	Mandarin	ni hao	nee how
Colombia	Spanish	hola	OH-lah
Germany	German	guten tag	GOO-ten tahg
Kenya	Swahili	jambo	JAHM-boh
India	Sanskrit	namaste	NAH-mah-stay
Israel	Hebrew	shalom	shah-LOHM
Pakistan	Arabic	salam	sah-lahm
Portugal	Portuguese	oi	oy
Ukraine	Ukrainian	pryvit	PRAY-vit
Turkey/Türkiye	Turkish	merhaba	MAR-hah-bah

Stop and Think

If you're traveling to another country, why might it be important to learn some of the language spoken there?

CHAPTER 8
ENVIRONMENT

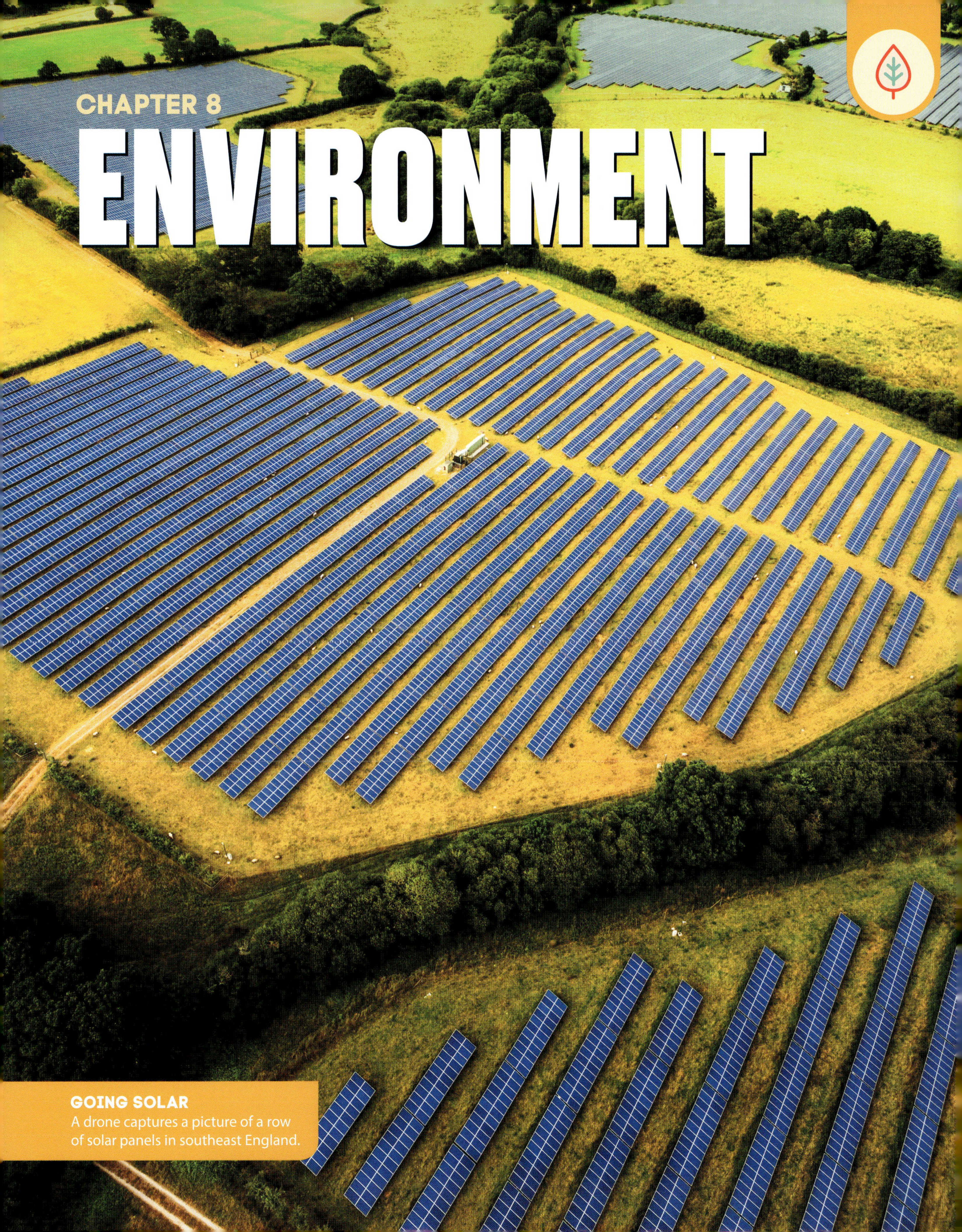

GOING SOLAR
A drone captures a picture of a row of solar panels in southeast England.

Word Play

You'll want to reuse these environmentally friendly definitions as much as possible!

BIODIVERSITY: the existence of different types of plants and animals within an environment

CARBON DIOXIDE (CO_2): a gas released by burning energy sources such as oil and coal, which can trap heat in the atmosphere

CARBON FOOTPRINT: the amount of carbon dioxide produced by a person in a year by using CO_2-emitting items such as gas-powered cars

CLIMATE: a large area's pattern of weather conditions over a very long time

CLIMATE CHANGE: long-term changes in the Earth's weather and climate patterns

COMPOST: a mix of organic waste, like paper or vegetables, that turns into nutrient-rich fertilizer after it decays

CONSERVATION: protecting and preserving natural resources

DEFORESTATION: cutting down so many trees in a forest that the ecosystem is harmed

ECOSYSTEM: the living and nonliving things that make up an environment and affect one another

ENDANGERED SPECIES: animals or plants at risk of extinction

ENDEMIC SPECIES: plants or animals that live in only one place

FOSSIL FUEL: an energy source like coal or oil that forms from the breakdown of prehistoric plants and animals

GREENHOUSE GASES: gases, such as CO_2, that trap heat in the atmosphere

GLOBAL WARMING: the increase of Earth's average temperature over a very long time

HABITAT: the natural home of a plant or animal, where it lives and grows

MICROPLASTICS: tiny, almost-invisible particles of plastic that have entered the ecosystem as a pollutant

NATURAL RESOURCE: things people can use that have been provided by nature, like water, wind, and energy from the sun

ORGANIC (AS IN COMPOST): something made up of carbon compounds that will eventually break down naturally (like plants)

ORGANIC (AS IN FOOD): grown or raised without pesticides or other chemicals

OZONE LAYER: a layer in the atmosphere that blocks harmful ultraviolet rays from the sun from entering Earth's lower atmosphere, where humans live

PRECIPITATION: deposits of wetness such as rain, snow, sleet, or hail

RENEWABLE ENERGY: energy from natural sources that don't run out, like the sun or wind

RENEWABLE RESOURCES: resources that can be replaced naturally over time

SUSTAINABILITY: using resources in a way that makes sure the resource is not damaged or depleted over time

TEMPERATURE: the degree of hotness or coldness

WEATHER: the day-to-day state of a place related to precipitation, temperature, and other conditions

Creative Crabs

FROM THE PAGES OF

Hermit crabs in the wild are ditching their shells and finding new homes—in our plastic litter.

Plastic is everywhere. About 2,000 garbage trucks' worth of plastic waste is dumped into oceans, rivers, and lakes each day. That's according to the United Nations. There's plastic at the bottom of the ocean. There's plastic at the top of Mount Everest.

Now plastic has been found in another unlikely place: on the backs of hermit crabs. They're using it as shells.

Zuzanna Jagiello is a biologist at the University of Warsaw, in Poland. She's the lead author of a study on the subject. "For me, a hermit crab in a plastic shell could be an **icon** of our times," Jagiello told TIME for Kids. "They don't have homes, so they use rubbish."

Jagiello studies the Anthropocene age. That's the **geologic** age we're in now. It's the period when human activity has made a big impact on the environment. Hermit crabs using plastic waste as shells is one example of this.

Hermit crab inside a pen cap

Internet Ecology

To study hermit crabs, researchers used iEcology, or Internet Ecology. It's a way of doing research. It uses information on the Internet to spot patterns in the natural world. For this study, researchers looked at photos of hermit crabs that people had posted online.

iEcology isn't perfect. The data can be biased. For example, people are more likely to take and post a photo of a hermit crab in a plastic shell than a snail shell, because it's more surprising.

NEW HOMES

Hermit crabs are small. They have soft bodies and live near oceans. For protection, they typically wear seashells. They find shells left behind by dead sea snails.

But according to the study, at least 386 hermit crabs have been documented wearing garbage. There are 16 species of hermit crabs that live on land. Ten species were seen wearing trash. Nearly 9 out of every 10 of those crabs were wearing plastic waste, such as bottle caps. The others wore glass or metal, such as broken light bulbs or soda cans.

Jagiello and her team saw photos online of hermit crabs wearing garbage. They decided to conduct research. (See "Internet Ecology.")

The researchers scanned the Internet for photos of hermit crabs wearing trash. They found photos from all over the world. Some were from scientists. Some were from nature photographers. Many were from people who were just curious.

WHAT DOES IT MEAN?

Scientists aren't sure why hermit crabs are choosing litter instead of snail shells. But they have theories.

Some sea snail populations are declining. It's possible that hermit crabs can't find enough seashells. It's also possible that crabs choose plastic because it's light and easy to carry. Or they're drawn to flashy colors.

Scientists agree that plastic pollution harms wildlife and habitats. But it isn't clear that the crabs are in any danger. "It's really an amazing example of the beauty of adaptation," Jagiello says. "What are the long-term consequences of these adaptations? We don't know."

—By Shay Maunz

POWER WORDS

icon *noun:* someone or something that has important meaning

geologic *adjective:* relating to the age of rock and its history

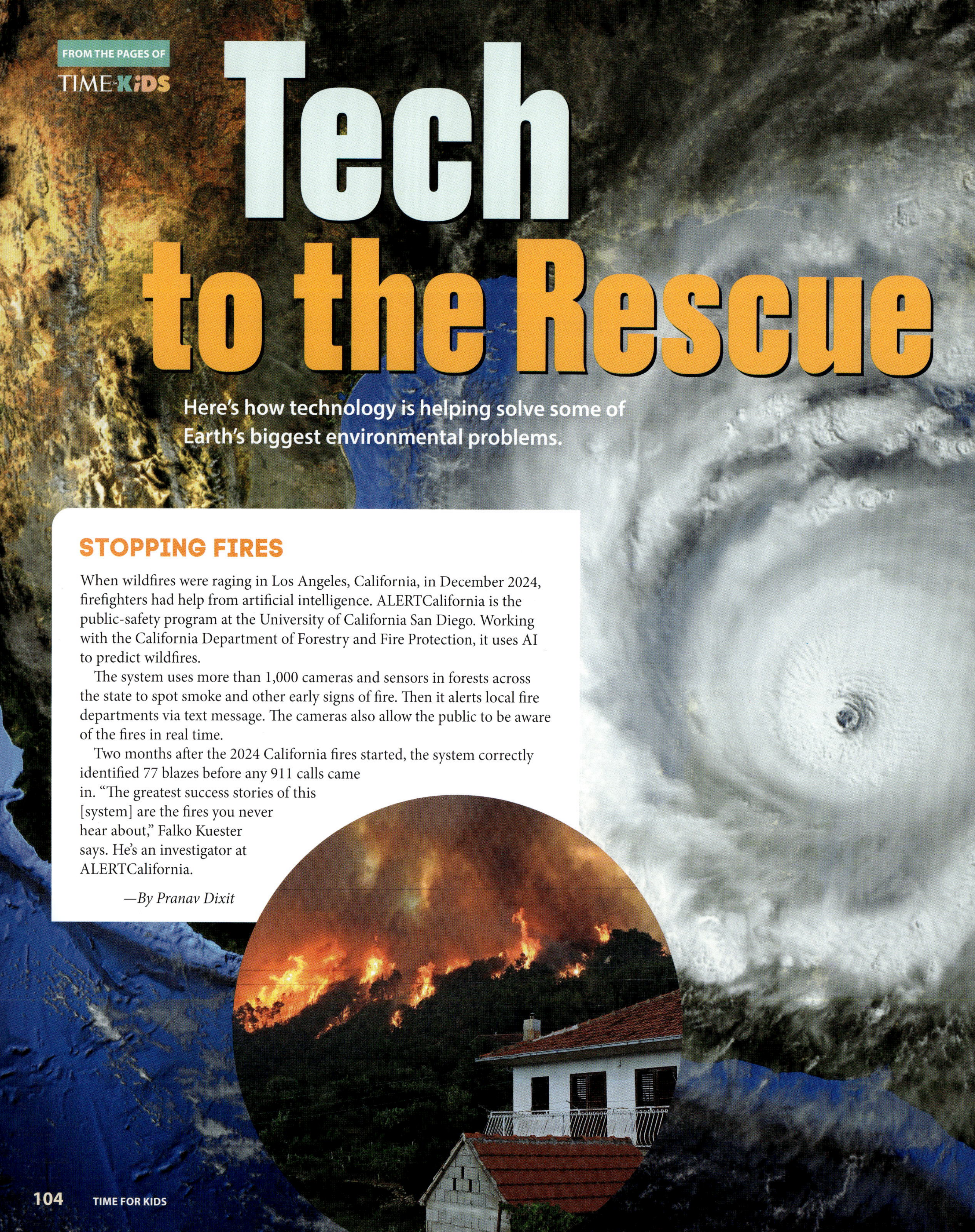

FROM THE PAGES OF TIME KIDS

Tech to the Rescue

Here's how technology is helping solve some of Earth's biggest environmental problems.

STOPPING FIRES

When wildfires were raging in Los Angeles, California, in December 2024, firefighters had help from artificial intelligence. ALERTCalifornia is the public-safety program at the University of California San Diego. Working with the California Department of Forestry and Fire Protection, it uses AI to predict wildfires.

The system uses more than 1,000 cameras and sensors in forests across the state to spot smoke and other early signs of fire. Then it alerts local fire departments via text message. The cameras also allow the public to be aware of the fires in real time.

Two months after the 2024 California fires started, the system correctly identified 77 blazes before any 911 calls came in. "The greatest success stories of this [system] are the fires you never hear about," Falko Kuester says. He's an investigator at ALERTCalifornia.

—By Pranav Dixit

FORECASTING WITH AI

Hurricanes have become more frequent and intense. Artificial intelligence is playing a big role in helping meteorologists forecast and track the storms. AI models use data from previous storms to find patterns. They quickly detect trends that most humans can't. AI models can make accurate predictions within seconds. And they can do so days in advance.

This is different from older models, which gather data by planes, satellites, and buoys. That can take hours and isn't always accurate. But AI programs like GraphCast are different. For instance, GraphCast predicted that Hurricane Beryl would hit Texas on July 8, 2024. An older model predicted Beryl would hit Mexico. GraphCast was right.

AI models still struggle to predict a storm's intensity and how much precipitation will fall. And the impacts to the environment can be huge. For instance, according to the Harvard Business Review, a large AI model can use thousands of megawatt hours of electricity, release tons of carbon, and waste fresh water that cools off data centers. For now, it's important for meteorologists to use AI along with other forecasting tools.

—By Andrew R. Chow

GOING SOLAR

Scientists from the California Institute of Technology are building solar panels that would collect the sun's energy from space. The scientists hope to gather the sun's energy in giant satellites orbiting Earth and beam it down to the power grid to produce a constant stream of power. And they would work even when it was cloudy on Earth. "In space, it's always noon on a sunny day," Ali Hajimiri says. He's one of the scientists leading the project.

These panels would be made out of lightweight material instead of heavy glass and use ultrathin antennas instead of bulky ones. This will make it easier to launch the panels into space. A recent experiment proved that the technology works in space. With more research, it could reach commercial use in the coming decades.

—By Brian S. McGrath

What Do You Think?

We asked TFK readers to tell us if they think AI is good for society. Here are four of their responses. Where do you stand?

YES

RIME LEE, 10

Winnipeg, Manitoba, Canada

"AI can help in health care, education, robotics, and more. Some people might think AI is bad because students can cheat. But AI doesn't just give students the answers. It can help them solve problems step by step, which is a great way to learn."

YES

THOMAS MCGIBBON, 9

Pelham, New York

"Without AI, some helpful websites wouldn't exist. It's also good because sometimes you might have a question and your parents don't know the answer. Then you can ask artificial intelligence. Plus, what's the percentage chance of AI actually taking over the world?"

NO

MAREN ALTRUP, 10

Springfield, Missouri

"With AI, it can be hard to know what is real and what is made-up. Also, students could stop thinking for themselves and rely too much on AI. But AI isn't going away. So we need to be careful how we use it."

NO

ELLIE MCBEE, 12

Georgetown, South Carolina

"In order to generate images, AI bots take images from people and combine them. It steals the artists' hard work. It's cool to look at book characters that were generated by artificial intelligence—but it's not cool enough for AI to steal an artist's work."

Stormy Seasons

These weather events can happen anytime in the United States. But they're most common during certain times of the year. Learn more about them—and how to stay safe.

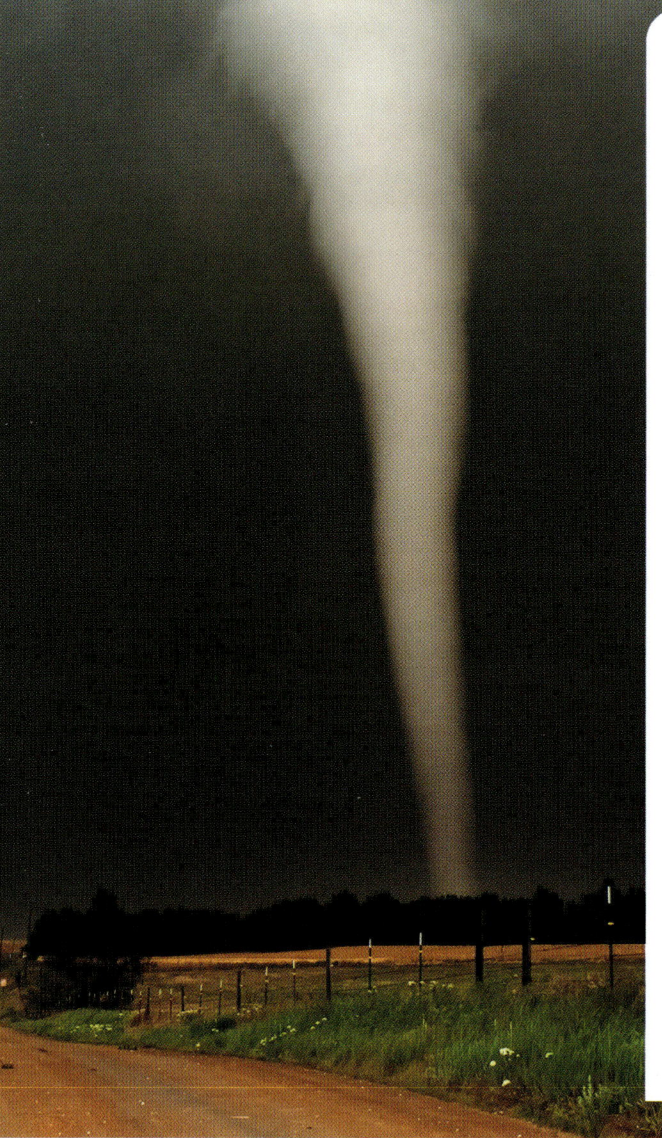

TORNADO SEASON

WHEN: March through July

WHAT THEY ARE: Formed from thunderstorms, tornadoes are violent funnels that can bring high winds, hail, and lightning.

DANGER ZONE: Tornadoes are so destructive because of their wind speed, which can be up to 300 miles an hour (483 km/h).

NOTABLE EVENT: On May 21, 2024, in Greenfield, Iowa, a tornado with winds up to 185 miles an hour (298 km/h) traveled 44 miles (71 km) in 47 minutes. (Most tornadoes last from 5 to 10 minutes.)

STAYING SAFE: Pay attention to tornado watches and tornado warnings. If a warning has been issued in your area, head to a basement or the lowest level of your home away from outer walls or windows, like a closet or bathroom.

When the warm, humid air of a thunderstorm passes through the cold, dry air above it, that updraft can cause a change in the wind direction. When those winds constantly shift speed and direction, the updraft starts to rotate. Drawing in more warm air results in even faster speeds, creating a forceful funnel from the storm cloud to the ground.

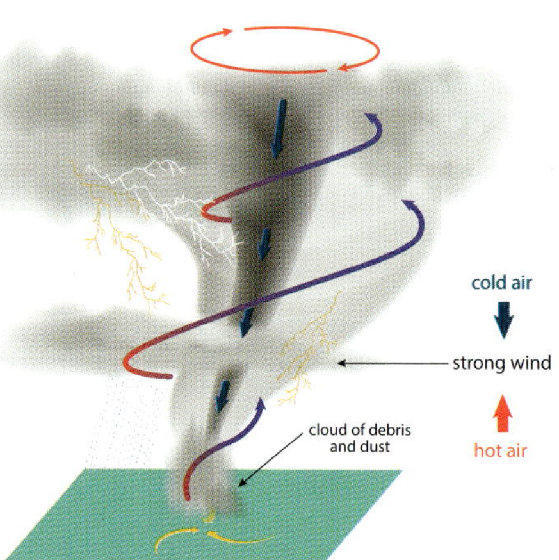

DEC	JAN	FEB	MAR	APR	MAY
			TORNADO SEASON		
POLAR VORTEX SEASON					

HURRICANE SEASON

WHEN: June through November (in the Atlantic Ocean)

WHAT THEY ARE: Fueled by warm ocean waters, a hurricane is a rotating low-pressure weather system with high, sustained winds.

DANGER ZONE: Hurricanes not only bring powerful winds gusting from 74 to more than 155 miles an hour (119 to 250 km/h), but they also create storm surges, or high levels of ocean water that are pushed ashore.

NOTABLE EVENT: Though not the most powerful hurricane of 2024, Hurricane Helene caused massive flooding in September, especially in the North Carolina mountains, an area not often affected by these storms. The hurricane had gusts up to 106 miles an hour (171 km/h) and storm surges of 15 feet (4.6 m).

STAYING SAFE: Meteorologists are experts at predicting when and where these storms will hit. If officials recommend leaving the area, do it.

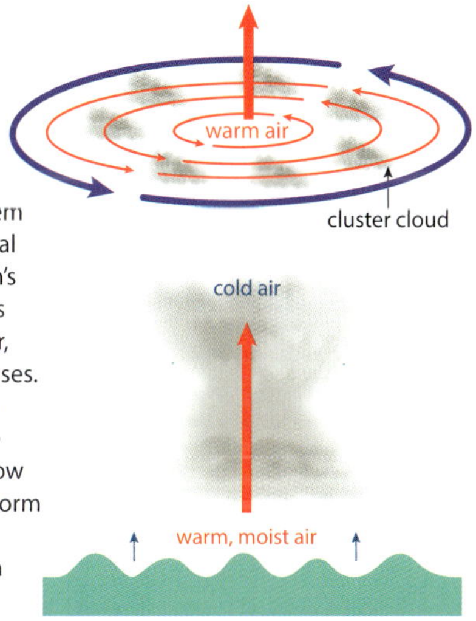

As a weather system passes over tropical waters, the system's low pressure sucks up warm, moist air, which cools as it rises. But as more warm air is pulled in, the winds begin to blow in a circle. They'll form a cluster of clouds that will become a hurricane.

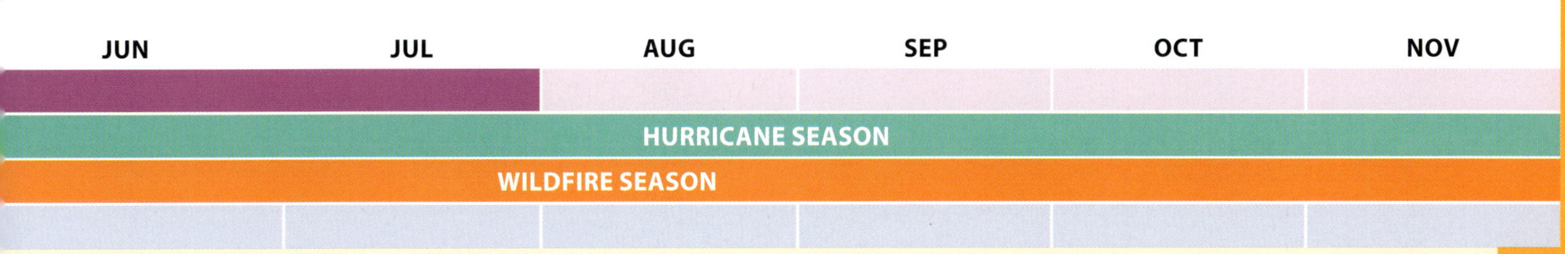

JUN	JUL	AUG	SEP	OCT	NOV

HURRICANE SEASON

WILDFIRE SEASON

ENVIRONMENT

WILDFIRE SEASON

WHEN: May through November

WHAT THEY ARE: Fueled by high winds and dry vegetation often caused by drought, wildfires are large, uncontrolled fires that begin burning in forests or grasslands.

DANGER ZONE: Depending on wind conditions, a wildfire can unexpectedly change directions and travel at speeds of 14 miles an hour (23 km/h). Their temperatures can reach 2200°F (1204°C).

NOTABLE EVENT: In January 2025, at least 255 wildfires raged in and around Los Angeles, California, burning nearly 60,000 acres (24,000 ha) and destroying entire neighborhoods.

STAYING SAFE: If you live where wildfires are common, make sure your family has two escape plans for when officials tell people to leave. Decide on a meeting spot in case your family is separated, and don't forget about your pets.

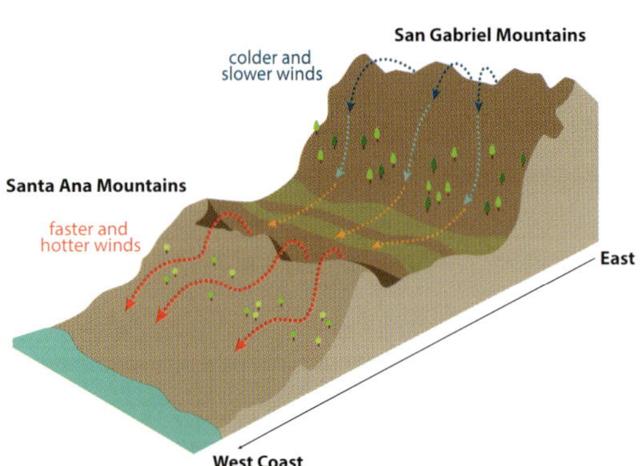

In Los Angeles, the Santa Ana winds helped fuel the wildfire. These winds develop over Nevada and Utah deserts and gather speed as they're pushed through the Santa Ana mountain range toward Southern California. In 2025, the winds gusted up to 100 miles an hour (161 km/h), and the dry, warm air created perfect wildfire conditions.

DEC	JAN	FEB	MAR	APR	MAY
			TORNADO SEASON		
POLAR VORTEX SEASON					

POLAR VORTEX SEASON

WHEN: December through March

WHAT THEY ARE: Polar vortexes are like giant cyclones always spinning above the north and south polar regions. When they break down, they can cause extremely cold temperatures in other regions.

DANGER ZONE: The polar vortex can cause dangerously low temperatures that are as much as 30°F (16.7°C) below average and windchills that feel even colder.

NOTABLE EVENT: The polar vortex might have contributed to frigid temperatures in the United States in January 2025, with temperatures dropping below zero in some places and affecting states as far south as Florida and Texas.

STAYING SAFE: Extremely low temperatures and windchills can cause your skin to quickly freeze (called frostbite) and your body temperature to drop dangerously low (called hypothermia). It's important to stay inside during these events. If you must go outside, dress in warm layers that cover as much of your body as possible.

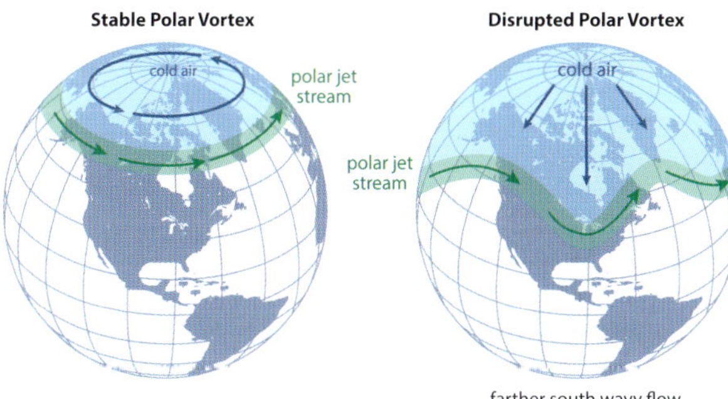

In the Northern Hemisphere, the polar vortex spins counterclockwise and strengthens during winter. When the winds are disrupted, the cold air is no longer locked over the polar region and can push south.

JUN	JUL	AUG	SEP	OCT	NOV

HURRICANE SEASON

WILDFIRE SEASON

Ecosystems

Nature is divided into five main biomes: aquatic, forest, grassland, desert, and tundra. Each biome has many different kinds of incredibly biodiverse ecosystems. Here are a few.

Sea otter

CORAL REEF

DEFINITION: A large living structure in the ocean made up of millions of organisms called corals

WHERE YOU'LL FIND THEM: They grow and thrive in warm, shallow waters around the world where they have access to sunlight and algae.

SCIENCE STUFF: Corals attach to hard surfaces such as rocks. Each coral has polyps, which eat, grow, and secrete a skeleton of calcium carbonate. Over thousands of years, other corals attach to these skeletons, and the reef keeps growing.

FAMOUS RESIDENT: Clownfish live in stinging anemones for protection. In return, they protect the anemone from small predators.

BY THE NUMBERS: Stretching 1,429 miles (2,300 km), Australia's Great Barrier Reef is the longest living structure in the world.

WHY THEY'RE IMPORTANT: About 25 percent of all marine life depend on coral reefs to find food, protect themselves, and raise their young. Coral reefs also protect coastlines from storms.

Clownfish and anemone

KELP FORESTS

DEFINITION: An underwater area containing clusters of large brown algae that grow from the bottom of the ocean to the surface

WHERE YOU'LL FIND THEM: Temperate and polar coasts of California, Alaska, Nova Scotia (Canada), South Africa, Japan, Australia, New Zealand, Iceland, Norway, the United Kingdom, and Chile

SCIENCE STUFF: Although they grow in forests, kelp are not trees. They're algae. Like plants, algae create food from the sun (called **photosynthesis**). Unlike plants, algae don't have true roots, leaves, or stems.

FAMOUS RESIDENT: Sea otters eat clams living in kelp forests and often wrap kelp around their babies so they won't float away while sleeping.

BY THE NUMBERS: Growing up to 18 inches (46 cm) a day, the average giant kelp stretches 100 feet (30 m) tall.

WHY THEY'RE IMPORTANT: Kelp forests are often called the "lungs of the ocean" because they breathe in CO_2 and breathe out oxygen. That helps regulate greenhouse gases.

Inland taipan

HOT DESERTS

DEFINITION: A large area of land that receives less than 10 inches (25 cm) of rain a year, is warm throughout the year, and is extremely hot in summer

WHERE YOU'LL FIND THEM: Near the Equator in places like western North and South America, northern and southern Africa, central Asia, and central Australia

SCIENCE STUFF: Dry air means that the desert surface absorbs more of the sun's heat during the day. But because there's no moisture to trap the heat, nights are cold. For instance, the Sahara in Africa averages 100°F (38°C) during the day and 25°F (–4°C) at night.

FAMOUS RESIDENT: The inland taipan is considered the world's most venomous snake, but the shy reptile is rarely seen in its Australian desert habitat. When it's not hiding, it's filling up on long-tailed rats, helping to control that population.

BY THE NUMBERS: Only 20 percent of Earth's deserts are covered in sand.

WHY THEY'RE IMPORTANT: Hot deserts are homes to plants and animals that have adapted to live with very little water. Scientists study these creatures to come up with solutions for humans living in similar conditions.

COLD DESERTS

DEFINITION: A large area of land—often in mountainous areas on or plateaus—that receives less than 10 inches (25 cm) of precipitation (usually snow) a year, is cool throughout the year, and is extremely cold in winter

WHERE YOU'LL FIND THEM: Central Asia, western North America, southeastern South America

SCIENCE STUFF: Found in Nevada's Great Basin, big sagebrush has a root system that can extend 90 feet (27 m) below the surface to catch water. The leaves' hairs and waxy coat help prevent evaporation.

FAMOUS RESIDENT: Native to China and Mongolia, the mouselike jerboa can hop up to 10 feet (3 m) in one leap as it looks for food and escapes predators.

BY THE NUMBERS: Even though Asia's Gobi Desert can reach 113°F (45°C) in summer, it's still considered a cold desert because of the plunging temperatures in winter: an average –40°F (–40°C) in January.

WHY THEY'RE IMPORTANT: Like hot deserts, cold deserts provide scientists a chance to study the amazing animals and plants that have adapted to extreme habitats.

Jerboa

POWER WORDS

biome *noun:* a big region with a specific climate and specific plants and animals that live there. It's sort of like a giant neighborhood.

photosynthesis *noun:* a process in which plants, algae, and microorganisms convert sunlight into energy that is used as food

Ecosystems

ARCTIC TUNDRAS

DEFINITION: Snow-and-ice-covered lands that have long winters, little precipitation, and no trees

WHERE YOU'LL FIND THEM: Above the Arctic Circle in places like Alaska, Canada, Russia, Greenland, Iceland, and Scandinavia

SCIENCE STUFF: Most soil in the Arctic tundra is frozen all year round (called permafrost). The growing season—when temperatures are warm enough to thaw a thin layer of soil—is only 6 to 10 weeks.

FAMOUS RESIDENT: Arctic foxes have white coats in winter but brown or bluish-gray fur for spring and summer.

BY THE NUMBERS: Winter temperatures can dip to −30°F (−34°C), but the average summer temperature is 37°F to 54°F (3°C to 12°C).

WHY THEY'RE IMPORTANT: Many arctic tundra animals live nowhere else on Earth. The snowy ecosystem also reflects solar radiation, which helps protect against global warming.

Arctic fox

Ibex

ALPINE TUNDRA

DEFINITION: Flat land at high altitudes, with no trees

WHERE YOU'LL FIND THEM: Just beyond the tree lines atop mountains all over the world

SCIENCE STUFF: CO_2 is a necessary ingredient for plants to convert sunlight into food. But the thin air of alpine tundras means less CO_2. So alpine plants have adapted to become much more efficient when it comes to photosynthesis.

FAMOUS RESIDENT: Scaling mountains in Europe, Asia, and northern Africa, ibex have special hooves that act like suction cups to help them grip the rocky cliffs.

BY THE NUMBERS: Wind speeds in some alpine tundras can reach 125 miles an hour (200 km/h).

WHY THEY'RE IMPORTANT: Rain and snowmelt draining from alpine tundras provide important water sources to the ecosystems below.

TROPICAL RAINFORESTS

DEFINITION: A hot and steamy forested area that receives a high amount of rain and little change of seasons

WHERE YOU'LL FIND THEM: South and Central America, West and Central Africa, Indonesia, Southeast Asia, and tropical Australia

SCIENCE STUFF: A rainforest has four layers where different animals thrive: the emergent layer at the very top, where a few trees have grown up to 200 feet (60 m) tall; the canopy, a dense network of leaves and branches that provides a roof over the rest of the forest; the understory, a dark and humid world; and the forest floor, where leaves fall and then decompose in the soil.

FAMOUS RESIDENT: Found in Central American rainforests, the red-eyed tree frog can flash its red eyes, blue legs, and orange feet to startle predators just enough to escape.

BY THE NUMBERS: Average rainfall in tropical forests is usually more than 70 to 100 inches (178 to 254 cm) a year.

WHY THEY'RE IMPORTANT: More than half of the world's animal and plant species call rainforests home. And by storing extra CO_2 in their trees and soil instead of releasing it into the atmosphere, the forests help regulate the world's climate.

Red-eyed tree frog

DECIDUOUS FORESTS

DEFINITION: A forest in a region that isn't extremely hot or cold and experiences spring, summer, winter, and fall

WHERE YOU'LL FIND THEM: Eastern North America, western Eurasia, northeastern Asia

SCIENCE STUFF: Deciduous leaves are green because of the **chlorophyll** they use for photosynthesis. But when less light is available in fall and winter, the chlorophyll breaks down, and the leaves change color.

FAMOUS RESIDENT: Unlike its cousins, the Eurasian green woodpecker doesn't often peck into deciduous forest trees for food. Instead, it prefers eating on the ground.

BY THE NUMBERS: Deciduous forests get about half the rainfall of rainforests. But they still receive enough rain to grow big trees—some are as tall as 100 feet (30 m).

WHY THEY'RE IMPORTANT: Up to a third of all migratory bird species depend on deciduous forests for food, rest, and mates at some point in their lives.

Eurasian green woodpecker

POWER WORD

chlorophyll *noun:* a green pigment that absorbs energy from sunlight

Ecosystems

Crocodile

RIVERS

DEFINITION: A natural body of water that flows over land and has banks on either side

WHERE YOU'LL FIND THEM: All over the world

SCIENCE STUFF: Rivers begin as dribbles from rainfall, snowfall, or underground sources. Flowing down from high ground, the dribbles meet up with other dribbles and form a creek, brook, or stream. Those grow into a river, which eventually empties out into a larger body of water, such as a lake or ocean.

FAMOUS RESIDENT: Crocodiles living in Africa's Nile River are fearsome predators but also caring parents. Both mom and dad guard the nest of eggs and sometimes roll the eggs in their mouths to help them hatch.

BY THE NUMBERS: NASA scientists estimate that all the world's rivers carry about 539 cubic miles (2,246 km^3) of water. But that's only 0.006 percent of all Earth's fresh water.

WHY THEY'RE IMPORTANT: Rivers impact humans' everyday lives. They provide drinking water, irrigation, and transportation, and they can be an important source of hydropower to create electricity.

SWAMPS

DEFINITION: A type of wetland dotted with trees whose land is always saturated, or filled, with water—and sometimes covered by it

WHERE YOU'LL FIND THEM: Low-lying areas with poor drainage and a nearby water supply, like a river

SCIENCE STUFF: Because swamp waters are so still, the mud is low in oxygen. That means dead stuff doesn't decay completely, which is why swamp water often appears yellow or dark brown.

FAMOUS RESIDENT: Allen's swamp monkeys have webbed feet to swim in the wetlands of their west Central African home.

BY THE NUMBERS: Sprawling over Brazil, Bolivia, and Paraguay, the Pantanal is the world's largest wetland. It supports about 3,500 plant species, 656 bird species, 325 fish species, 159 mammals, 53 amphibians, and 98 reptiles.

WHY THEY'RE IMPORTANT: All wetlands play an important role in protecting nearby areas from flood and erosion.

Allen's swamp monkey

Giraffe

SAVANNAS

DEFINITION: A hot, dry grassland with scattered trees

WHERE YOU'LL FIND THEM: Africa, South America, Australia, Asia

SCIENCE STUFF: Savannas are considered transition zones between rainforests near the Equator and deserts at higher latitudes.

FAMOUS RESIDENT: A giraffe's long tongue is like an extra finger that can wrap around the leaves of tall, thorny acacia trees in African savannas.

BY THE NUMBERS: A whopping 30 percent of dead matter in savannas is decomposed by termites.

WHY THEY'RE IMPORTANT: Savannas are the source of many of the world's most important rivers. The soil and plant roots also lock in carbon to help regulate the planet's temperature.

PRAIRIES

DEFINITION: Large space of flat grasslands with mild temperatures and few trees

WHERE YOU'LL FIND THEM: North America

SCIENCE STUFF: Prairies formed after mountains grew so tall that little rain fell on the eastern sides of their slopes. Trees couldn't grow, so grasslands did instead.

FAMOUS RESIDENT: Monarch butterflies lay their eggs only on milkweed plants, which are common on the prairie. The butterflies are important pollinators and help crops grow.

BY THE NUMBERS: Tallgrass prairies have more than 300 species of flowers and herbs; 100 species of lichens, liverworts, trees, and shrubs; and 40 to 60 species of grasses.

WHY THEY'RE IMPORTANT: Many prairie animals contribute to the health of this important agricultural ecosystem. For instance, the American bison "plows" the land by walking over it with its pointy hooves. This helps the soil hold more water.

Bison

FROM THE PAGES OF TIME for KIDS

Heroes for the Planet

Get inspired by these four young people who have taken action to help the environment.

RECYCLING ROLE MODEL

When Mateo Lange was 11, he wanted to raise money for his baseball team to travel. So he and his teammates collected bottles and aluminum cans to recycle for cash. It was so successful that Mateo thought, "Why don't we keep this going?"

Mateo, who lives in Indian River, Michigan, now runs a community recycling program. His efforts have collected more than two million bottles and cans and raised more than $350,000. The money is donated to youth groups, and the recycling helps keep trash out of rivers and lakes.

"Just do a little bit to help make the world a little bit of a better place," Mateo says. "Have an idea and build on it."

—By Jaime Joyce

WILDLIFE WARRIOR

Ava Toomey knew she had to do something. She had learned that birds like owls and hawks were being poisoned after eating rodents killed by rat poison, also called rodenticide. When she was 11, she reached out to two of her elected state officials in Massachusetts. They were sponsoring a bill that would make these poisons against the law.

With her Girl Scout troop, Ava is now inspiring her community to support the bill. She even spoke in front of the state legislature. "It's a long process. A bill might not always get passed [the first time]," she says. "Then you just have to try again."

—By TFK Kid Reporter Harper Carroll

SEA STAR

Miles Fetherston-Resch loves collecting shark teeth along the Florida coastline where he lives. He loves it so much that when he was six years old, he wanted to donate his weekly allowance to help the marine predators.

Now Miles runs Kids Saving Oceans, which sells T-shirts, hats, and stickers made out of recycled plastic found in the ocean. A portion of every sale—more than $40,000 so far—is donated to causes that support clean waterways.

"If you have an idea, go for it," Miles says. "The worst thing you can do is have it not work out. And that's not a loss."

—By Brian S. McGrath

BATTERY BATTLER

On his 10th birthday, Sri Nihal Tammana learned that each year, 15 billion batteries are thrown out. They wind up in landfills. They pollute groundwater and harm the environment. He started Recycle My Battery to provide recycling bins for batteries.

Recycle My Battery has a team of 250 student volunteers around the world. In just three years, they helped recycle more than 260,000 batteries.

"My biggest goal for this organization is to bring the 15 billion batteries being thrown away each year worldwide to zero," he says.

—By Cristina Fernandez

ENVIRONMENT

Be a Planet Protector

The more we work together, the healthier we can keep Earth. Try these easy tips to get started.

Instead of getting a car ride, which emits greenhouse gases, start a giant bike-pool. Gather all your neighborhood friends. With the guidance of an adult, bicycle to class in one big group. (You can do this with walking, too.)

Stay on trails and paths when you're exploring outside. Trampling over nature can disturb wildlife and damage the plants they rely on.

The next time your family goes to a restaurant, try ordering a plant-based meal. Farm animals expel a lot of methane, which traps heat in the atmosphere. Instead, try main dishes made with beans, lentils, and chickpeas, which are high in protein.

Hold a swap meet at school. Once a month, everyone brings stuff they no longer want—books, video games, clothes, toys—then swaps them for other unwanted items. This helps keep items out of the landfill and keeps you from buying new things that have been created with precious resources.

A party's still a party without balloons. Skip decorating with items that can entangle wildlife or be accidentally swallowed by them.

Turn off unnecessary lights at night. The lights can confuse birds, causing them to crash into windows or tire out from flying in circles. This is especially important during spring and fall, when many birds are migrating.

Only flush human waste and toilet paper down the toilet. Things like cotton balls, medicine, dental floss, and even hair can end up in waterways and harm animals.

Use your high-tech devices as long as possible, and always recycle them when you're done. Tablets, cell phones, and laptops contain minerals mined from gorilla habitats, so the more everyone uses and recycles them, the less those habitats are disturbed.

Always keep your dog on a leash when you're outside (unless you're at a dog park). Dogs have a natural chase instinct and will run after squirrels and birds, which can disturb them while they're hunting or raising their young.

Cats prey on more than one billion birds each year, so keep your furry feline inside.

Drink from reusable water bottles, shop with cloth bags, and skip the plastic straws. Single-use plastic items often end up in waterways, where animals mistake them for food.

Take a trip to a local farmers market. Buying food that's been grown nearby cuts down on the emissions needed to transport groceries from far away. Plus, you'll be supporting local business owners.

Stop and Think

What would happen if we stopped recycling?

CHAPTER 9

ENTERTAINMENT AND CULTURE

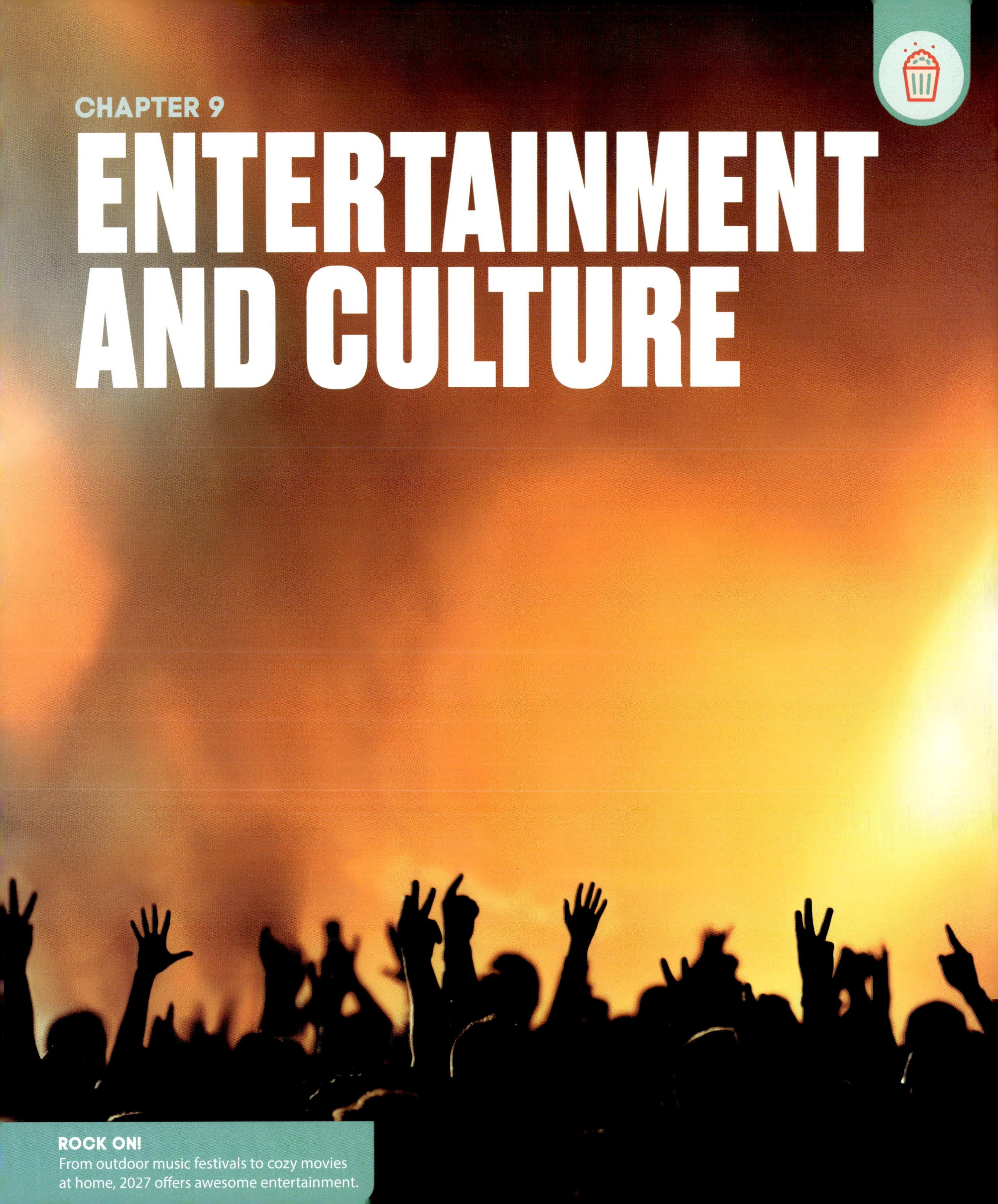

ROCK ON!
From outdoor music festivals to cozy movies at home, 2027 offers awesome entertainment.

And the Award Goes to . . .

A look at some of the entertainment world's best performances

Adrien Brody

Mikey Madison

MOVIE AWARDS

ACADEMY AWARD

BEST PICTURE

2020: *Parasite*

2021: *Nomadland*

2022: *CODA*

2023: *Everything Everywhere All at Once*

2024: *Oppenheimer*

2025: *Anora*

ACADEMY AWARD

BEST ACTOR IN A LEADING ROLE

2020: Joaquin Phoenix

2021: Anthony Hopkins

2022: Will Smith

2023: Brendan Fraser

2024: Cillian Murphy

2025: Adrien Brody

ACADEMY AWARD

BEST ACTRESS IN A LEADING ROLE

2020: Renée Zellweger

2021: Frances McDormand

2022: Jessica Chastain

2023: Michelle Yeoh

2024: Emma Stone

2025: Mikey Madison

Jack Black

MOVIE AWARDS

KIDS' CHOICE AWARD

FAVORITE MOVIE

2020: *Avengers: Endgame*

2021: *Wonder Woman 1984*

2022: *Spider-Man: No Way Home*

2023: *Sonic the Hedgehog 2*

2024: *Barbie*

2025: *Wicked*

KIDS' CHOICE AWARD

FAVORITE MOVIE ACTOR

2020: Dwayne Johnson

2021: Robert Downey, Jr.

2022: Tom Holland

2023: Dwayne Johnson

2024: Timothée Chalamet

2025: Jack Black

KIDS' CHOICE AWARD

FAVORITE MOVIE ACTRESS

2020: Dove Cameron

2021: Millie Bobby Brown

2022: Zendaya

2023: Millie Bobby Brown

2024: Margot Robbie

2025: Ariana Grande

KIDS' CHOICE AWARD

FAVORITE ANIMATED MOVIE

2020: *Frozen II*

2021: *Soul*

2022: *Encanto*

2023: *Minions: The Rise of Gru*

2024: *Spider-Man: Across the Spider-Verse*

2025: *Inside Out 2*

Ariana Grande

TELEVISION AWARDS

KIDS' CHOICE AWARD

FAVORITE KIDS TV SHOW

2020: *Henry Danger*

2021: *Alexa & Katie*

2022: *High School Musical: The Musical: The Series*

2023: *The Fairly OddParents: Fairly Odder*

2024: *Percy Jackson and the Olympians*

2025: *The Thundermans: Undercover*

KIDS' CHOICE AWARD

FAVORITE FEMALE TV STAR (KIDS)

2020: Millie Bobby Brown

2021: Millie Bobby Brown

2022: Olivia Rodrigo

2023: Olivia Rodrigo

2024: Olivia Rodrigo

2025: Kira Kosarin

KIDS' CHOICE AWARD

FAVORITE MALE TV STAR (KIDS)

2020: Jace Norman

2021: Jace Norman

2022: Joshua Bassett

2023: Joshua Bassett

2024: Walker Scobell

2025: Jack Griffo

Kira Kosarin and Jack Griffo

Olivia Rodrigo

Arianna McDonald and John Tartaglia

EMMY AWARD

OUTSTANDING CHILDREN'S OR FAMILY VIEWING

2020: *Jim Henson's The Dark Crystal: Age of Resistance*

2021: *The Power of We: A Sesame Street Special*

2022: *The Baby-Sitters Club*

2023: *The Muppets Mayhem*

2024: *Fraggle Rock: Back to the Rock*

EMMY AWARD

OUTSTANDING COMEDY SERIES

2020: *Schitt's Creek*

2021: *Ted Lasso*

2022: *Ted Lasso*

2023: *The Bear*

2024: *Hacks*

2025: *The Studio*

MUSIC AWARDS

GRAMMY AWARD

ALBUM OF THE YEAR

2020: *When We All Fall Asleep, Where Do We Go?*, Billie Eilish

2021: *Folklore*, Taylor Swift

2022: *We Are*, Jon Batiste

2023: *Harry's House*, Harry Styles

2024: *Midnights*, Taylor Swift

2025: *Cowboy Carter*, Beyoncé

Kendrick Lamar

Beyoncé

GRAMMY AWARD

SONG OF THE YEAR

2020: "Bad Guy," Billie Eilish

2021: "I Can't Breathe," H.E.R.

2022: "Leave the Door Open," Silk Sonic

2023: "Just Like That," Bonnie Raitt

2024: "What Was I Made For?," Billie Eilish

2025: "Not Like Us," Kendrick Lamar

GRAMMY AWARD

RECORD OF THE YEAR

2020: "Bad Guy," Billie Eilish

2021: "Everything I Wanted," Billie Eilish

2022: "Leave the Door Open," Silk Sonic

2023: "About Damn Time," Lizzo

2024: "Flowers," Miley Cyrus

2025: "Not Like Us," Kendrick Lamar

KIDS' CHOICE AWARD
FAVORITE MUSIC GROUP

2020: BTS

2021: BTS

2022: BTS

2023: BTS

2024: Imagine Dragons

2025: Stray Kids

KIDS' CHOICE AWARD
FAVORITE FEMALE ARTIST

2020: Ariana Grande

2021: Ariana Grande

2022: Ariana Grande

2023: Taylor Swift

2024: Taylor Swift

2025: SZA

KIDS' CHOICE AWARD
FAVORITE MALE ARTIST

2020: Shawn Mendes

2021: Justin Bieber

2022: Ed Sheeran

2023: Harry Styles

2024: Post Malone

2025: Bruno Mars

Stray Kids

BOOK AWARDS

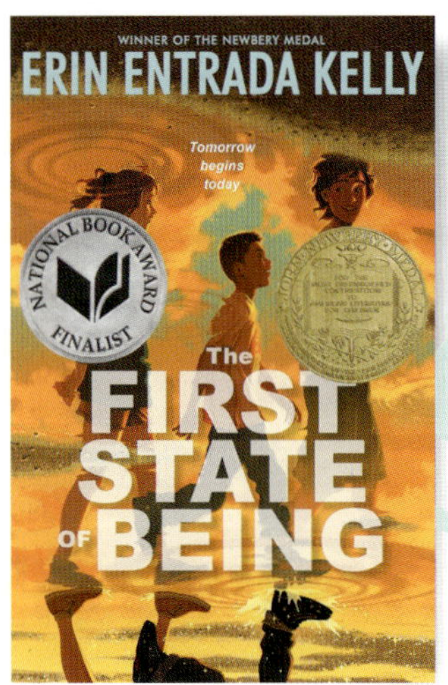

JOHN NEWBERY MEDAL

DISTINGUISHED AUTHOR

2020: *New Kid*, by Jerry Craft

2021: *When You Trap a Tiger*, by Tae Keller

2022: *The Last Cuentista*, by Donna Barba Higuera

2023: *Freewater*, by Amina Luqman-Dawson

2024: *The Eyes and the Impossible*, by Dave Eggers

2025: *The First State of Being*, by Erin Entrada Kelly

RANDOLPH CALDECOTT MEDAL

DISTINGUISHED ILLUSTRATOR

2020: *The Undefeated*, illustrated by Kadir Nelson, written by Kwame Alexander

2021: *We Are Water Protectors*, illustrated by Michaela Goade, written by Carole Lindstrom

2022: *Watercress*, illustrated by Jason Chin, written by Andrea Wang

2023: *Hot Dog*, illustrated and written by Doug Salati

2024: *Big*, illustrated and written by Vashti Harrison

2025: *Chooch Helped*, illustrated by Rebecca Lee Kunz, written by Andrea L. Rogers

DIGITAL AWARDS

KIDS' CHOICE AWARD

FAVORITE VIDEO GAME

2020: *Minecraft*

2021: *Among Us*

2022: *Minecraft*

2023: *Minecraft*

2024: *Roblox*

2025: *Roblox*

WEBBY AWARD

BEST KIDS AND FAMILY APP

2020: Toca Life: World

2021: Duolingo ABC

2022: PBS KIDS Video

2023: PBS KIDS Games

2024: PBS KIDS Games

2025: Good Inside Mobile App

WEBBY AWARD

BEST KIDS AND FAMILY PODCAST

2020: *Story Pirates*

2021: *Dope Black Dads*

2022: *Story Pirates*

2023: *Million Bazillion*

2024: *Story Pirates*

2025: *Grimm, Grimmer, Grimmest*

CORETTA SCOTT KING AWARD

OUTSTANDING WORK BY AN AFRICAN AMERICAN AUTHOR AND ILLUSTRATOR

2020: *New Kid*, by Jerry Craft

2021: *Before the Ever After*, by Jacqueline Woodson

2022: *Unspeakable: The Tulsa Race Massacre*, by Carole Boston Weatherford

2023: *Freewater*, by Amina Luqman-Dawson

2024: *Nigeria Jones*, by Ibi Zoboi

2025: *Twenty-Four Seconds from Now ...*, by Jason Reynolds

Fashion Statement

The annual Met Gala shows off celebrities' most creative styles.

Alton Mason

The Met Gala in New York City is one of the hottest tickets in the world. The invitation-only fashion event is attended by A-list actors, musicians, models, and clothing designers—and everyone wants to know, "What will they wear?"

The exclusive event started in 1948 to raise money for the Metropolitan Museum of Art's Costume Institute and launch the museum's annual fashion exhibit. In 2025, the gala raised a record $31 million. And no wonder—tickets cost $75,000 a person!

Attendees come in one-of-a-kind, eye-popping looks. Sometimes they're elegant, floor-length gowns studded with crystals. Other outfits are unusual, like dresses that are covered in giant, poofy flowers. Some even have political messages, like one creation with "Tax the Rich" on its back.

Every Met Gala has a theme that matches the fashion exhibit opening at the museum. The 2025 theme was "Superfine: Tailoring Black Style" to celebrate Black men's fashion throughout history. The dress code was "Tailored for You." How well do you think the fashion on these pages matches the theme and dress code? Take a look!

Teyana Taylor

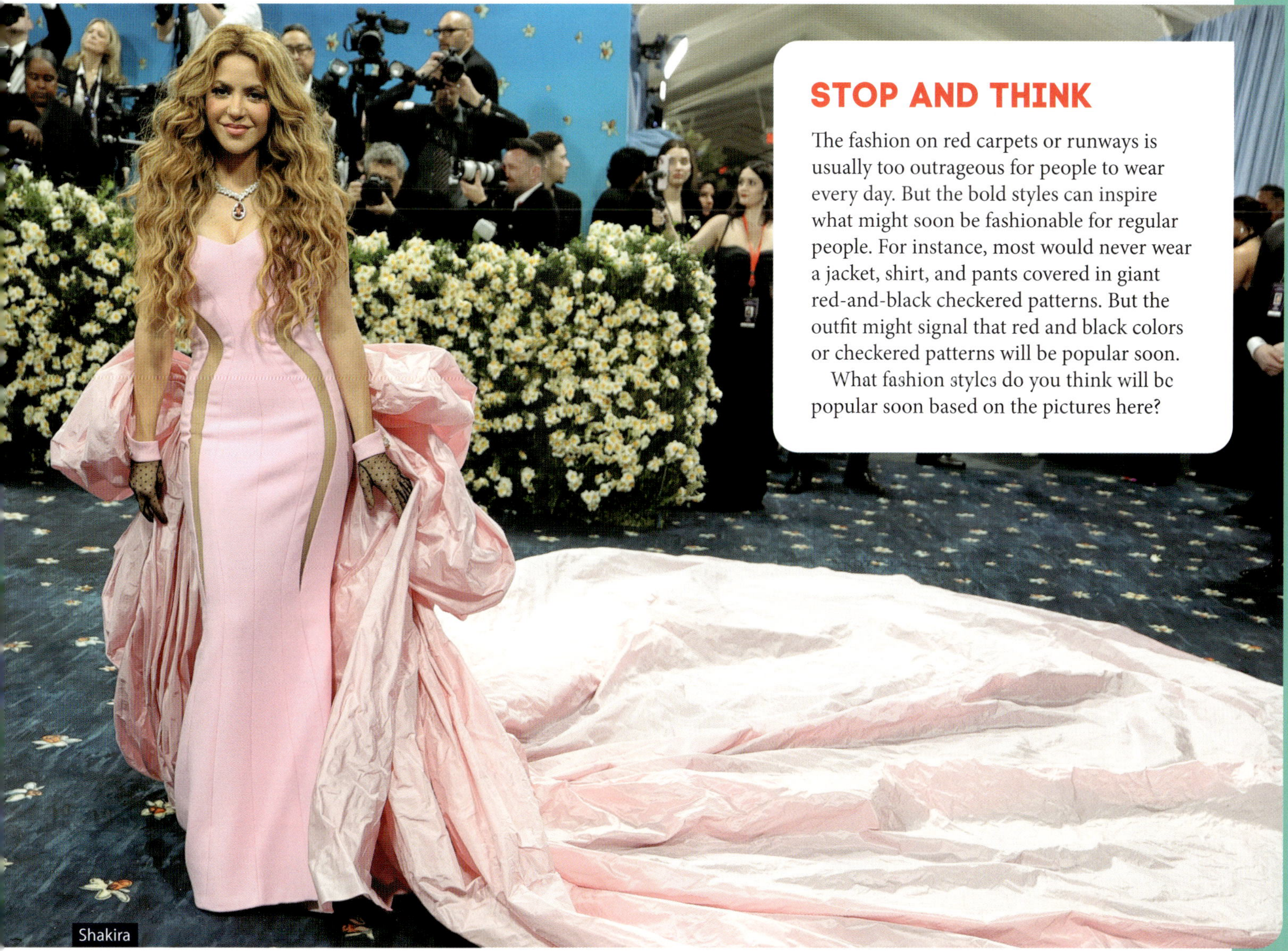

STOP AND THINK

The fashion on red carpets or runways is usually too outrageous for people to wear every day. But the bold styles can inspire what might soon be fashionable for regular people. For instance, most would never wear a jacket, shirt, and pants covered in giant red-and-black checkered patterns. But the outfit might signal that red and black colors or checkered patterns will be popular soon.

What fashion styles do you think will be popular soon based on the pictures here?

Shakira

The Taylor Effect

FROM THE PAGES OF

Taylor Swift stays true to herself despite smashing records.

When Taylor Swift tells a story, you listen. This one is about a time when she got her heart broken.

She was 17. She had booked the biggest opportunity of her life so far: opening for country star Kenny Chesney on tour. But a couple of weeks later, Taylor's mom gave her bad news. Plans for the tour had shifted. Taylor was too young to join. "I was devastated," she says.

For her 18th birthday, Chesney wrote her a card. It read: "I'm sorry that you couldn't come on the tour, so I wanted to make it up to you." With the note was a check. "It was for more money than I'd ever seen in my life," Swift says. "I was able to fuel my dreams."

A lot has changed since then. At 36, Swift is a pop superstar. She's also a businesswoman. "This is the proudest and happiest I've ever felt," she says.

AN EPIC TOUR

When Swift arrives in a city, a mini economic boom takes place. Hotels get more visitors. So do restaurants. Some people call this the "Taylor effect."

The Eras Tour kicked off in Glendale, Arizona. Businesses in the city made more money than they did during the 2023 Super Bowl, which was also held there.

This can be a lot of pressure for one person. After she plays a run of shows, Swift takes a day to rest. "I can barely speak because I've been singing for three shows straight," she says.

MOVIE MAYHEM

The movie version of Swift's Eras Tour took an uncommon route. It was released directly to theaters. No Hollywood studio was involved. "I did what I tend to do more and more often these days," she says. "[I] bet on myself."

The premiere took place in Los Angeles, California, in October 2023. Swift packed 13 theaters with fans. She went into each one, thanking people. During the movie, she sat with her fans. She sang along and danced in her seat.

Since then, the movie became the highest-grossing concert film of all time, bringing in more than $261 million. Swift is "so good at making her personal experience relate to millions of people," says McCall, 20, a fan. "When I listen to her songs, I think about what I've been through—not what she's been through."

—By Sam Lansky for TIME

End of an Era

In December 2024, Taylor Swift wrapped up the highest-grossing concert tour of all time. It was the first concert tour to make more than a billion dollars. Then, after 21 months and 149 shows, Swift smashed her own record: The Eras Tour sold more than $2 billion in tickets, per *The New York Times.*

Swift's touring company told the *Times* that a total of 10,168,008 people attended the tour. During her final show, Swift described the tour as "the most thrilling chapter of my entire life to date." She told fans: "You're why this is so special."

—By Lillian Stone

Overheard

We asked TIME for Kids reporters for their predictions about trends we might see 30 years from now. Here's what they said.

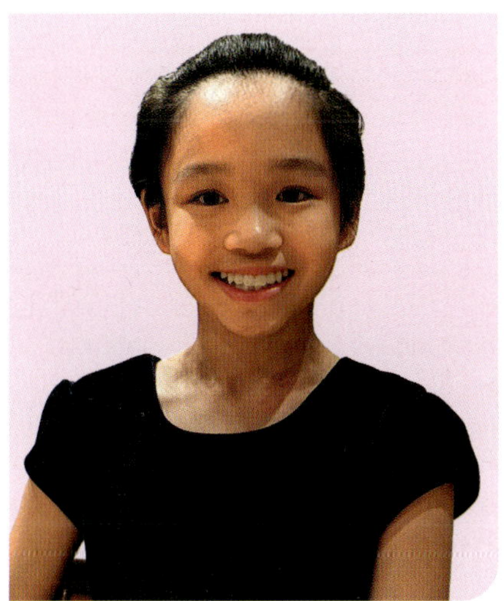

EVELYN PENG

12, New York

Brushing your teeth could be faster, easier, and even tasty. You could chew a flavorful piece of gum (or maybe suck on a mint for those with braces or limited mouth muscles) and your teeth would be plaque-free and shiny white.

DYLAN LANDAW

10, New York

Instead of VR headsets, we'll play games in special rooms where you can play games and interact with people anywhere in the world without wearing anything on your head.

MILO BHUSHAN

10, South Carolina

Most kids will be learning online from home. If kids do go to classes in person, they'll be taking smaller and more specialized classes. Computer science and robotics will be required.

Virtual reality systems will be so advanced that we can use them for vacations. We might vacation underwater in the Mariana Trench, visit Antarctica wearing shorts and T-shirts, or even time travel in VR and vacation in the time of dinosaurs!

Clothes will protect us from extreme weather and pollution. They'll be able to sense things like body temperature and hydration status, and they'll change color and design like a chameleon. These "smart clothes" will even sync with the smart devices we'll probably have implanted in our bodies.

Stop and Think

What do *you* think life will be like 30 years from now? Ask your parents the same question, then compare your answers.

GAME

Double Trouble

See if you can spot the 15 differences in these two photos of Katseye performing at the 2025 Kids' Choice Awards. (The real picture is on the top.)

Answers on page 200

CHAPTER 10
SCIENCE

PUTTING IT TOGETHER
A young boy holds a glucose molecular model in a chemistry lab.

Experiment Like a Scientist

Researchers think about questions they want science to answer, then act like detectives to gather clues and make observations. Some run experiments to test their ideas and predictions. Follow these steps to conduct your own scientific experiment.

MATERIALS

2 glass jars

2 thermometers

white vinegar

baking soda

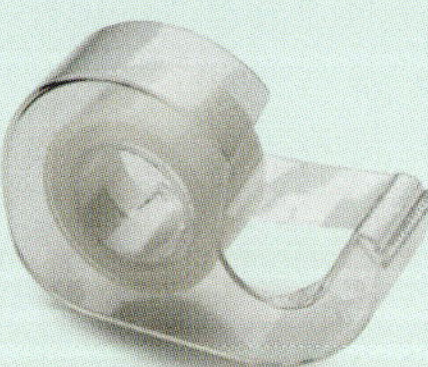

tape

STEP 1:

ASK A QUESTION AND DEFINE THE PROBLEM.

The first step is to ask questions that can be tested and lead to a possible explanation. Think about something you're interested in learning more about and how an experiment could give you answers.

For instance, maybe you want to learn how greenhouse gases like carbon dioxide trap heat in the atmosphere. Your experiment would show how heat behaves in different environments, with and without CO_2.

STEP 2:

DEVELOP YOUR MODEL.

A model is a tool that represents your idea and possible explanation. This can include drawings, diagrams, or physical representations.

Here, your model might be two jars that represent Earth's atmosphere. One will have normal air (called the control), and the other will have extra CO_2 (the experimental jar).

POWER WORDS

analyze *verb:* to thoroughly study something to understand it better

interpret *verb:* to explain the meaning of something

SCIENCE

STEP 3:

PLAN AND CARRY OUT YOUR INVESTIGATION.

This explains things like what materials you'll need and how you'll use those materials. Scientists also define what data they'll be looking for.

For your greenhouse gas experiment, you'll need two clear glass jars with lids, two thermometers that will fit inside the jar, tape, white vinegar and baking soda (for the CO_2), and a sunny spot.

Then you'll map out the process:

1. Place the thermometers inside the jars. Tape them so you can read the temperatures.
2. Seal the control jar with nothing in it except the thermometer.
3. In the other jar, add a little baking soda and pour vinegar over it. Quickly seal the jar.
4. Place both jars in a sunny spot for 15 minutes.

The data will be the temperatures in each jar.

STEP 4:

ANALYZE AND INTERPRET THE DATA.

This is where scientists try to figure out what the data means. They also think about potential mistakes, or what would happen if the experiment were changed a little bit.

In your CO_2 experiment, write down the temperatures for each jar. What has happened? Is one temperature higher than the other? What do you think that means? What would happen if a hole was in the lid of the control jar? What would the new data mean?

STEP 5:

DO SOME MATH.

Math helps scientists understand the data's relationship to each other. This can lead to even deeper analysis—and more knowledge.

For instance, calculate each jar's temperature difference by subtracting the final temperature from the starting temperature. How much more heat did the CO_2 jar retain?

Did you forget to plan to record each jar's starting temperature in Step 3? That's OK—it's all a part of science. Scientists often have to refine their process to fix mistakes.

STEP 6:

DRAW CONCLUSIONS.

Scientists then take all the data and their observations to make explanations about what happened in the experiment and how it relates to real life.

Here, try to explain why the jar with the CO_2 heated up more. How does that relate to greenhouse gases in Earth's atmosphere?

STEP 7:

EXPLAIN YOUR EVIDENCE.

Scientists use all their evidence and observations to explain what happened, and what it might mean. Other scientists might have questions, which is why it's important that explanations are based on evidence, not opinion.

In the greenhouse gas experiment, the evidence should explain why the jar with the CO_2 behaved differently. Young scientists might also connect the model to real-world global warming.

STEP 8:

SHARE WHAT YOU'VE LEARNED.

Scientists put all these steps and results into a presentation for others to comment on. Being open to different explanations is an important part of finding out the truth.

How would you like to communicate your findings? An infographic? A poster? A video? Science should be fun, so think about what will be the most exciting.

SCIENCE

FROM THE PAGES OF TIME for KIDS

Science Careers

These people use science in their jobs every day.

ANDREA CARTER
Agronomist

Andrea Carter is a scientist who studies how plants grow. This kind of researcher is also called a crop scientist. She uses this knowledge to help farmers produce better crops in larger quantities.

Carter focuses on plants that grow in desert regions. That includes crops like corn, beans, and squash that have been grown by Indigenous farmers for centuries. Many are at risk of disappearing. With a group called Native Seeds / SEARCH in Arizona, she works with farmers to grow these crops and harvest their seeds. The group is devoted to preserving seeds that are adapted to the dry climates of the American Southwest and to sharing knowledge about how to grow them. The seeds are then stored in a seed bank for future use.

"Indigenous people have these time-honored and proven ways of growing out of these landscapes and with these crops," Carter says. "Our goal is just reconnecting with that and supporting it."

—By Nathalie Alonso

CORE CLASSES
biology, chemistry, math, environmental science, geography

FRANK RUBIO
Astronaut

Many astronauts are scientists. "We conduct tons of experiments," says astronaut Frank Rubio, a surgeon who spent 371 days on the International Space Station. "I think there were more than 300 experiments that our crew was a part of while I was there."

A typical day in space also means performing maintenance [on the station]. You also might get to do something cool, like a space walk. But it can be challenging, especially being away from family. "But you're able to call [Earth] anytime you want," Rubio says.

Rubio says it takes two or three months to feel "normal" after returning to Earth. But he says the whole experience is incredible. "The fact that you're able to live in space for a full year is mind-blowing," he says.

—By Solcyré Burga for TIME, with reporting by Jeffrey Kluger

CORE CLASSES
math, physics, chemistry, biology, engineering

DANIELLE BELLENY

Wildlife Biologist

As a wildlife biologist, Danielle Belleny surveys birds to keep track of different species. The survey points she visits are studied by different researchers over time. She also searches for signs of what other animals in the area are doing. This helps scientists like her understand what's going on in the ecosystem so they can help if something's not right.

"It's basically knowing how to read the landscape," she says, "based on what plants and different characteristics are there."

Belleny has advice for young people thinking about careers. "Try everything you're interested in," she says. "You don't know every job that exists out there, so keep asking questions."

—By Cristina Fernandez

CORE CLASSES
biology, chemistry, math, environmental science, geography

Science Careers

KAMAL BELL

Beekeeper

Kamal Bell knows a lot about the science of plants and how they grow. He also knows a lot about the science of bugs. He's a beekeeper.

Bees are vital to fruit and vegetable pollination on farms. In fact, honeybees pollinate more than 130 types of fruits, vegetables, and nuts. The insects are important to the crops Bell grows on Sankofa Farms, which he founded in Cedar Grove, North Carolina.

While he checks the human-made beehives, Bell wears a beekeeper suit and gloves to protect himself from stings. He's checking the bees' honey production, and looking for eggs, larvae, and pupae. "If I see the eggs," he says, "I then look for the queen [bee] to make sure she's laying and productive."

—By Alexis Benveniste

CORE CLASSES

biology, environmental science, chemistry, math, botany

ASHLEY RUIZ

Meteorologist

When you think about a city's safety, do you think about your local meteorologist? That's the career Ashley Ruiz chose. She predicts the weather in Seattle, Washington, to help people prepare for what's coming and stay safe.

Meteorology can be challenging, she says, because weather patterns are changing everywhere as the planet warms. There are more frequent droughts, stronger storms, and increasing temperature changes.

Her advice to kids? "Even if you struggle with STEM, just keep trying," she says. "I struggled so hard with math and wanted to give up. But I kept pushing and working hard."

—By TFK Kid Reporter Cash Daniels

CORE CLASSES
physics, math, earth science, geography, computer science

MYRIA PEREZ

Paleontologist

Myria Perez is a fossil preparator at the Smithsonian National Museum of Natural History in Washington, DC. She removes rocks from fossils and also glues fossils together.

"I like that it's a combination of art and science," Perez says. "Each fossil kind of has its own personality. It needs glue here, or it needs to be fixed." Sometimes fossils erode and pieces go missing. So Perez adds some putty to fill holes—but scientists know not to study that part.

"The past is the key to the present," she says. "If we learn how ancient ecosystems worked, we can prepare for what's going to happen to them in the future."

—By TFK Kid Reporter Elisha Lee

CORE CLASSES
biology, geology, chemistry, physics, math

The Periodic Table

The chemical elements arranged by atomic number

Element groups

- Alkali Metals
- Alkaline Earth Metals
- Transition Metals
- Other Metals
- Non-metals
- Metalloids
- Halogens
- Noble Gases
- Lanthanides
- Actinides

H 1  Hydrogen

Li 3  Lithium

Be 4  Beryllium

Na 11  Sodium

Mg 12  Magnesium

K 19 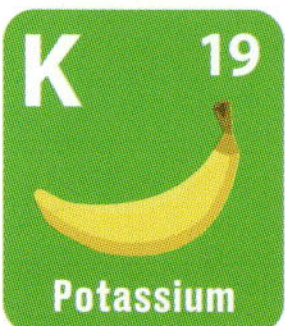 Potassium

Ca 20 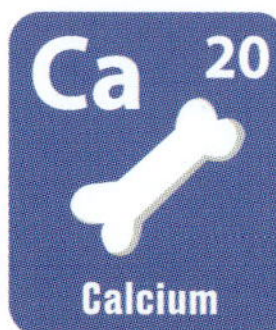 Calcium

Sc 21  Scandium

Ti 22  Titanium

V 23  Vanadium

Cr 24  Chromium

Mn 25  Manganese

Fe 26  Iron

Co 27  Cobalt

Rb 37  Rubidium

Sr 38  Strontium

Y 39 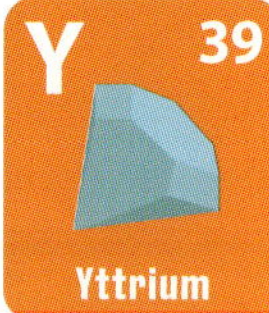 Yttrium

Zr 40 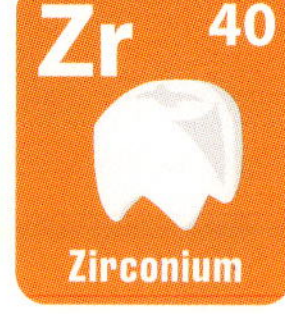 Zirconium

Nb 41  Niobium

Mo 42  Molybdenum

Tc 43 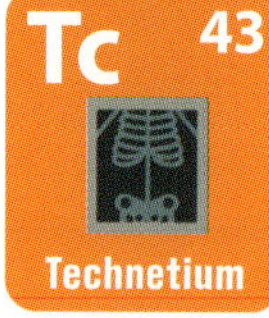 Technetium

Ru 44  Ruthenium

Rh 45  Rhodium

Cs 55 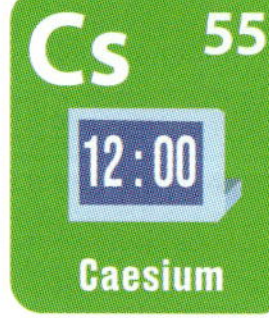 Caesium

Ba 56  Barium

 57–71

Hf 72  Hafnium

Ta 73  Tantalum

W 74  Tungsten

Re 75  Rhenium

Os 76  Osmium

Ir 77 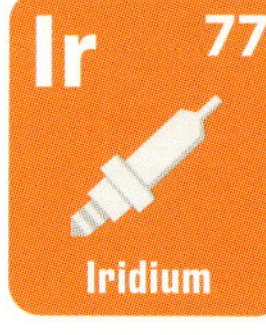 Iridium

Fr 87  Francium

Ra 88  Radium

 89–103

Rf 104  Rutherfordium

Db 105  Dubnium

Sg 106   Seaborgium

Bh 107  Bohrium

Hs 108  Hassium

Mt 109  Meitnerium

La 57 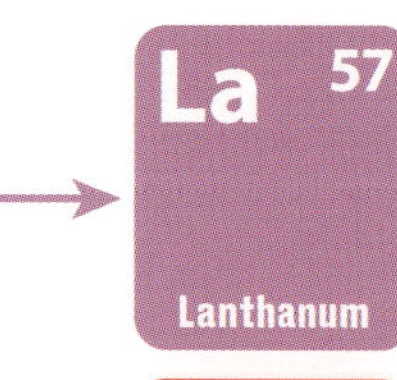 Lanthanum

Ce 58 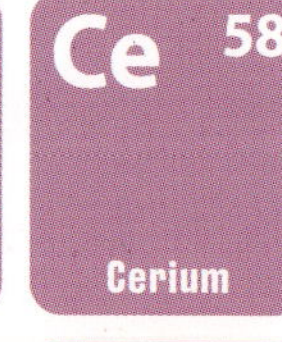 Cerium

Pr 59 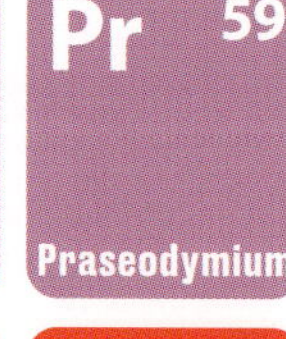 Praseodymium

Nd 60  Neodymium

Pm 61  Promethium

Sm 62  Samarium

Ac 89 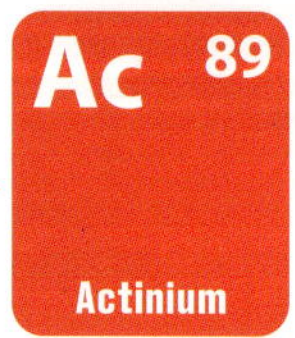 Actinium

Th 90 Thorium

Pa 91  Protactinium

U 92  Uranium

Np 93  Neptunium

Pu 94  Plutonium

Element name

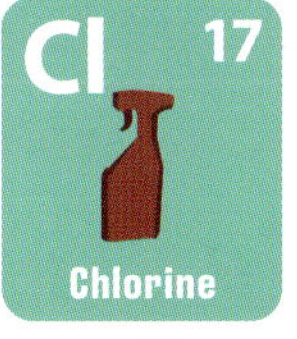

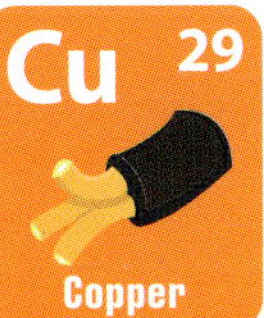

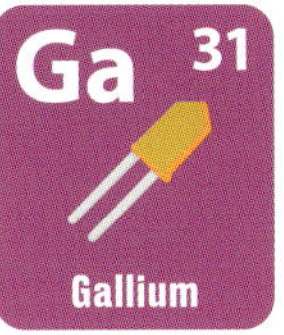

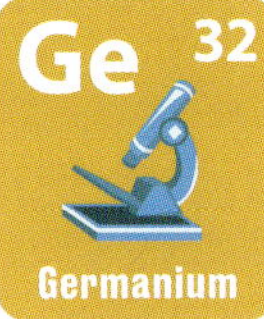

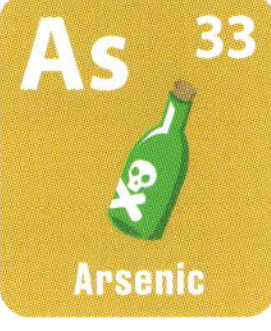

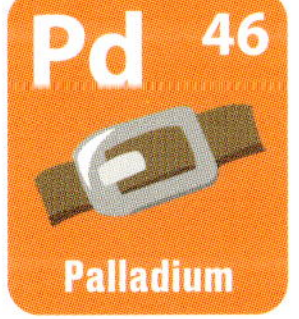

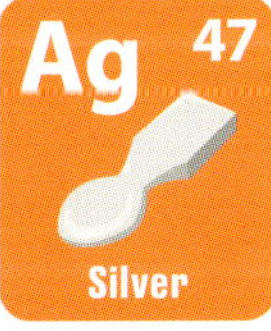

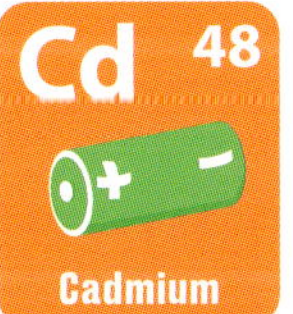

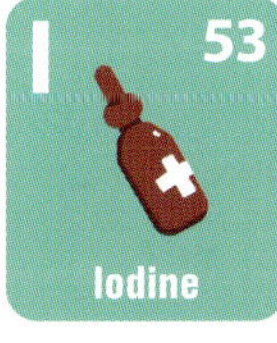

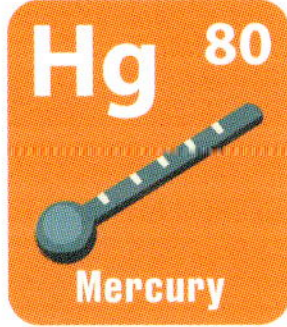

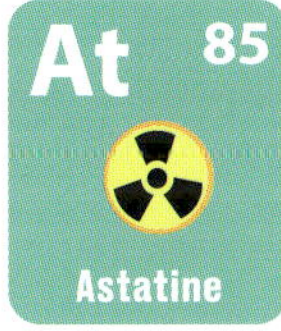

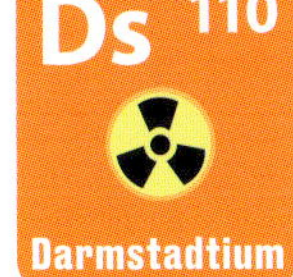

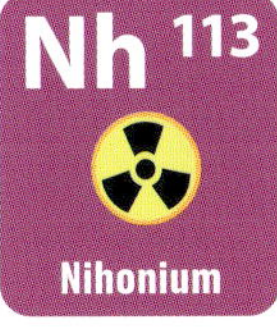

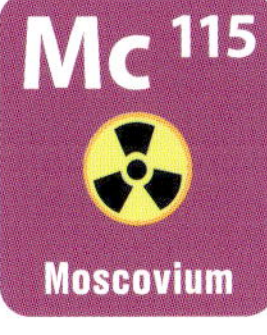

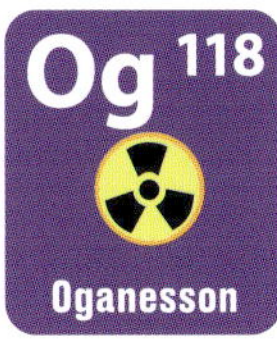

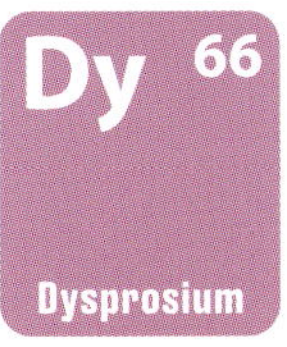

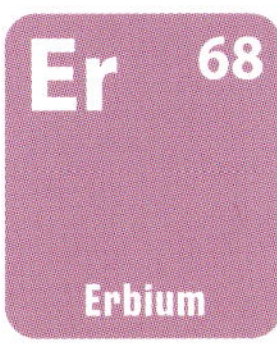

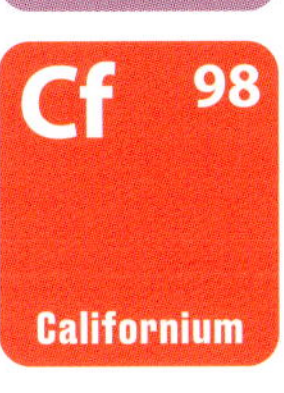

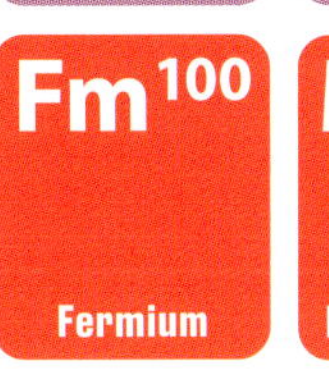

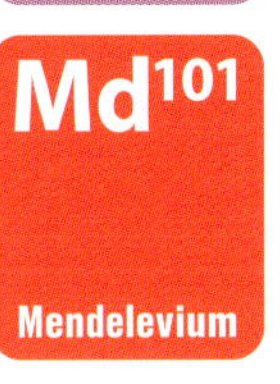

Lr 103
Lawrencium

Dino Derby

Match each fact with the correct image of these amazing dinosaurs.

SPINOSAURUS

TITANOSAURUS

MAIASAURA

MICRORAPTOR

ANKYLOSAURUS

TYRANNOSAURUS

NIGERSAURUS

1 Stretching up to 28 feet (9 m) tall and 122 feet (37 m) long, this dinosaur is the biggest species ever found.

____

2 This plant-eating dino likely used its clubbed tail for side-swiping predators.

____

3 This toothy plant-eater had more than 500 teeth to help it grab plants from the ground.

____

4 Thought to be a good parent, this dinosaur probably brought plants to its young to eat.

____

5 Theropods like this dinosaur had pointy teeth that curved backward and were serrated like knives.

____

6 Not much bigger than a Chihuahua, this flying dinosaur was a fierce predator … of small lizards, fish, and other animals.

____

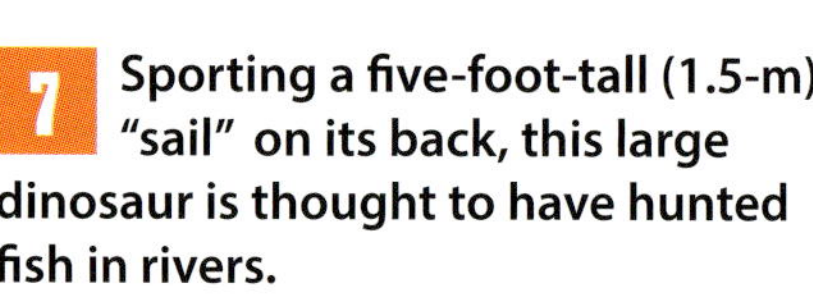

7 Sporting a five-foot-tall (1.5-m) "sail" on its back, this large dinosaur is thought to have hunted fish in rivers.

____

Answers on page 200

CHAPTER 11

SPACE

STARSTRUCK
With the Milky Way galaxy above, a radio telescope "listens" for radio waves from space.

Astro Events 2027

Zoom in on these cosmic happenings.

January 3–4: Quadrantids meteor shower peak

January 22: Supermoon

January / February: The spacecraft *Hera* is scheduled to enter the orbit of the asteroid Didymos and its moon, Dimorphos.

February 6: Annular solar eclipse over much of Africa, South America, Antarctica, and the Pacific and Atlantic Oceans

February 20: Supermoon

March 20: March equinox, with equal amounts of day and night

May 6–7: Eta Aquarids meteor shower peak

May 20: Blue moon

June: As part of the Dragonfly mission, a spacecraft will launch to deliver a robotic hovercraft to Saturn's largest moon, Titan, by 2034.

June 21: June solstice, the longest day of the year

August 2: Total solar eclipse over Europe, southern and western Asia, eastern North America, and the Atlantic and Indian Oceans

August 12: The spacecraft *Lucy* is scheduled to fly by the asteroid Eurybates.

August 12–13: Perseids meteor shower peak

September 15: The spacecraft *Lucy* is expected to fly past the asteroid Polymele.

September 23: September equinox, with equal amounts of day and night

October 21–22: Orionids meteor shower peak

December 13–14: Geminids meteor shower peak

December 22: December solstice, the shortest day of the year

Supermoon

Space Smarts

Annular solar eclipse: when the moon appears as a dark disk on top of a larger, bright disk (the sun), creating what looks like a ring around the moon

Blue moon: a second full moon in a calendar month

Supermoon: when a full moon also happens to be closest to Earth during its 27-day orbit and looks unusually big

Total solar eclipse: when the moon passes between the sun and Earth, completely blocking the face of the sun

A NASA artist's illustration of Artemis astronauts on the moon

Sometime in 2027

- The Nancy Grace Roman Space Telescope will launch. It will have a field of view at least 100 times larger than Hubble's and will survey the cosmos 1,000 times faster.
- As part of the Artemis III mission, a spacecraft will deliver special scientific equipment near the moon's south pole.
- Two Artemis III astronauts will spend a week on the moon's south pole conducting science experiments.

Astronauts Return Home

These astronauts spent an unexpected nine months living in space.

Suni Williams and Butch Wilmore are NASA astronauts. They spent more than nine months in space for what was supposed to be an eight-day mission.

On June 5, 2024, Williams and Wilmore were the first people to blast off on Boeing's new Starliner spacecraft. Their trip was supposed to be eight days long. But the craft had problems and couldn't carry them home. So the two had to wait at the International Space Station (ISS) until a SpaceX Dragon craft arrived on March 16, 2025, to fly them back to Earth.

SAFE LANDING The SpaceX capsule parachutes into the ocean on March 18, 2025.

WELCOME HOME A member of a support team works to steady the SpaceX capsule on March 18, 2025. Those are dolphins near the capsule.

STUCK AT WORK

Astronauts train a long time to prepare for space missions. But Williams and Wilmore's long mission came as a surprise. Fortunately, they had plenty to do on the ISS. They went for space walks. They conducted experiments. "We came up prepared to stay long, even though we [planned] to stay short," Wilmore said in an air-to-ground press conference.

ZERO GRAVITY Wilmore (top) and Williams pose for a photo on June 13, 2024.

Being home was filled with challenges. "The toughest thing about returning to Earth after many months in space is adapting to gravity," retired astronaut Terry Virts says. Williams and Wilmore went through medical tests. They also did special workouts to help them readjust.

SPLASHING DOWN

Wilmore and Williams returned to Earth on March 18, 2025—that's 278 days later than planned. After their SpaceX capsule splashed down in the ocean, they received a message. "On behalf of SpaceX, welcome home," radioed mission control in California.

—By Jeffrey Kluger for TIME

Spectacular Space

Peer into the past with these amazing space images.

Launched in 2021, the James Webb Space Telescope (JWST) is the most powerful space telescope ever. It can see galaxies forming, stars exploding, and distant planets orbiting distant suns.

Looking into space is like time traveling. That's because of light-years, or the amount of time it takes for light traveling from space to get to Earth for humans to see. For instance, in 2024, the JWST took a picture of five possible galaxies 13.6 billion light-years away. That means that what scientists were seeing were the galaxies forming 13.6 billion years ago. And they would be among the first galaxies ever in the universe.

Take a look at these images from the JWST—and do some time traveling yourself.

A pillar of gas and dust from a newly forming star, nicknamed the "cosmic tornado"

Two galaxies, one in the center and one that appears to be wrapped around the other

A young star cluster in a galaxy called the Small Magellanic Cloud

Spectacular Space

Gas and dust from a pair of actively forming stars

Jupiter

Fingerlike gas and dust called the Pillars of Creation

The Ring Nebula, a dying star throwing off its outer layers

Galaxies IC 2163 and NGC 2207

A NEW TELESCOPE

The universe is always expanding. But scientists have noticed that it's expanding even faster than they thought—and they want to know why. They hope that the Nancy Grace Roman Space Telescope will help them do that. Scheduled to launch by May 2027, the telescope will explore dark matter and dark energy, and help scientists answer questions about the universe.

The Solar System

A solar system is a collection of celestial bodies that include planets, moons, comets, and asteroids that orbit a star. Learn more about the solar system you live in.

NEPTUNE

Distance from the Sun: 2.8 billion miles (4.5 billion km)

Size / Diameter: 30,775 miles (49,528 km)

Orbit Time: 165 Earth years

Moons: 16

Average Surface Temperature: –330°F (–201°C)

Fun Fact: Scientists think Neptune might have a giant, superhot ocean under its clouds.

URANUS

Distance from the Sun: 1.8 billion miles (2.9 billion km)

Size / Diameter: 31,763 miles (51,118 km)

Orbit Time: 84 Earth years

Moons: 28

Average Surface Temperature: –320°F (–196°C)

Fun Fact: Because of the way Uranus rotates, the planet appears to spin sideways, more like a rolling ball than a spinning top.

SATURN

Distance from the Sun: 886 million miles (1.4 billion km)

Size / Diameter: 74,897 miles (120,500 km)

Orbit Time: 29.4 Earth years

Moons: 146, but scientists are always discovering more

Average Surface Temperature: –220°F (–140°C)

Fun Fact: Saturn's rings are made of billions of chunks of rock and ice that came from moons, comets, and asteroids shattered by the planet's intense gravity.

JUPITER

Distance from the Sun: 484 million miles (778 million km)

Size / Diameter: 86,881 miles (139,822 km)

Orbit Time: 11.9 Earth years

Moons: 95

Average Surface Temperature: 166°F (74°C)

Fun Fact: The largest planet in the solar system, Jupiter could fit 1,000 Earths inside it (if Jupiter were hollow).

THE SUN

Distance from Earth: 93.3 million miles (150.2 million km)

Size / Diameter: 865,000 miles (1.4 million km)

Average Surface Temperature: 10,000°F (5538°C)

Fun Fact: Like all stars, the sun will one day run out of energy and die. But scientists think that won't happen for about five billion years.

MERCURY

Distance from the Sun: 36 million miles (58 million km)

Size / Diameter: 3,032 miles (4,880 km)

Orbit Time: 88 Earth days

Moons: 0

Average Surface Temperature: 333°F (167°C)

Fun Fact: Mercury's surface kind of looks like Earth's moon, with lots of craters made by meteoroid and comet impacts.

VENUS

Distance from the Sun: 67 million miles (108 million km)

Size / Diameter: 7,521 miles (12,104 km)

Orbit Time: 225 Earth days

Moons: 0

Average Surface Temperature: 867°F (464°C)

Fun Fact: Even though Mercury is closer to the sun, Venus is actually the hottest planet in the solar system because its dense atmosphere full of CO_2 traps heat from the sun.

EARTH

Distance from the Sun: 93.3 million miles (150.2 million km)

Size / Diameter: 7,926 miles (12,760 km)

Orbit Time: 365.3 Earth days

Moons: 1

Average Surface Temperature: 59°F (15°C)

Fun Fact: Earth is the only planet in the solar system that has liquid water on the surface, which provided a great place for life to begin 3.8 million years ago.

MARS

Distance from the Sun: 142 million miles (228 million km)

Size / Diameter: 4,212 miles (6,780 km)

Orbit Time: 1.9 Earth years

Moons: 2

Average Surface Temperature: –85°F (–65°C)

Fun Fact: Mars's surface looks red because the iron minerals in its rocks, dirt, and dust rust and give off a reddish color to the atmosphere.

Cosmic Neighbors

ASTEROIDS are rocky leftovers from the earliest time of our solar system. They hang out mostly in the "asteroid belt" between Mars and Jupiter as they orbit the sun.

MOONS are natural satellites made of rock or ice that orbit planets (and sometimes asteroids).

COMETS are huge bunches of frozen gases, rock, and dust that orbit the sun. When they're close to the sun, the heat creates a tail that can be millions of miles long.

METEOROIDS are pieces of asteroids or comets, often created by a collision. When a meteoroid enters Earth's atmosphere, it becomes a meteor. When it lands on Earth, it's a meteorite.

GALAXIES are collections of stars, planets, and lots of gassy and dusty clouds held together by gravity. Scientists estimate that anywhere from 100 billion to 2 trillion galaxies could be in the universe; ours is called the Milky Way.

STARS are giant balls of hot, mostly hydrogen gas that often have planets orbiting them. Scientists think up to one septillion (a one followed by 24 zeros) could be in the universe.

What's Your Planet Personality?

Take this just-for-fun quiz to see which planet you're most like.

1 What's your ideal vacation activity?
A. Hanging out on a hot, sunny beach
B. Taking a ride in a hot-air balloon
C. Skiing down a mountain

2 It's the weekend—what are your plans?
A. I'm just going to stay home and read a book.
B. I'm having a few friends over for a sleepover.
C. I'm going to a big birthday party with tons of friends.

3 You're a climatologist—which weather phenomenon would you choose to study?
A. Heat waves
B. Tornadoes and hurricanes
C. Ice storms

4 Which best describes your fashion style?
A. Classic—I don't go for trends and just wear whatever I want.
B. Vibrant—I love colors and patterns.
C. Cozy—Give me sweats and pj's any day.

5 Which phrase are you most likely to say to your friends?
A. "Let's go!"
B. "Let's crush this!"
C. "Let's party!"

6 How would your friends describe you most of the time?
A. Sunny and happy
B. Spirited—I say what I think.
C. Quiet and shy—until you get to know me

MOSTLY *A'S*

You're Mercury!

Sort of like the planet closest to the sun, you're a warm person who's just fine hanging out by themselves. You're always in a hurry to try something new, kind of like how Mercury's in a hurry to orbit around the sun in just 88 Earth days.

MOSTLY *B'S*

You're Jupiter!

You're loyal to your close group of friends, who appreciate your honest and spirited opinions that swirl like Jupiter's many cyclones. You work hard to crush nearly everything you do, sort of like how gassy Jupiter's pressure would crush anything caught in its atmosphere.

MOSTLY *C'S*

You're Neptune!

Your reserved nature makes you mysterious, so like Neptune's many moons, people can't help but want to orbit around you. You're a night owl and love to have fun when it's dark—sort of like this planet, where high noon always looks like twilight.

This quiz is just for fun, so it's OK if your answer doesn't match your personality.

CHAPTER 12

SPORTS

MAKING WAVES
A swimmer competes in a freestyle event.

We Are the Champions

The winners of some of the sports world's major events

NATIONAL FOOTBALL LEAGUE (NFL) SUPER BOWL WINNERS

2020: Kansas City Chiefs

2021: Tampa Bay Buccaneers

2022: Los Angeles Rams

2023: Kansas City Chiefs

2024: Kansas City Chiefs

2025: Philadelphia Eagles

NFL MOST VALUABLE PLAYERS

2020: Aaron Rodgers, Green Bay Packers

2021: Aaron Rodgers, Green Bay Packers

2022: Patrick Mahomes, Kansas City Chiefs

2023: Lamar Jackson, Baltimore Ravens

2024: Josh Allen, Buffalo Bills

2025: Josh Allen, Buffalo Bills

Philadelphia Eagles

NATIONAL BASKETBALL ASSOCIATION (NBA) FINALS WINNERS

2020: Los Angeles Lakers

2021: Milwaukee Bucks

2022: Golden State Warriors

2023: Denver Nuggets

2024: Boston Celtics

2025: Oklahoma City Thunder

NBA MOST VALUABLE PLAYERS

2020: Giannis Antetokounmpo, Milwaukee Bucks

2021: Nikola Jokić, Denver Nuggets

2022: Nikola Jokić, Denver Nuggets

2023: Joel Embiid, Philadelphia 76ers

2024: Nikola Jokić, Denver Nuggets

2025: Shai Gilgeous-Alexander, Oklahoma City Thunder

Oklahoma City Thunder and Indiana Pacers

Will Smith of the Los Angeles Dodgers tags out Giancarlo Stanton of the New York Yankees.

MAJOR LEAGUE BASEBALL (MLB) WORLD SERIES WINNERS

2020: Los Angeles Dodgers

2021: Atlanta Braves

2022: Houston Astros

2023: Texas Rangers

2024: Los Angeles Dodgers

2025: Los Angeles Dodgers

Shohei Ohtani and his dog Decoy

MLB MOST VALUABLE PLAYERS, AMERICAN LEAGUE

2020: José Abreu, Chicago White Sox

2021: Shohei Ohtani, Los Angeles Angels

2022: Aaron Judge, New York Yankees

2023: Shohei Ohtani, Los Angeles Angels

2024: Aaron Judge, New York Yankees

MLB MOST VALUABLE PLAYERS, NATIONAL LEAGUE

2020: Freddie Freeman, Atlanta Braves

2021: Bryce Harper, Philadelphia Phillies

2022: Paul Goldschmidt, St. Louis Cardinals

2023: Ronald Acuña Jr., Atlanta Braves

2024: Shohei Ohtani, Los Angeles Dodgers

NATIONAL HOCKEY LEAGUE (NHL) STANLEY CUP WINNERS

2020: Tampa Bay Lightning

2021: Tampa Bay Lightning

2022: Colorado Avalanche

2023: Vegas Golden Knights

2024: Florida Panthers

2025: Florida Panthers

NHL MOST VALUABLE PLAYERS

2020: Leon Draisaitl, Edmonton Oilers

2021: Connor McDavid, Edmonton Oilers

2022: Auston Matthews, Toronto Maple Leafs

2023: Connor McDavid, Edmonton Oilers

2024: Nathan MacKinnon, Colorado Avalanche

2025: Connor Hellebuyck, Winnipeg Jets

Aleksander Barkov

A'ja Wilson

WOMEN'S NATIONAL BASKETBALL ASSOCIATION (WNBA) FINALS WINNERS

2020: Seattle Storm

2021: Chicago Sky

2022: Las Vegas Aces

2023: Las Vegas Aces

2024: New York Liberty

2025: Las Vegas Aces

WNBA MOST VALUABLE PLAYERS

2020: A'ja Wilson, Las Vegas Aces

2021: Jonquel Jones, Connecticut Sun

2022: A'ja Wilson, Las Vegas Aces

2023: Breanna Stewart, New York Liberty

2024: A'ja Wilson, Las Vegas Aces

2025: A'ja Wilson, Las Vegas Aces

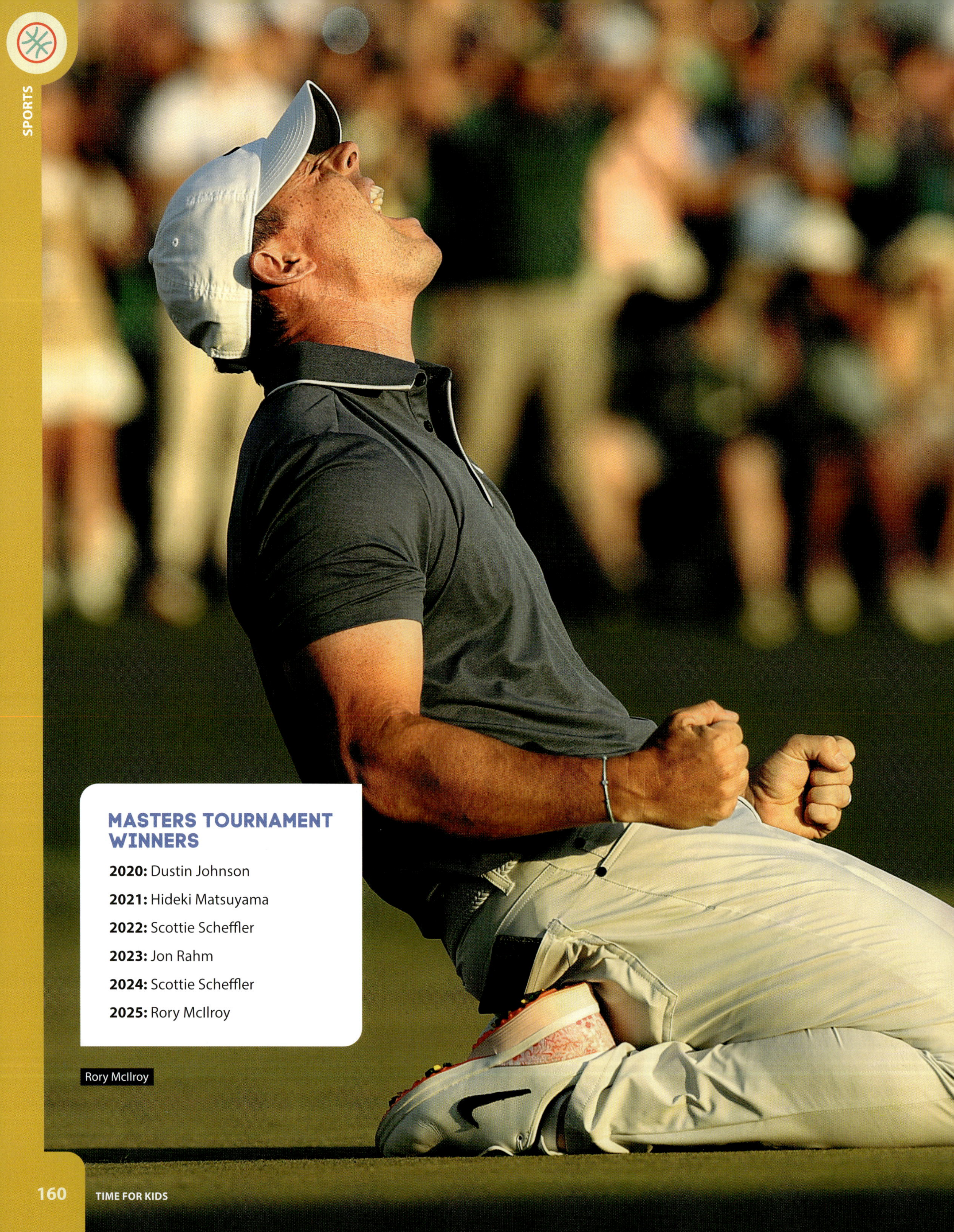

MASTERS TOURNAMENT WINNERS

2020: Dustin Johnson

2021: Hideki Matsuyama

2022: Scottie Scheffler

2023: Jon Rahm

2024: Scottie Scheffler

2025: Rory McIlroy

Rory McIlroy

US WOMEN'S OPEN WINNERS

2020: A Lim Kim

2021: Yuka Saso

2022: Minjee Lee

2023: Allisen Corpuz

2024: Yuka Saso

2025: Maja Stark

US OPEN WINNERS, WOMEN'S SINGLES

2020: Naomi Osaka

2021: Emma Raducanu

2022: Iga Świątek

2023: Coco Gauff

2024: Aryna Sabalenka

2025: Aryna Sabalenka

US OPEN WINNERS, MEN'S SINGLES

2020: Dominic Thiem

2021: Daniil Medvedev

2022: Carlos Alcaraz

2023: Novak Djokovic

2024: Jannik Sinner

2025: Carlos Alcaraz

Maja Stark

Barbra Banda of the Orlando Pride dribbles past Leicy Santos of the Washington Spirit.

NATIONAL WOMEN'S SOCCER LEAGUE (NWSL) CHAMPIONSHIP WINNERS

(2020 canceled due to COVID)

2021: Washington Spirit

2022: Portland Thorns

2023: New Jersey / New York Gotham

2024: Orlando Pride

MAJOR LEAGUE SOCCER CUP WINNERS

2020: Columbus Crew

2021: New York City Football Club

2022: Los Angeles Football Club

2023: Columbus Crew

2024: Los Angeles Galaxy

FROM THE PAGES OF

TIME KIDS AMAZING ATHLETES
101 STARS YOU NEED TO KNOW!

Amazing Athletes

These athletes show you don't have to play football or basketball to be a star.

—By James Buckley, Jr.

NATHAN CHEN

Figure Skating

Growing up in Salt Lake City, Utah, Chen started skating when he was three. Later, he added ballet training—that's why he's so graceful and flowing on the ice. Chen won a record six US national senior championships in a row, then earned a bronze in the team event at the 2018 Olympics. He soared to gold in the individual skate at the 2022 Olympics.

ERICA ENDERS

Auto Racing

Enders is one of the overall best drivers in drag racing, a sport with few women competitors. Since 2005, she's been winning titles in the Pro Stock Division. Her car reaches more than 210 miles an hour (338 km/h) in only 1,000 feet (305 m). In 2022, Enders had the fastest race in Pro Stock history at only 6.45 seconds, and she earned six national championships through 2023.

TATYANA MCFADDEN

Track and Field

McFadden began her life in a Russian orphanage with spina bifida, a spinal condition that left her paralyzed from the waist down. When she was six, she was adopted by US parents—and found she loved going fast. Her breakthrough came with three gold medals at the 2012 Paralympics. McFadden's career includes 20 Paralympic medals in wheelchair racing and 24 marathon wins.

CHLOE KIM

Snowboarding

Kim was only 14 when she burst onto the snowboarding scene with a SuperPipe gold at the 2015 X Games. She took home awards at the world championship and the Junior Olympics, thrilling fans with her high-flying, twisting, creative skills on the half-pipe. In 2018, she won a Winter Olympics gold medal—then she repeated gold in 2022.

NYJAH HUSTON

Skateboarding

Few skaters have been as successful as Huston. He first made news by reaching the X Games when he was only 11 years old. He's been among the world's best street skaters since, winning a record 13 X Games gold medals and six World Championships. He even won a bronze medal at the 2024 Olympics in Paris, France.

LYLE THOMPSON

Lacrosse

Lacrosse grew out of an Indigenous American game that's been played for hundreds of years. Thompson grew up playing in his Haudenosaunee (a group of six Native American nations) community in New York. At the University of Albany, he set an all-time college record with 400 goals. As a pro, he's a three-time Premier Lacrosse League All-Star and a league MVP. Playing for the Haudenosaunee Nationals team, he's taken part in three World Championships.

SPORTS

GAME

Unbreakable

Match the athlete with the record that some experts think won't be broken anytime soon.

1. Most Career Points
2. Most Points by a Rookie
3. Most Career Stolen Bases
4. Most Assists
5. Most World Championship Gold Medals
6. Most Career Rushing Yards
7. Most Grand Slam Titles
8. Most Olympic Medals

CAITLIN CLARK

RICKEY HENDERSON

SERENA WILLIAMS

MICHAEL PHELPS

MIA HAMM

EMMITT SMITH

WAYNE GRETZKY

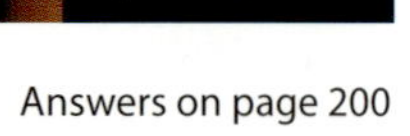

SIMONE BILES

Answers on page 200

CHAPTER 13

THE UNITED STATES

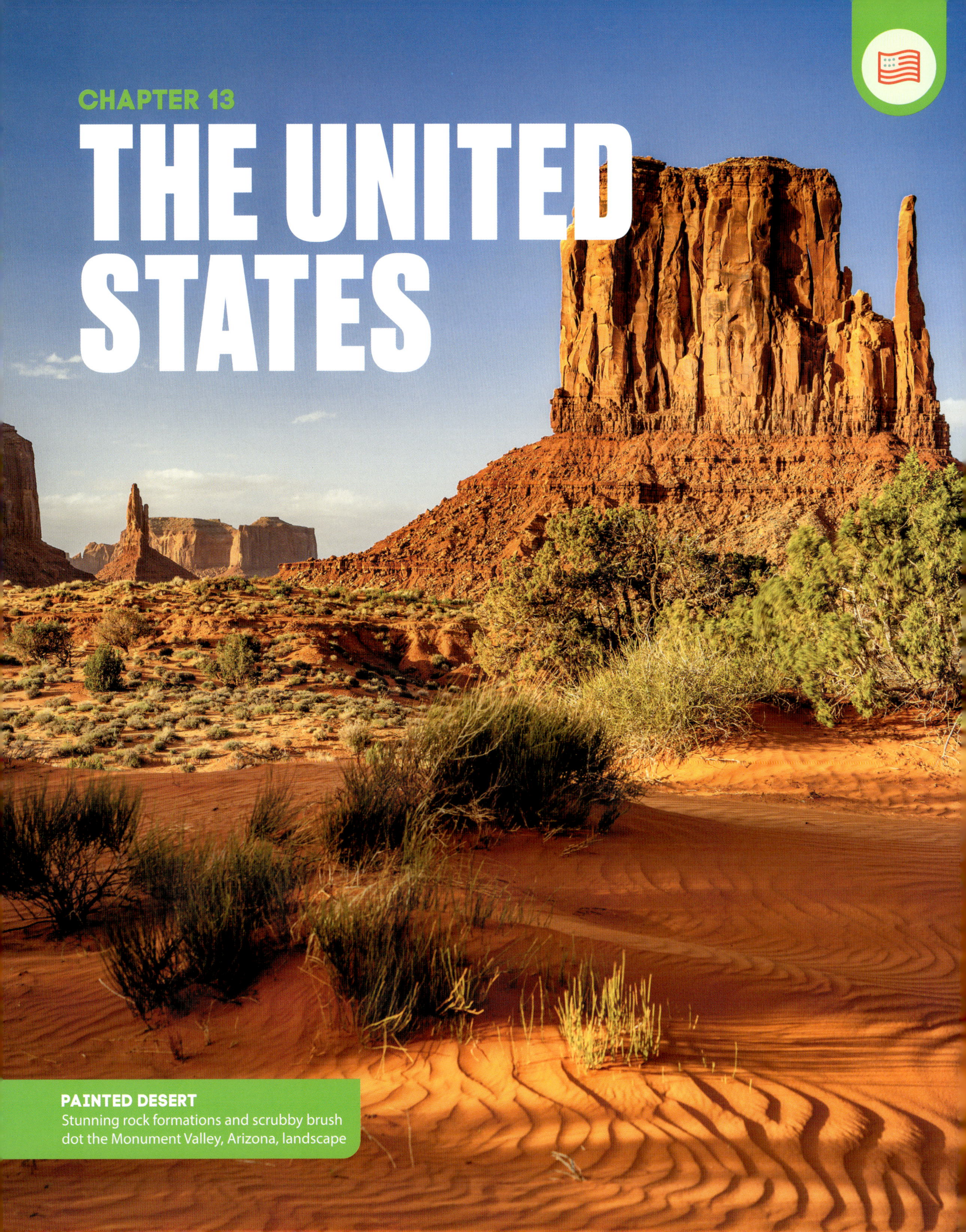

PAINTED DESERT
Stunning rock formations and scrubby brush dot the Monument Valley, Arizona, landscape

United Regions of America

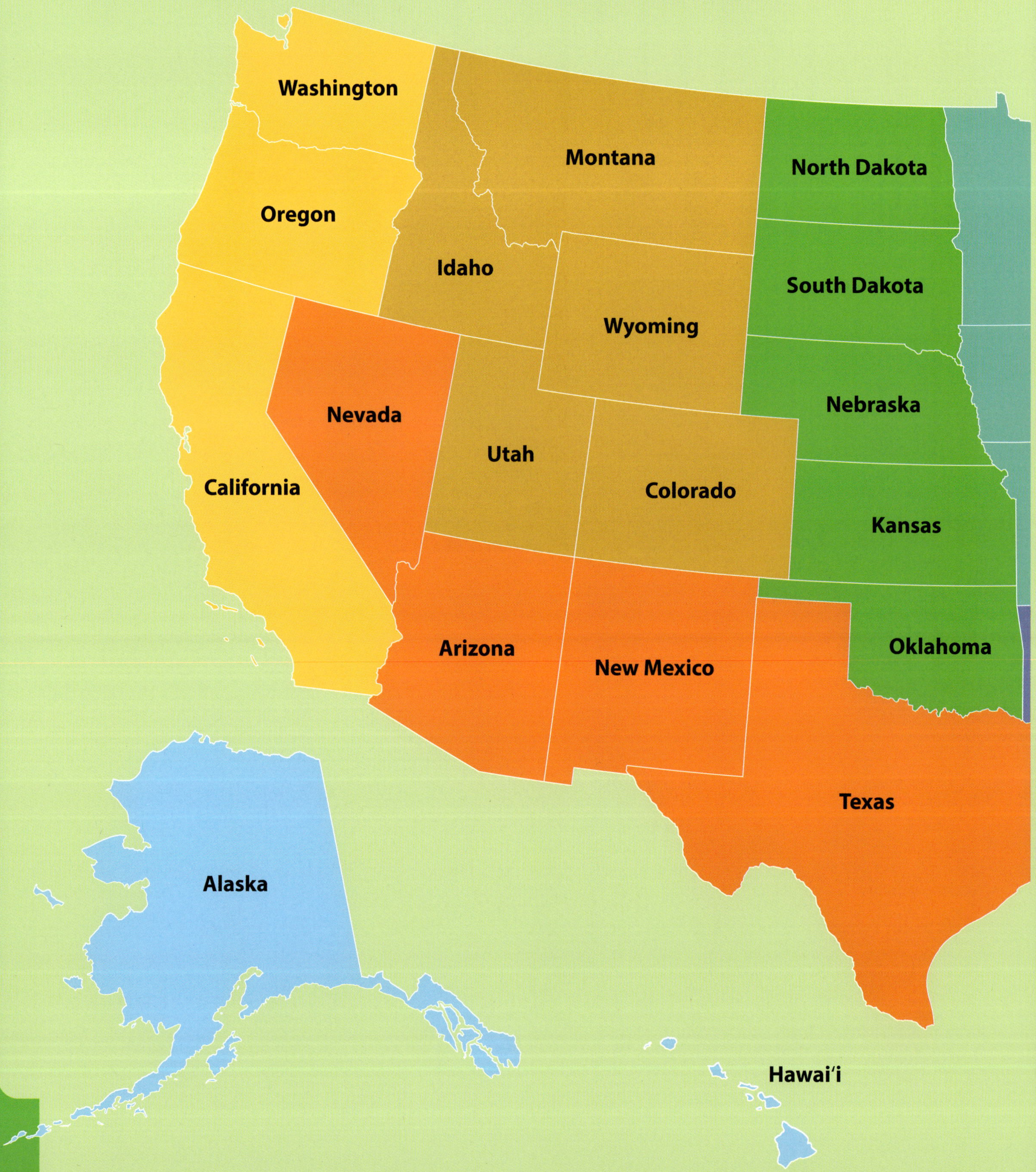

Washington
Montana
North Dakota
Oregon
Idaho
South Dakota
Wyoming
Nevada
Nebraska
Utah
California
Colorado
Kansas
Arizona
New Mexico
Oklahoma
Texas
Alaska
Hawai'i

Many people group the continental US into seven geographic regions. (And don't forget Alaska and Hawai'i!)

REGIONS

- NEW ENGLAND
- MID-ATLANTIC
- SOUTH
- MIDWEST
- GREAT PLAINS
- SOUTHWEST
- ROCKY MOUNTAIN
- WEST COAST
- ALASKA & HAWAI'I

Alaska and Hawai'i are not shown in actual position or to scale.

ALABAMA

CAPITAL: Montgomery

LARGEST CITY: Huntsville

POSTAL CODE: AL

LAND AREA: 50,645 square miles (131,171 sq km)

POPULATION ESTIMATE (2020): 5,024,279

MOTTO: *Audemus jura nostra defendere.* (We dare maintain our rights.)

TREE: Longleaf pine

FLOWER: Camellia

BIRD: Yellowhammer

NICKNAMES: Yellowhammer State, Cotton State

PEOPLE BORN HERE: Rosa Parks, civil rights leader; Jesse Owens, Olympic track-and-field athlete; Harper Lee, author; Courteney Cox, actress

The sun sets over Alabama's Mobile Bay, which leads out to the Gulf of Mexico.

FUN FACT: The Natural Bridge is a sandstone-and-iron-ore bridge formed two million years ago.

ALASKA

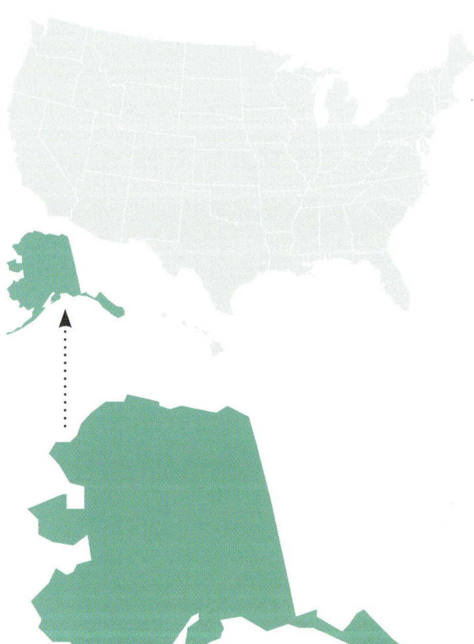

CAPITAL: Juneau

LARGEST CITY: Anchorage

POSTAL CODE: AK

LAND AREA: 570,641 square miles (1,477,953 sq km)

POPULATION ESTIMATE (2020): 733,391

MOTTO: North to the future.

TREE: Sitka spruce

FLOWER: Alpine forget-me-not

BIRD: Willow ptarmigan

NICKNAMES: The Last Frontier

PEOPLE BORN HERE: Peter the Aleut, Orthodox saint; William Paul, Native American activist; Irene Bedard, actress, voice of Pocahontas

A playful whale dives down into the ocean waters off Alaska.

FUN FACT: More than 98 percent of the country's brown bears live in Alaska.

ARIZONA

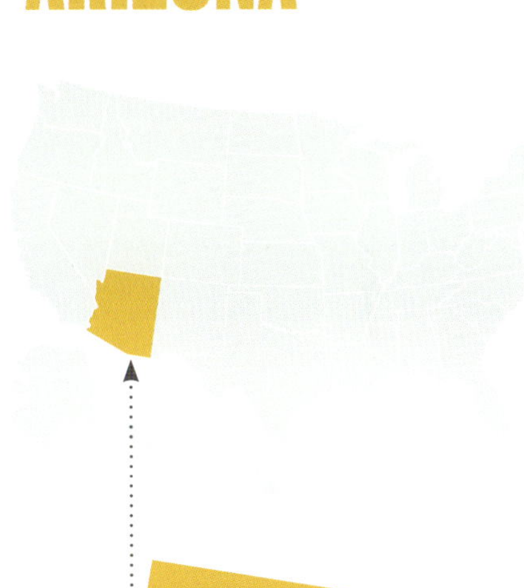

CAPITAL: Phoenix

LARGEST CITY: Phoenix

POSTAL CODE: AZ

LAND AREA: 113,594 square miles (294,207 sq km)

POPULATION ESTIMATE (2020): 7,151,502

MOTTO: *Ditat deus.* (God enriches.)

TREE: Palo verde

FLOWER: Saguaro cactus blossom

BIRD: Cactus wren

NICKNAMES: Grand Canyon State

PEOPLE BORN HERE: Cesar Chavez, labor leader, activist; Joan Ganz Cooney, co-creator, *Sesame Street*; Emma Stone, actress

Horseshoe Bend is a stunning river-and-rock formation near the town of Page, Arizona.

FUN FACT: About 50 feet (15 m) tall, the saguaro cactus grows only in the Sonoran Desert.

ARKANSAS

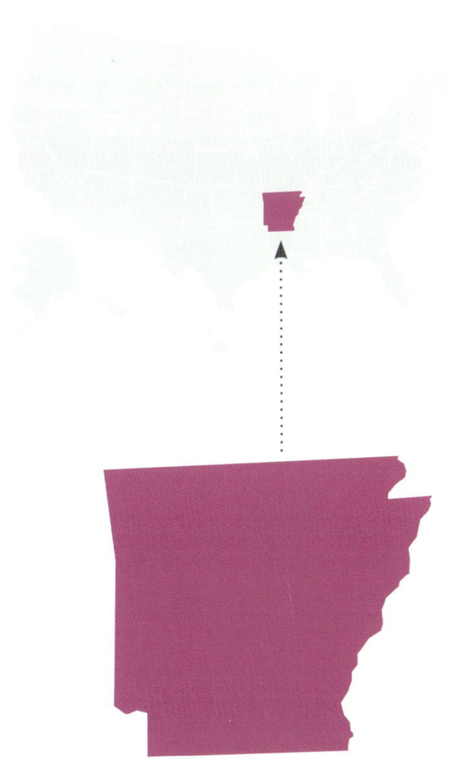

CAPITAL: Little Rock

LARGEST CITY: Little Rock

POSTAL CODE: AR

LAND AREA: 52,035 square miles (134,771 sq km)

POPULATION ESTIMATE (2020): 3,011,524

MOTTO: *Regnat populus.* (The people rule.)

TREE: Loblolly pine

FLOWER: Apple blossom

BIRD: Northern mockingbird

NICKNAMES: Natural State

PEOPLE BORN HERE: Bill Clinton, US president; Johnny Cash, singer-songwriter; Bo Nix, football player

The Old Mill is a reproduction of an 1880s grain mill in North Little Rock, Arkansas.

FUN FACT: In 1957, nine Black students known as the Little Rock Nine integrated a high school.

CALIFORNIA

CAPITAL: Sacramento

LARGEST CITY: Los Angeles

POSTAL CODE: CA

LAND AREA: 155,779 square miles (403,466 sq km)

POPULATION ESTIMATE (2020): 39,538,223

MOTTO: *Eureka*. (I found it.)

TREE: Coastal redwood

FLOWER: California poppy

BIRD: California quail

NICKNAMES: Golden State

PEOPLE BORN HERE: William Randolph Hearst, newspaper publisher; Julia Child, chef, author; Aaron Judge, baseball player; Billie Eilish, singer; Olivia Rodrigo, actress, singer-songwriter

Surfing in the Pacific Ocean is a popular activity in California.

FUN FACT: The Golden Gate Bridge in San Francisco is painted a color called International Orange.

COLORADO

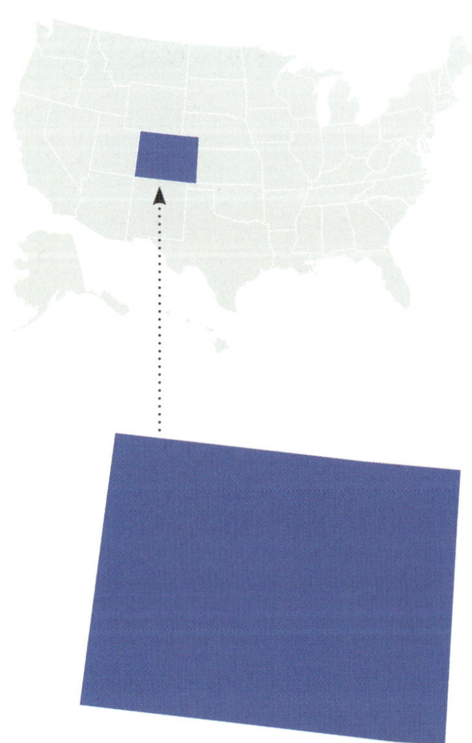

CAPITAL: Denver

LARGEST CITY: Denver

POSTAL CODE: CO

LAND AREA: 103,642 square miles (268,431 sq km)

POPULATION ESTIMATE (2020): 5,773,714

MOTTO: *Nil sine numine.* (Nothing without providence or deity.)

TREE: Colorado blue spruce

FLOWER: Rocky mountain columbine

BIRD: Lark bunting

NICKNAMES: Centennial State

PEOPLE BORN HERE: Ruth Handler, creator of Barbie; Scott Carpenter, astronaut, second American to orbit Earth; Sophia Smith, soccer player

Drivers cruising through Colorado can spot spectacular colors in the fall.

FUN FACT: The Eisenhower-Johnson Memorial Tunnel bores through nearly two miles (3.2 km) of a mountain.

CONNECTICUT

CAPITAL: Hartford

LARGEST CITY: Bridgeport

POSTAL CODE: CT

LAND AREA: 4,842 square miles (12,542 sq km)

POPULATION ESTIMATE (2020): 3,605,944

MOTTO: *Qui transtulit sustinet.* (He who transplanted still sustains.)

TREE: The Charter oak

FLOWER: Mountain laurel

BIRD: American robin

NICKNAMES: Constitution State, Nutmeg State

PEOPLE BORN HERE: Benedict Arnold, Revolutionary War figure; J. P. Morgan, business leader; Charli D'Amelio, social media personality; Gaten Matarazzo, actor

Part of the Saville Dam, this 1940s tower is a must-see spot in Connecticut.

FUN FACT: Connecticut's Weir Farm National Historic Park is the only national park dedicated to a painter.

DELAWARE

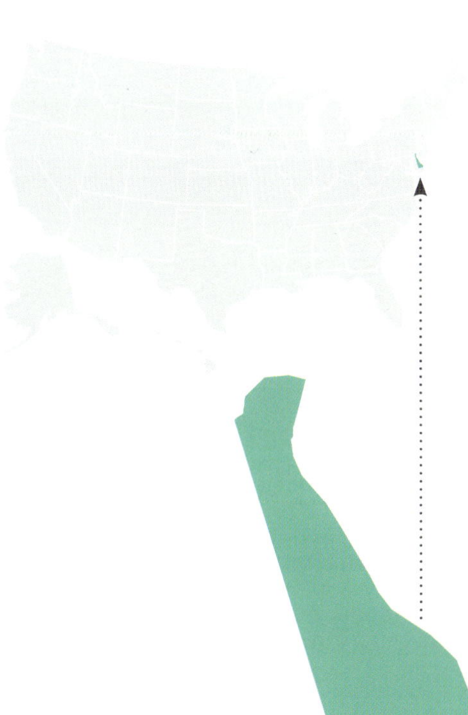

CAPITAL: Dover

LARGEST CITY: Wilmington

POSTAL CODE: DE

LAND AREA: 1,949 square miles (5,047 sq km)

POPULATION ESTIMATE (2020): 989,948

MOTTO: Liberty and independence.

TREE: American holly

FLOWER: Peach blossom

BIRD: Blue hen chicken

NICKNAMES: First State, Diamond State

PEOPLE BORN HERE: Eldridge R. Johnson, creator of the Victrola, an early record player; Stephen Marley, reggae artist; Aubrey Plaza, actress

A sandy trail leads to the beach in Cape Henlopen State Park in Delaware.

FUN FACT: Delaware was the first state to ratify, or approve, the US Constitution, on December 7, 1787.

FLORIDA

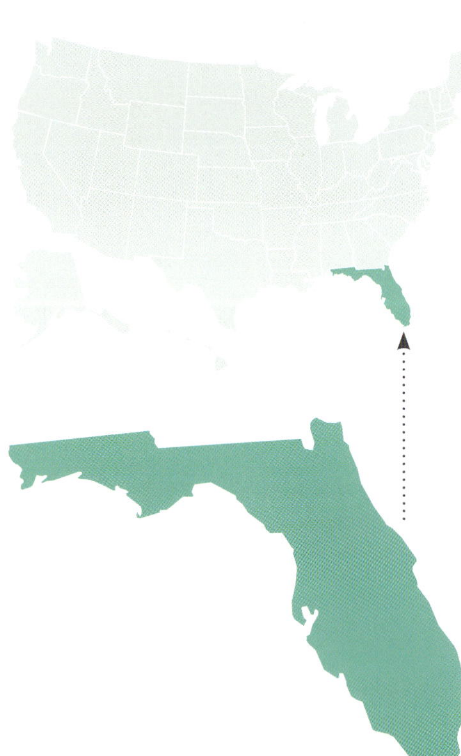

CAPITAL: Tallahassee

LARGEST CITY: Jacksonville

POSTAL CODE: FL

LAND AREA: 53,625 square miles (138,887 sq km)

POPULATION ESTIMATE (2020): 21,538,187

MOTTO: In God we trust.

TREE: Sabal palm

FLOWER: Orange blossom

BIRD: Northern mockingbird

NICKNAMES: Sunshine State

PEOPLE BORN HERE: Peyton List, actress; Coco Gauff, Olympic tennis player; Caeleb Dressel, Olympic swimmer

Lifeguards posted in colorful towers on Miami Beach watch over swimmers.

FUN FACT: You can spot the rare grass-hopper sparrow at Kissimmee Prairie Preserve State Park.

GEORGIA

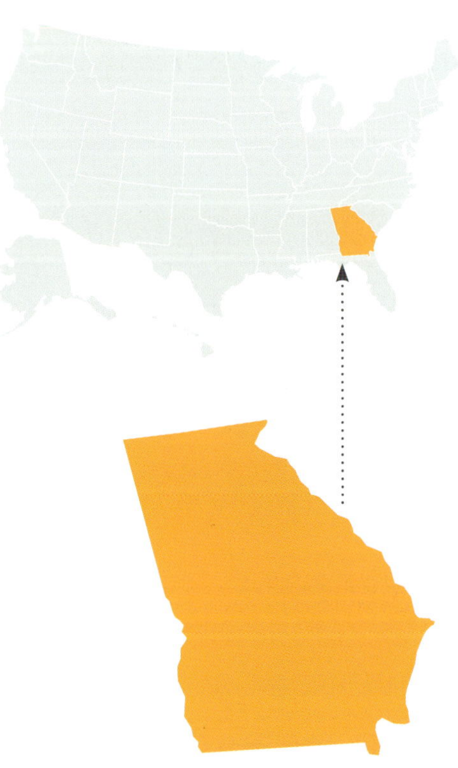

CAPITAL: Atlanta

LARGEST CITY: Atlanta

POSTAL CODE: GA

LAND AREA: 57,513 square miles (148,959 sq km)

POPULATION ESTIMATE (2020): 10,711,908

MOTTO: Wisdom, justice, and moderation.

TREE: Southern live oak

FLOWER: Cherokee rose

BIRD: Brown thrasher

NICKNAMES: Peach State, Empire State of the South

PEOPLE BORN HERE: Martin Luther King, Jr., civil rights leader; Halle Bailey, actress; Iain Armitage, actor

Built in the 1920s, Swan House is now a popular place for events like weddings.

FUN FACT: A local Cherokee named Sequoyah developed a syllable-based Cherokee alphabet with 86 characters.

HAWAIʻI

CAPITAL: Honolulu

LARGEST CITY: Honolulu

POSTAL CODE: HI

LAND AREA: 6,423 square miles (16,635 sq km)

POPULATION ESTIMATE (2020): 1,455,271

MOTTO: *Ua mau ke ea o ka ʻāina I ka pono.* (The life of the land is perpetuated in righteousness.)

TREE: Kukui

FLOWER: Yellow hibiscus

BIRD: Nene

NICKNAMES: Aloha State

PEOPLE BORN HERE: Daniel Inouye, US senator, WWII hero; Barack Obama, US president; Jason Momoa, actor

The Nāpali Coast on the island of Kauai is mountainous and rugged.

FUN FACT: ʻIolani Palace is the only royal palace in the United States.

IDAHO

CAPITAL: Boise

LARGEST CITY: Boise

POSTAL CODE: ID

LAND AREA: 82,643 square miles (214,045 sq km)

POPULATION ESTIMATE (2020): 1,839,106

MOTTO: *Esto perpetua.* (Let it be perpetual.)

TREE: Western white pine

FLOWER: Western syringa

BIRD: Mountain bluebird

NICKNAMES: Gem State

PEOPLE BORN HERE: Ezra Pound, poet; Lana Turner, actress

Farm machinery sprays water to irrigate a potato field in Idaho.

FUN FACT: The state capital uses heat generated from local volcanic activity.

ILLINOIS

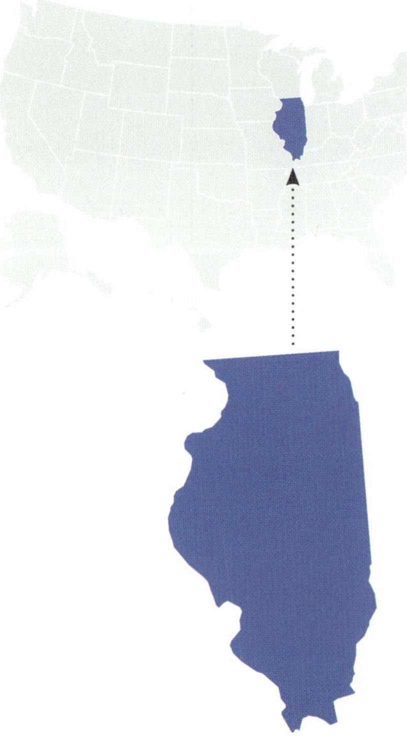

CAPITAL: Springfield

LARGEST CITY: Chicago

POSTAL CODE: IL

LAND AREA: 55,519 square miles (143,793 sq km)

POPULATION ESTIMATE (2020): 12,812,508

MOTTO: State sovereignty, national union.

TREE: White oak

FLOWER: Violet

BIRD: Northern cardinal

NICKNAMES: Prairie State, Land of Lincoln

PEOPLE BORN HERE: Walt Disney, animator, business leader; Melissa McCarthy, actress; Sam Altman, founder of OpenAI (ChatGPT)

***Cloud Gate* is a famous mirrored sculpture in Chicago's Millennium Park.**

FUN FACT: In 1900, engineers reversed the flow of the Chicago River to avoid polluting Lake Michigan.

INDIANA

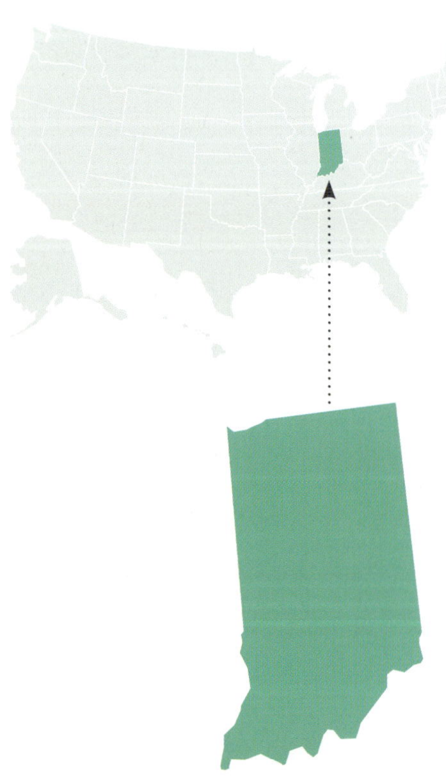

CAPITAL: Indianapolis

LARGEST CITY: Indianapolis

POSTAL CODE: IN

LAND AREA: 35,826 square miles (92,789 sq km)

POPULATION ESTIMATE (2020): 6,785,528

MOTTO: The crossroads of America.

TREE: Tulip tree (yellow poplar)

FLOWER: Peony

BIRD: Northern cardinal

NICKNAMES: Hoosier State

PEOPLE BORN HERE: Orville Redenbacher, popcorn business leader; James Dean, actor; Jim Davis, *Garfield* creator

Cornfields like this one are common throughout Indiana.

FUN FACT: Indiana Dunes National Park has sand dunes, woodlands, wetlands, and prairies.

IOWA

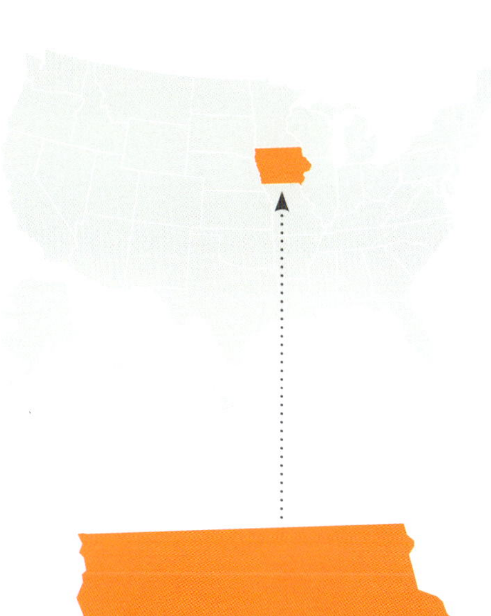

CAPITAL: Des Moines

LARGEST CITY: Des Moines

POSTAL CODE: IA

LAND AREA: 55,857 square miles (144,669 sq km)

POPULATION ESTIMATE (2020): 3,190,369

MOTTO: Our liberties we prize, and our rights we will maintain.

TREE: Oak

FLOWER: Wild rose

BIRD: American goldfinch

NICKNAMES: Hawkeye State, Corn State

PEOPLE BORN HERE: William "Buffalo Bill" Cody, Wild West entertainer; Peggy A. Whitson, astronaut; Caitlin Clark, basketball player

The shining dome of the Iowa state capitol has stood since 1886.

FUN FACT: Iowa gets 64 percent of its electricity from wind sources.

KANSAS

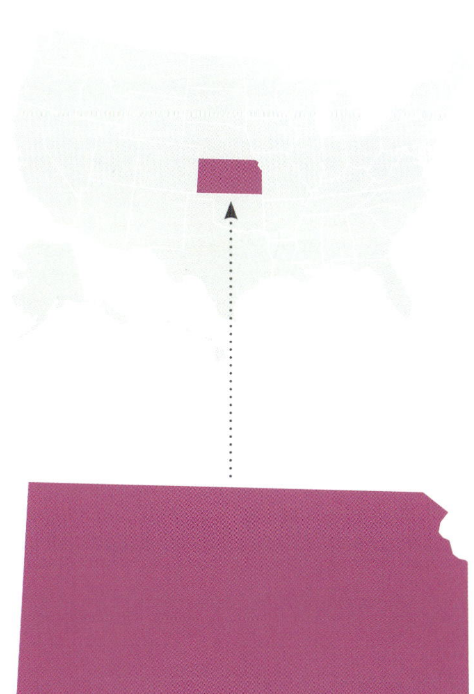

CAPITAL: Topeka

LARGEST CITY: Wichita

POSTAL CODE: KS

LAND AREA: 81,759 square miles (211,754 sq km)

POPULATION ESTIMATE (2020): 2,937,880

MOTTO: *Ad astra per aspera.* (To the stars through difficulties.)

TREE: Cottonwood

FLOWER: Wild native sunflower

BIRD: Western meadowlark

NICKNAMES: Sunflower State, Jayhawker State

PEOPLE BORN HERE: Hattie McDaniel, first Black Oscar winner, *Gone with the Wind*; Amelia Earhart, aviator; MrBeast (Jimmy Donaldson), YouTube personality

Brightly colored sunflowers dot the landscape in a Kansas field.

FUN FACT: Smith County is the geographic center of the contiguous, or connected, United States.

KENTUCKY

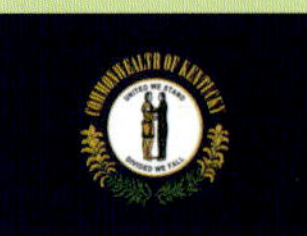

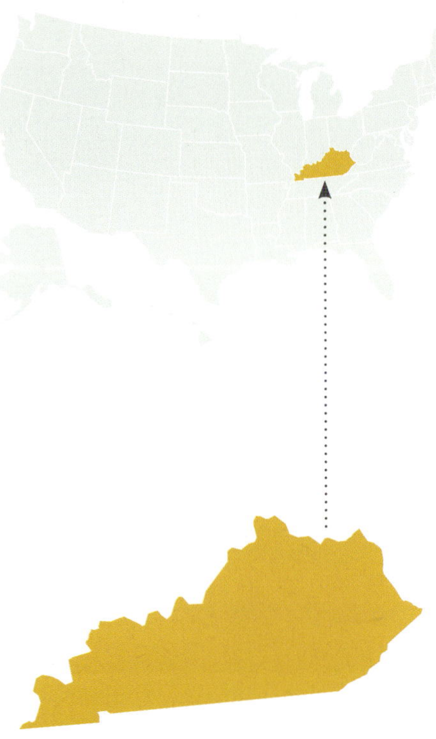

CAPITAL: Frankfort

LARGEST CITY: Louisville

POSTAL CODE: KY

LAND AREA: 39,486 square miles (102,269 sq km)

POPULATION ESTIMATE (2020): 4,505,836

MOTTO: United we stand, divided we fall.

TREE: Tulip poplar

FLOWER: Goldenrod

BIRD: Northern cardinal

NICKNAMES: Bluegrass State

PEOPLE BORN HERE: Abraham Lincoln, US president; Louis Brandeis, Supreme Court justice; Jack Harlow, rapper

This sandstone arch is one of many natural bridges in Kentucky.

FUN FACT: Bluegrass—high-pitched music played on stringed instruments like the banjo—originated here.

LOUISIANA

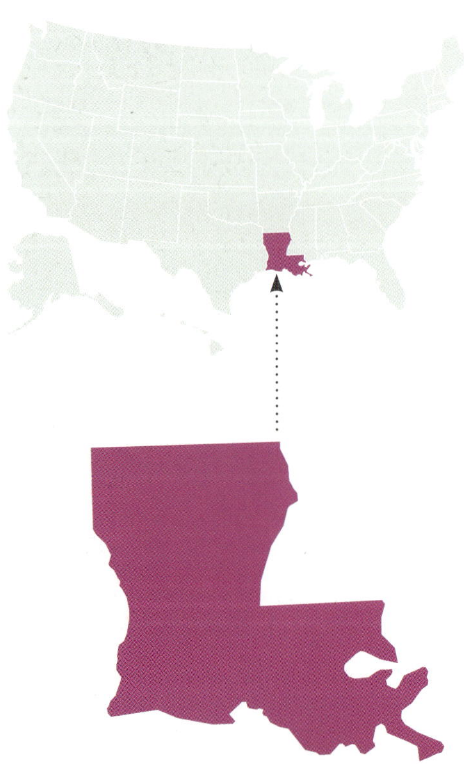

CAPITAL: Baton Rouge

LARGEST CITY: New Orleans

POSTAL CODE: LA

LAND AREA: 43,204 square miles (111,898 sq km)

POPULATION ESTIMATE (2020): 4,657,757

MOTTO: Union, justice, confidence.

TREE: Bald cypress

FLOWER: Magnolia

BIRD: Brown pelican

NICKNAMES: Pelican State, Creole State

PEOPLE BORN HERE: Louis Armstrong, jazz musician; Tyler Perry, entertainment mogul; Brenna Huckaby, Paralympic snowboarder

Jackson Square in New Orleans, Louisiana, is a popular gathering place.

FUN FACT: Cajuns descended from 18th-century French Canadians who settled in Louisiana.

MAINE

CAPITAL: Augusta

LARGEST CITY: Portland

POSTAL CODE: ME

LAND AREA: 30,843 square miles (79,883 sq km)

POPULATION ESTIMATE (2020): 1,362,359

MOTTO: *Dirigo*. (I lead.)

TREE: White pine

FLOWER: White pine cone and tassel

BIRD: Black-capped chickadee

NICKNAMES: Pine Tree State

PEOPLE BORN HERE: Milton Bradley, board game producer; Jessica McClintock, fashion designer; Patrick Dempsey, actor

Maine is famous for lighthouses like the Bass Harbor Head Light Station.

FUN FACT: Maine produces 99 percent of the blueberries in the United States.

MARYLAND

CAPITAL: Annapolis

LARGEST CITY: Baltimore

POSTAL CODE: MD

LAND AREA: 9,707 square miles (25,142 sq km)

POPULATION ESTIMATE (2020): 6,177,224

MOTTO: *Fatti maschii, parole femine*. (Strong deeds, gentle words.)

TREE: White oak

FLOWER: Black-eyed Susan

BIRD: Baltimore oriole

NICKNAMES: Free State, Old Line State

PEOPLE BORN HERE: Harriet Tubman, abolitionist; Jeff Kinney, author, Diary of a Wimpy Kid series; Tim Sweeney, founder, Epic Games (*Fortnite*)

The Bay Bridge stretches nearly 4.5 miles (7 km) across the Chesapeake Bay.

FUN FACT: Francis Scott Key wrote the lyrics to "The Star-Spangled Banner" in 1814 in Baltimore.

MASSACHUSETTS

CAPITAL: Boston

LARGEST CITY: Boston

POSTAL CODE: MA

LAND AREA: 7,800 square miles (20,202 sq km)

POPULATION ESTIMATE (2020): 7,029,917

MOTTO: *Ense petit placidam sub libertate quietem*. (By the sword we seek peace, but peace only under liberty.)

TREE: American elm

FLOWER: Mayflower

BIRD: Black-capped chickadee

NICKNAMES: Bay State, Old Colony State

PEOPLE BORN HERE: Crispus Attucks, Revolutionary War hero; Amy Poehler, actress

A ship rests in the coastal waters off of Salem, Massachusetts.

FUN FACT: Alexander Graham Bell's famous first phone call was made in Boston.

MICHIGAN

CAPITAL: Lansing

LARGEST CITY: Detroit

POSTAL CODE: MI

LAND AREA: 56,539 square miles (146,435 sq km)

POPULATION ESTIMATE (2020): 10,077,331

MOTTO: *Si quaeris peninsulam amoenam circumspice*. (If you seek a pleasant peninsula, look about you.)

TREE: White pine

FLOWER: Apple blossom

BIRD: American robin

NICKNAMES: Great Lakes State, Wolverine State

PEOPLE BORN HERE: Charles Lindbergh, aviator; Keegan-Michael Key, actor and comedian; Lizzo, singer and flutist

An icy and snowy walkway leads to a lighthouse on Lake Michigan.

FUN FACT: Michigan has a floating post office that delivers mail to passing ships in the Detroit River.

MINNESOTA

CAPITAL: Saint Paul

LARGEST CITY: Minneapolis

POSTAL CODE: MN

LAND AREA: 79,627 square miles (206,232 sq km)

POPULATION ESTIMATE (2020): 5,706,494

MOTTO: *L'étoile du nord*. (Star of the North.)

TREE: Norway pine

FLOWER: Pink and white lady's slipper

BIRD: Common loon

NICKNAMES: North Star State, Land of 10,000 Lakes

PEOPLE BORN HERE: Judy Garland, actress and singer; Louise Erdrich, Native American author; Chris Pratt, actor

A canoe is ready for a paddling adventure in the Boundary Waters Canoe Area Wilderness.

FUN FACT: The Minnesota Timberwolves' name pays tribute to the state's gray wolves.

MISSISSIPPI

CAPITAL: Jackson

LARGEST CITY: Jackson

POSTAL CODE: MS

LAND AREA: 46,923 square miles (121,531 sq km)

POPULATION ESTIMATE (2020): 2,961,279

MOTTO: *Virtute et armis*. (By valor and arms.)

TREE: Magnolia

FLOWER: Magnolia

BIRD: Northern mockingbird

NICKNAMES: Magnolia State

PEOPLE BORN HERE: Elvis Presley, singer; Medgar Evers, civil rights leader; Hayley Nichole Williams, lead singer, Paramore

The Mississippi River winds its way through this state—and many others.

FUN FACT: The state is named for the Mississippi River, called the "great river" in the Ojibwe language.

MISSOURI

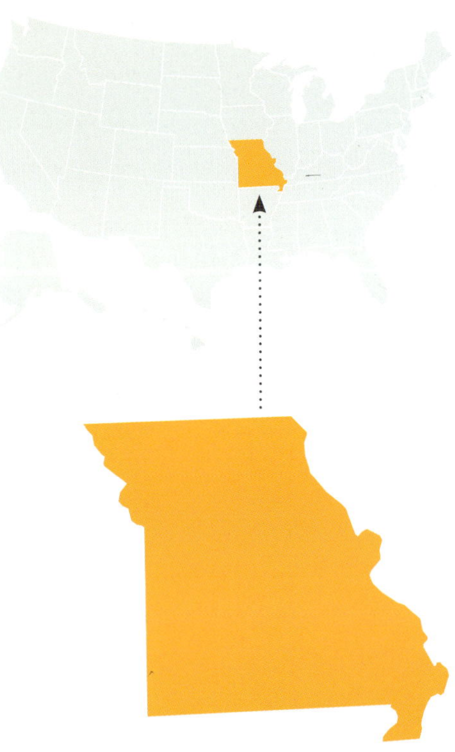

CAPITAL: Jefferson City

LARGEST CITY: Kansas City

POSTAL CODE: MO

LAND AREA: 68,742 square miles (178,040 sq km)

POPULATION ESTIMATE (2020): 6,154,913

MOTTO: *Salus populi suprema lex esto*. (The welfare of the people shall be the supreme law.)

TREE: Flowering dogwood

FLOWER: White hawthorn blossom

BIRD: Eastern bluebird

NICKNAMES: Show Me State

PEOPLE BORN HERE: George Washington Carver, scientist; Edwin Hubble, astronomer; Jayson Tatum, basketball player; Maya Angelou, poet

A popular attraction, the Gateway Arch in St. Louis rises up toward the Missouri sky.

FUN FACT: The 1904 Summer Olympics were moved to St. Louis, Missouri, from Chicago, Illinois.

MONTANA

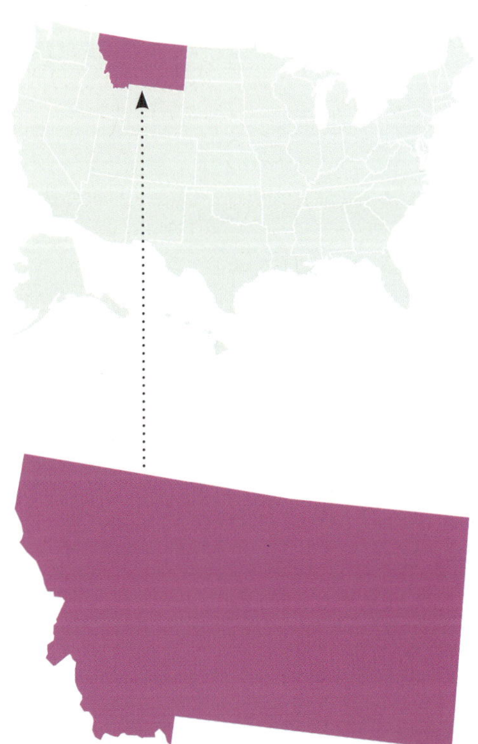

CAPITAL: Helena

LARGEST CITY: Billings

POSTAL CODE: MT

LAND AREA: 145,546 square miles (376,962 sq km)

POPULATION ESTIMATE (2020): 1,084,225

MOTTO: *Oro y plata*. (Gold and silver.)

TREE: Ponderosa pine

FLOWER: Bitterroot

BIRD: Western meadowlark

NICKNAMES: Big Sky Country, Treasure State

PEOPLE BORN HERE: Lily Gladstone, actress; Evel Knievel, stunt motorcyclist; Chief Washakie, Shoshone leader

Springtime offers stunning views in Montana's Glacier National Park.

FUN FACT: Montana claims its Roe River as the world's shortest, measuring just 201 feet (61 m) long.

NEBRASKA

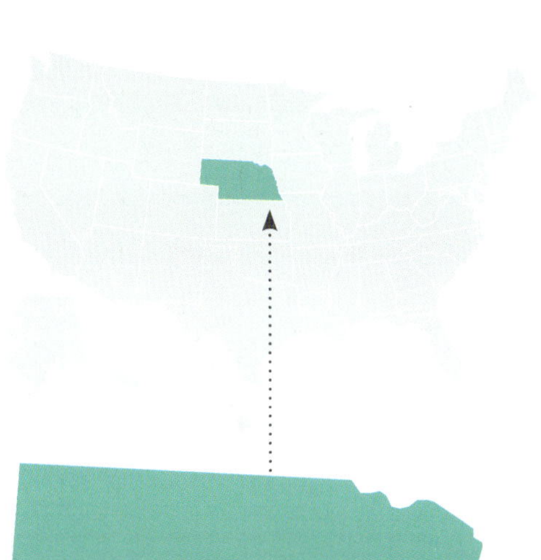

CAPITAL: Lincoln

LARGEST CITY: Omaha

POSTAL CODE: NE

LAND AREA: 76,824 square miles (198,974 sq km)

POPULATION ESTIMATE (2020): 1,961,504

MOTTO: Equality before the law.

TREE: Cottonwood

FLOWER: Golden rod

BIRD: Western meadowlark

NICKNAMES: Cornhusker State

PEOPLE BORN HERE: Warren Buffett, investor and philanthropist; Fred Astaire, dancer and actor; JoJo Siwa, singer

Covered wagons like this one once rolled through Scotts Bluff National Monument.

FUN FACT: On display in Lincoln, "Archie" is the largest mounted mammoth fossil in the world.

NEVADA

CAPITAL: Carson City

LARGEST CITY: Las Vegas

POSTAL CODE: NV

LAND AREA: 109,781 square miles (284,332 sq km)

POPULATION ESTIMATE (2020): 3,104,614

MOTTO: All for our country.

TREE: Single-leaf piñon, bristlecone pine

FLOWER: Sagebrush

BIRD: Mountain bluebird

NICKNAMES: Silver State, Sagebrush State

PEOPLE BORN HERE: Sarah Winnemucca, author and tribal leader; Edna Purviance, silent movie actress; Kyle Busch, NASCAR driver

Cholla cactus dot the landscape in Nevada's Red Rock Canyon.

FUN FACT: Nevada produces about 75 percent of the country's gold.

NEW HAMPSHIRE

CAPITAL: Concord

LARGEST CITY: Manchester

POSTAL CODE: NH

LAND AREA: 8,953 square miles (23,187 sq km)

POPULATION ESTIMATE (2020): 1,377,529

MOTTO: Live free or die.

TREE: White birch

FLOWER: Purple lilac

BIRD: Purple finch

NICKNAMES: Granite State

PEOPLE BORN HERE: Horace Greeley, newspaper journalist; Sarah Josepha Hale, writer, Thanksgiving advocate; Sarah Silverman, comedian

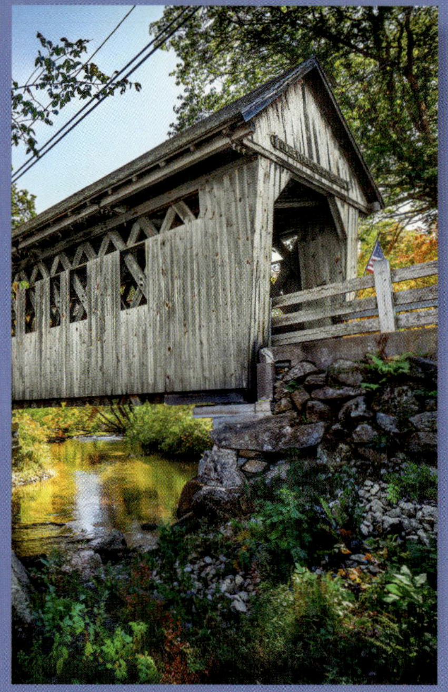

Covered bridges like the Cilleyville Bog Bridge are seen throughout New Hampshire.

FUN FACT: New Hampshire is the only state in which ski jumping is an official high school sport.

NEW JERSEY

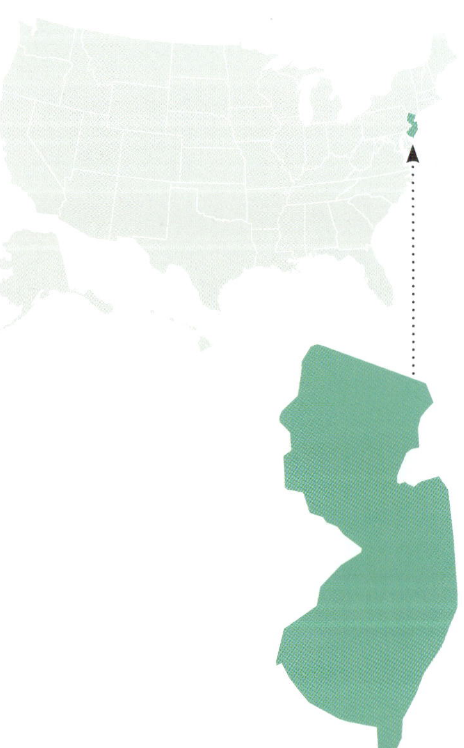

CAPITAL: Trenton

LARGEST CITY: Newark

POSTAL CODE: NJ

LAND AREA: 7,354 square miles (19,047 sq km)

POPULATION ESTIMATE (2020): 9,288,994

MOTTO: Liberty and prosperity.

TREE: Northern red oak

FLOWER: Violet

BIRD: American goldfinch

NICKNAMES: Garden State

PEOPLE BORN HERE: Frank Sinatra, singer; Judy Blume, author; Scottie Scheffler, golfer; Jalen Brunsen, basketball player

Beachgoers can take a short ferry ride to reach Cape May, New Jersey.

FUN FACT: More than 90 percent of New Jersians live in cities and urban areas.

NEW MEXICO

CAPITAL: Santa Fe

LARGEST CITY: Albuquerque

POSTAL CODE: NM

LAND AREA: 121,298 square miles (314,161 sq km)

POPULATION ESTIMATE (2020): 2,117,522

MOTTO: *Crescit eundo*. (It grows as it goes.)

TREE: Piñon pine

FLOWER: Yucca

BIRD: Roadrunner

NICKNAMES: Land of Enchantment, Sunshine State

PEOPLE BORN HERE: Dolores Huerta, migrant farmworker leader; Jeff Bezos, founder of Amazon; Demi Lovato, singer and actress

Some buildings at Taos Pueblo are more than 1,000 years old.

FUN FACT: The Gila Cliff Dwellings National Monument is an example of ancient people's cliff homes.

NEW YORK

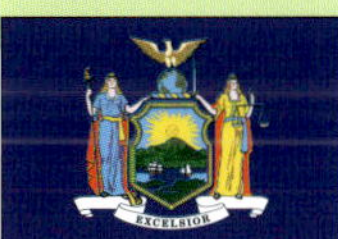

CAPITAL: Albany

LARGEST CITY: New York

POSTAL CODE: NY

LAND AREA: 47,126 square miles (122,057 sq km)

POPULATION ESTIMATE (2020): 20,201,249

MOTTO: *Excelsior*. (Ever upward.)

TREE: Sugar maple

FLOWER: Rose

BIRD: Eastern bluebird

NICKNAMES: Empire State

PEOPLE BORN HERE: Donald Trump, US president; Norman Rockwell, artist; Awkwafina, actress and comedian; Saquon Barkley, football player

Off the Hudson River, One World Trade Center soars above the New York City skyline.

FUN FACT: New York City was the first US capital, where President George Washington was sworn in in 1789.

NORTH CAROLINA

CAPITAL: Raleigh

LARGEST CITY: Charlotte

POSTAL CODE: NC

LAND AREA: 48,618 square miles (125,920 sq km)

POPULATION ESTIMATE (2020): 10,439,388

MOTTO: *Esse quam videri*. (To be, rather than to seem.)

TREE: Pine

FLOWER: Flowering dogwood

BIRD: Northern cardinal

NICKNAMES: Tar Heel State

PEOPLE BORN HERE: Virginia Dare, first English child born in the colonies; John Coltrane, saxophonist; Luke Combs, country singer

Bodie Island Light Station keeps an eye on ships off of Cape Hatteras National Seashore.

FUN FACT: In 1903, Orville Wright made the first powered, sustained, and controlled flight, in Kitty Hawk.

NORTH DAKOTA

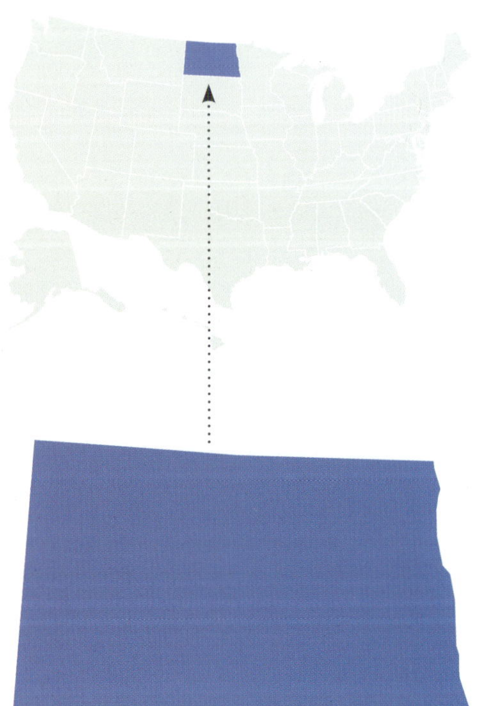

CAPITAL: Bismarck

LARGEST CITY: Fargo

POSTAL CODE: ND

LAND AREA: 69,001 square miles (178,711 sq km)

POPULATION ESTIMATE (2020): 779,094

MOTTO: Liberty and union now and forever, one and inseparable.

TREE: American elm

FLOWER: Wild prairie rose

BIRD: Western meadowlark

NICKNAMES: Peace Garden State, Flickertail State

PEOPLE BORN HERE: Lawrence Welk, accordionist, band leader; Louis L'Amour, writer of westerns; Peggy Lee, musician and actress

Wild bison roam throughout North Dakota's Theodore Roosevelt National Park.

FUN FACT: The Enchanted Highway is a stretch of road with gigantic metal sculptures.

OHIO

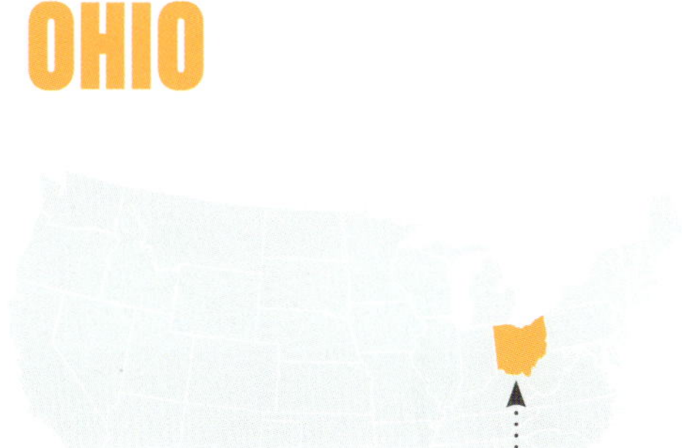

CAPITAL: Columbus

LARGEST CITY: Columbus

POSTAL CODE: OH

LAND AREA: 40,861 square miles (105,829 sq km)

POPULATION ESTIMATE (2020): 11,799,448

MOTTO: With God, all things are possible.

TREE: Ohio buckeye

FLOWER: Red carnation

BIRD: Northern cardinal

NICKNAMES: Buckeye State

PEOPLE BORN HERE: Thomas Edison, scientist and inventor; Dav Pilkey, Captain Underpants creator; Stephen Curry, basketball player; Simone Biles, Olympic gymnast

Bales of wheat and barley await a threshing machine to separate the grain from the stalks.

FUN FACT: Ohio is sometimes called the Mother of Presidents—seven US chiefs of state were born here.

OKLAHOMA

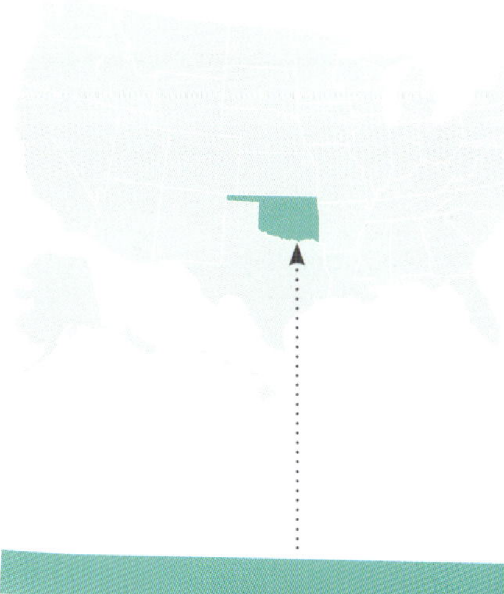

CAPITAL: Oklahoma City

LARGEST CITY: Oklahoma City

POSTAL CODE: OK

LAND AREA: 68,595 square miles (177,660 sq km)

POPULATION ESTIMATE (2020): 3,959,353

MOTTO: *Labor omnia vincit.* (Work conquers all.)

TREE: Redbud

FLOWER: Oklahoma rose

BIRD: Scissor-tailed flycatcher

NICKNAMES: Sooner State

PEOPLE BORN HERE: Joe Albertson, grocery store entrepreneur; Maria Tallchief, ballet dancer; Ryan Tedder, lead singer, OneRepublic

Storm clouds roll in over Oklahoma's Tallgrass Prairie Preserve.

FUN FACT: Oklahoma has a state meal that includes barbecued pork, fried okra, and grits.

OREGON

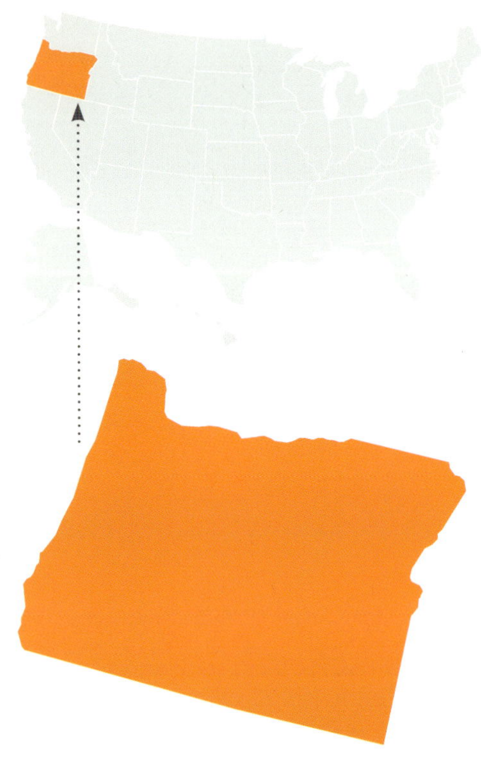

CAPITAL: Salem

LARGEST CITY: Portland

POSTAL CODE: OR

LAND AREA: 95,988 square miles (248,608 sq km)

POPULATION ESTIMATE (2020): 4,237,256

MOTTO: *Alis volat propiis*. (She flies with her own wings.)

TREE: Douglas fir

FLOWER: Oregon grape

BIRD: Western meadowlark

NICKNAMES: Beaver State

PEOPLE BORN HERE: Beverly Cleary, author; Matt Groening, *The Simpsons* creator; Rico Roman, Paralympic sled-hockey athlete; Justin Herbert, football player

Rocks formed by ancient lava flows jut out of the water at Oregon's Cannon Beach.

FUN FACT: Oregon's amazingly blue Crater Lake sits in a volcanic caldera that collapsed 7,700 years ago.

PENNSYLVANIA

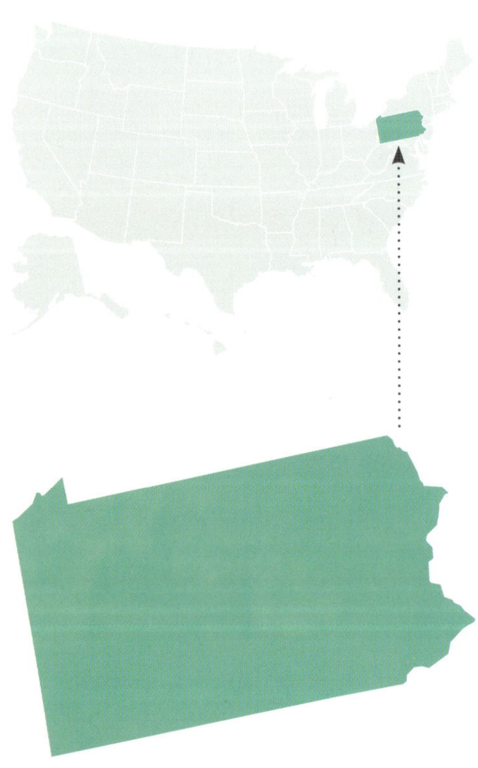

CAPITAL: Harrisburg

LARGEST CITY: Philadelphia

POSTAL CODE: PA

LAND AREA: 44,743 square miles (115,883 sq km)

POPULATION ESTIMATE (2020): 13,002,700

MOTTO: Virtue, liberty, and independence.

TREE: Eastern hemlock

FLOWER: Mountain laurel

BIRD: Ruffed grouse

NICKNAMES: Keystone State

PEOPLE BORN HERE: Andy Warhol, artist; Taylor Swift, singer; Bradley Cooper, actor; Kobe Bryant, basketball player

Horse-drawn carriages driven by the Amish are common in parts of Pennsylvania.

FUN FACT: Every February 2, a groundhog comes out of its Pennsylvania burrow to "predict" spring.

RHODE ISLAND

CAPITAL: Providence

LARGEST CITY: Providence

POSTAL CODE: RI

LAND AREA: 1,034 square miles (2,678 sq km)

POPULATION ESTIMATE (2020): 1,097,379

MOTTO: Hope.

TREE: Red maple

FLOWER: Violet

BIRD: Rhode Island red

NICKNAMES: Ocean State, Little Rhody

PEOPLE BORN HERE: Nathanael Greene, Revolutionary War hero; Gilbert Stuart, painter; Mena Suvari, actress

Scenic Newport Harbor in Rhode Island attracts ships and visitors alike.

FUN FACT: Dating to 1762, Touro Synagogue in Rhode Island is the oldest synagogue in the United States.

SOUTH CAROLINA

CAPITAL: Columbia

LARGEST CITY: Charleston

POSTAL CODE: SC

LAND AREA: 30,061 square miles (77,857 sq km)

POPULATION ESTIMATE (2020): 5,118,425

MOTTO: *Animis opibusque parati.* (Prepared in mind and resources.); *Dum spiro spero*. (While I breathe, I hope.)

TREE: Palmetto

FLOWER: Yellow jessamine

BIRD: Carolina wren

NICKNAMES: Palmetto State

PEOPLE BORN HERE: Jesse Jackson, civil rights leader; Jaimie Alexander, actress; A'ja Wilson, basketball player

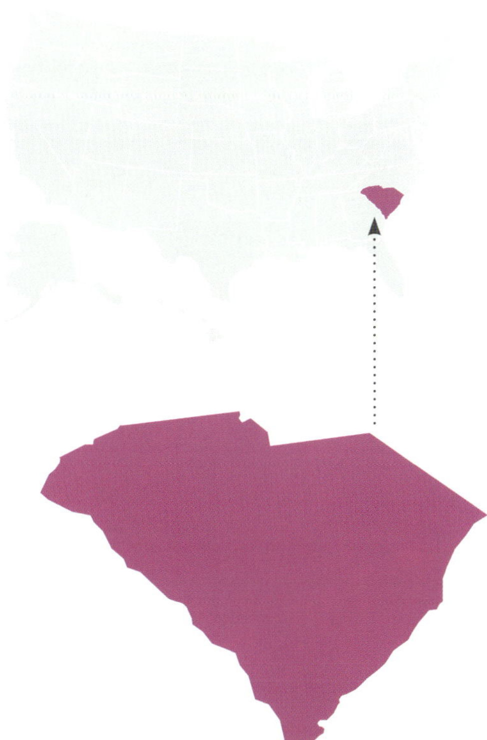

Historical Charleston is rich in both Revolutionary and Civil War–era sites.

FUN FACT: People called Gullah—descendants of enslaved Africans—are famous for their handmade baskets.

SOUTH DAKOTA

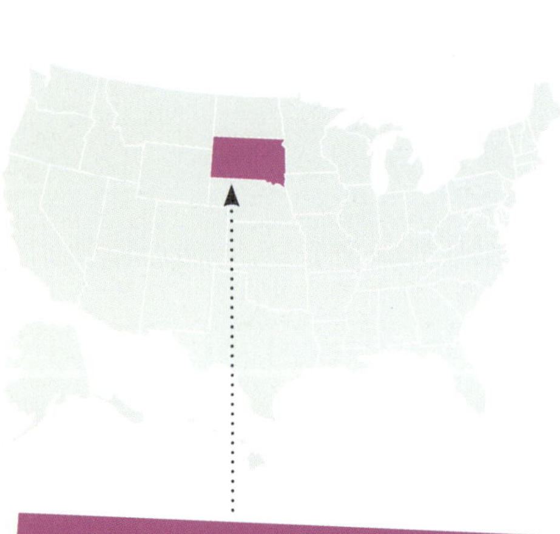

CAPITAL: Pierre

LARGEST CITY: Sioux Falls

POSTAL CODE: SD

LAND AREA: 75,811 square miles (196,350 sq km)

POPULATION ESTIMATE (2020): 886,667

MOTTO: Under God the people rule.

TREE: Black hills spruce

FLOWER: American pasque

BIRD: Ring-necked pheasant

NICKNAMES: Mount Rushmore State

PEOPLE BORN HERE: Crazy Horse (Tasunke Witco), Lakota leader; Tom Brokaw, TV journalist; January Jones, actress

The Mount Rushmore mountain was known as "Six Grandfathers" by the Lakota people.

FUN FACT: Artists use 275,000 ears of corn to create murals at South Dakota's Corn Palace.

TENNESSEE

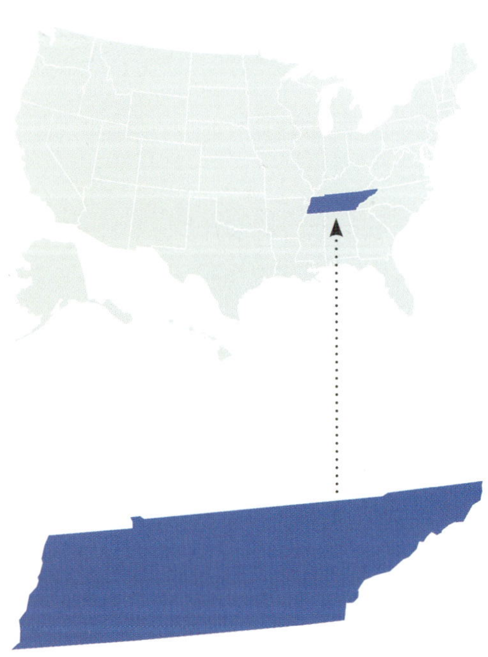

CAPITAL: Nashville

LARGEST CITY: Nashville

POSTAL CODE: TN

LAND AREA: 41,235 square miles (106,798 sq km)

POPULATION ESTIMATE (2020): 6,910,840

MOTTO: Agriculture and commerce.

TREE: Tulip poplar

FLOWER: Iris

BIRD: Northern mockingbird

NICKNAMES: Volunteer State

PEOPLE BORN HERE: Davy Crockett, frontiersman, politician; Minnie Pearl, country singer, comedian; Justin Timberlake, singer, actor

A giant guitar sits outside country music's legendary Grand Ole Opry in Nashville.

FUN FACT: The Lost Sea, an underground lake in Craighead Caverns, can be explored in a glass-bottom boat.

TEXAS

CAPITAL: Austin

LARGEST CITY: Houston

POSTAL CODE: TX

LAND AREA: 261,232 square miles (676,587 sq km)

POPULATION ESTIMATE (2020): 29,145,505

MOTTO: Friendship.

TREE: Pecan

FLOWER: Bluebonnet

BIRD: Northern mockingbird

NICKNAMES: Lone Star State

PEOPLE BORN HERE: José Antonio Navarro, Texas Revolution leader; Scott Joplin, ragtime composer; Selena Gomez, actress; Bobby Witt, Jr., baseball player

Cattle ranching is an important part of the Texas economy.

FUN FACT: Twice a day, cattle are driven through the Fort Worth Stockyards, just outside the city's downtown.

UTAH

CAPITAL: Salt Lake City

LARGEST CITY: Salt Lake City

POSTAL CODE: UT

LAND AREA: 82,170 square miles (212,818 sq km)

POPULATION ESTIMATE (2020): 3,271,616

MOTTO: Industry.

TREE: Quaking aspen

FLOWER: Sego lily

BIRD: Seagull

NICKNAMES: Beehive State

PEOPLE BORN HERE: Butch Cassidy (Robert LeRoy Parker), American outlaw; Nolan Bushnell, creator of Atari and Chuck E. Cheese; Wayne Sermon, lead guitarist, Imagine Dragons

Delicate Arch is the largest freestanding arch in Arches National Park.

FUN FACT: The east- and west-bound tracks of the Transcontinental Railroad were connected in 1869, in Utah.

VERMONT

CAPITAL: Montpelier

LARGEST CITY: Burlington

POSTAL CODE: VT

LAND AREA: 9,217 square miles (23,871 sq km)

POPULATION ESTIMATE (2020): 643,077

MOTTO: Freedom and unity.

TREE: Sugar maple

FLOWER: Red clover

BIRD: Hermit thrush

NICKNAMES: Green Mountain State

PEOPLE BORN HERE: Calvin Coolidge, US president; Rudy Vallee, singer; Noah Kahan, singer

Colorful fall foliage bursts over the quaint village of Waits River, Vermont.

FUN FACT: Some say a dinosaur-like creature named Champ lives in Lake Champlain, which borders Vermont.

VIRGINIA

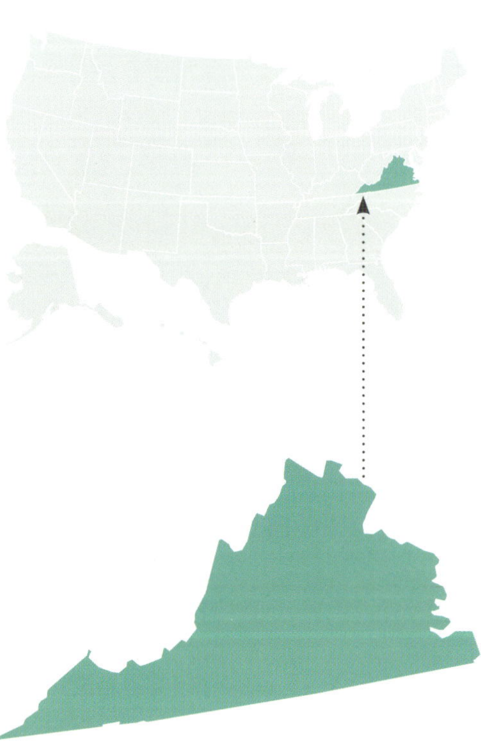

CAPITAL: Richmond

LARGEST CITY: Virginia Beach

POSTAL CODE: VA

LAND AREA: 39,490 square miles (102,279 sq km)

POPULATION ESTIMATE (2020): 8,631,393

MOTTO: *Sic semper tyrannis*. (Thus always to tyrants.)

TREE: American dogwood

FLOWER: American dogwood

BIRD: Northern cardinal

NICKNAMES: The Old Dominion, Mother of Presidents

PEOPLE BORN HERE: Pocahontas, Powhatan princess, peacekeeper; Meriwether Lewis and William Clark, explorers; Arthur Ashe, tennis player; Walker Scobell, actor

Virginia's Luray Caverns reveal 10-story-high ceilings, clear pools, and stunning stalactites.

FUN FACT: About 557 miles (896 km) of the 14-state Appalachian Trail cuts through Virginia.

WASHINGTON

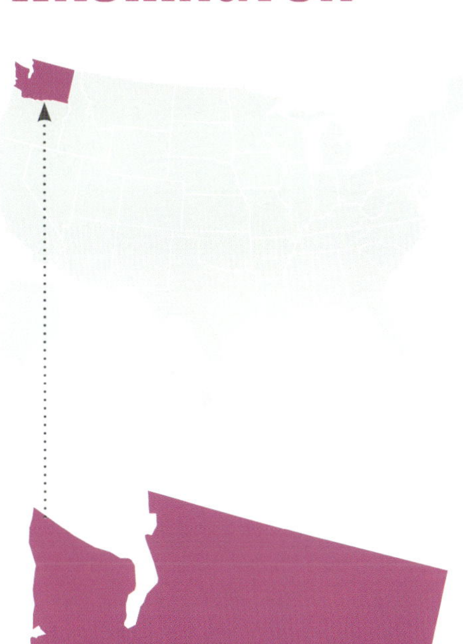

CAPITAL: Olympia

LARGEST CITY: Seattle

POSTAL CODE: WA

LAND AREA: 66,456 square miles (172,119 sq km)

POPULATION ESTIMATE (2020): 7,705,281

MOTTO: *Al-ki*. (This Chinook word translates to "By and by" or "Into the future.")

TREE: Western hemlock

FLOWER: Coast rhododendron

BIRD: Willow goldfinch

NICKNAMES: Evergreen State

PEOPLE BORN HERE: Bing Crosby, singer; Murray McCory, backpack creator; Dove Cameron, musician, actress

The views are amazing from the platform atop the 605-foot-tall (184-m) Space Needle.

FUN FACT: Three pods of orcas call Washington's Puget Sound home.

WEST VIRGINIA

CAPITAL: Charleston

LARGEST CITY: Charleston

POSTAL CODE: WV

LAND AREA: 24,038 square miles (62,259 sq km)

POPULATION ESTIMATE (2020): 1,793,716

MOTTO: *Montani semper liberi.* (Mountaineers are always free.)

TREE: Sugar maple

FLOWER: Rhododendron

BIRD: Northern cardinal

NICKNAMES: Mountain State

PEOPLE BORN HERE: Pearl S. Buck, author; Chuck Yeager, test pilot; Steve Harvey, comedian, TV personality

The Glade Creek Grist Mill in Babcock State Park grinds corn into cornmeal.

FUN FACT: The New River Gorge Bridge cut travel across a canyon from 40 minutes to just 1 minute.

WISCONSIN

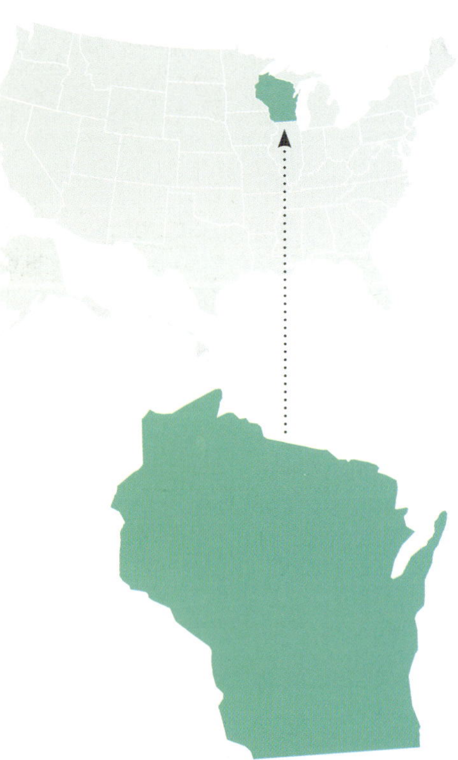

CAPITAL: Madison

LARGEST CITY: Milwaukee

POSTAL CODE: WI

LAND AREA: 54,158 square miles (140,268 sq km)

POPULATION ESTIMATE (2020): 5,893,718

MOTTO: Forward.

TREE: Sugar maple

FLOWER: Wood violet

BIRD: American robin

NICKNAMES: Badger State, America's Dairyland

PEOPLE BORN HERE: Laura Ingalls Wilder, author; Orson Welles, director; Les Paul, guitarist; Rachel Brosnahan, actress

Giant icicles form on the rocky structures dotting the beaches of Lake Superior.

FUN FACT: The Badger State refers to tough, strong people who lived and worked in lead mines.

WYOMING

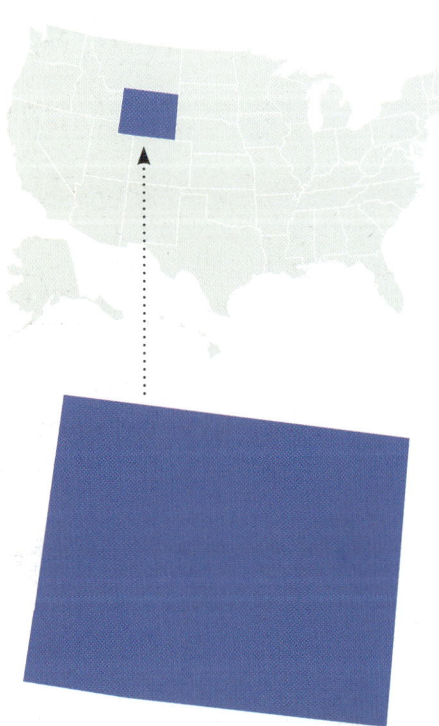

CAPITAL: Cheyenne

LARGEST CITY: Cheyenne

POSTAL CODE: WY

LAND AREA: 97,093 square miles (251,470 sq km)

POPULATION ESTIMATE (2020): 576,851

MOTTO: Equal rights.

TREE: Plains cottonwood

FLOWER: Indian paintbrush

BIRD: Western meadowlark

NICKNAMES: Equality State

PEOPLE BORN HERE: Jackson Pollock, artist; Patricia MacLachlan, author

The geyser Old Faithful erupts on schedule at Yellowstone National Park.

FUN FACT: Dino fossils are common in Wyoming and include near-complete skeletons like "Jimbo" the sauropod.

WASHINGTON, DC
THE NATION'S CAPITAL

The District of Columbia became the seat of the US government on December 1, 1800, after being moved from Philadelphia, Pennsylvania. It is not a state, but its residents pay federal taxes and vote for president. They're also governed by a locally elected mayor and city council.

LAND AREA: 61 square miles (158 sq km)

POPULATION ESTIMATE (2020): 689,545

MOTTO: *Justitia omnibus.* (Justice for all.)

TREE: Scarlet oak

FLOWER: American beauty rose

BIRD: Wood thrush

PEOPLE BORN HERE: Bill Nye, science TV host; Katie Ledecky, Olympic swimmer

Dawn rises over the Lincoln Memorial, the Washington Monument, and the United States Capitol.

US TERRITORIES

PUERTO RICO became part of the United States after the country took possession from Spain after the 1898 Spanish-American War. Sitting about 1,000 miles (1,609 km) from Miami, Florida, in the Caribbean Sea, Puerto Rico has a main island and three islets: Vieques, Culebra, and Mona. The capital, on the main island, is San Juan, and the entire population is 3.2 million.

AMERICAN SAMOA is about halfway between Hawai'i and New Zealand in the South Pacific Ocean. The group of islands has a land area of 76 square miles (198 sq km) and a population of about 49,710.

GUAM also became a US territory after it was transferred from Spain in 1898. Located in the North Pacific Ocean, its land area is about 210 square miles (543 sq km), and its population is about 153,836.

The **US VIRGIN ISLANDS** has about 50 islets and three main islands: Saint Croix, Saint Thomas, and Saint John. They're east of Puerto Rico in the Caribbean Sea and have a land area of 134 square miles (348 sq km). Its population is about 87,146.

The **NORTHERN MARIANA ISLANDS** became part of the United States when Japan ceded the territory after losing World War II. Located in the North Pacific Ocean, the group of 14 islands and islets has a land area of 182 square miles (472 sq km) and a population of about 47,329.

One of the US Virgin Islands, St. Thomas, was once a haven for pirates.

The Northern Mariana Islands are a chain of volcanic islands in the Pacific Ocean.

The La Perla neighborhood sits near the historic walls of San Juan, Puerto Rico.

A Japanese cannon reminds residents of Guam's important role during World War II.

US Presidents

1 GEORGE WASHINGTON
Served: 1789–1797
Political Party: Federalist
Lived: February 22, 1732–December 14, 1799
Vice President: John Adams
First Lady: Martha Washington

2 JOHN ADAMS
Served: 1797–1801
Political Party: Federalist
Lived: October 30, 1735–July 4, 1826
Vice President: Thomas Jefferson
First Lady: Abigail Adams

3 THOMAS JEFFERSON
Served: 1801–1809
Political Party: Democratic-Republican
Lived: April 13, 1743–July 4, 1826
Vice Presidents: Aaron Burr, George Clinton
First Lady: None

4 JAMES MADISON
Served: 1809–1817
Political Party: Democratic-Republican
Lived: March 16, 1751–June 28, 1836
Vice Presidents: George Clinton, Elbridge Gerry
First Lady: Dolley Madison

5 JAMES MONROE
Served: 1817–1825
Political Party: Democratic-Republican
Lived: April 28, 1758–July 4, 1831
Vice President: Daniel D. Tompkins
First Lady: Elizabeth Monroe

6 JOHN QUINCY ADAMS
Served: 1825–1829
Political Party: National Republican
Lived: July 11, 1767–February 23, 1848
Vice President: John C. Calhoun
First Lady: Louisa Adams

7 ANDREW JACKSON
Served: 1829–1837
Political Party: Democratic
Lived: March 15, 1767–June 8, 1845
Vice Presidents: John C. Calhoun, Martin Van Buren
First Lady: Emily Donelson (Jackson's niece)

8 MARTIN VAN BUREN
Served: 1837–1841
Political Party: Democratic
Lived: December 5, 1782–July 24, 1862
Vice President: Richard M. Johnson
First Lady: Angelica Van Buren (Van Buren's daughter-in-law)

9 WILLIAM HENRY HARRISON
Served: 1841
Political Party: Whig
Lived: February 9, 1773–April 4, 1841
Vice President: John Tyler
First Lady: Anna Harrison

10 JOHN TYLER
Served: 1841–1845
Political Party: Whig
Lived: March 29, 1790–January 18, 1862
Vice President: None
First Ladies: Letitia Tyler (died 1842), Julia Tyler

11 JAMES K. POLK
Served: 1845–1849
Political Party: Democratic
Lived: November 2, 1795–June 15, 1849
Vice President: George M. Dallas
First Lady: Sarah Polk

12 ZACHARY TAYLOR
Served: 1849–1850
Political Party: Whig
Lived: November 24, 1784–July 9, 1850
Vice President: Millard Fillmore
First Lady: Margaret Taylor

13 MILLARD FILLMORE
Served: 1850–1853
Political Party: Whig
Lived: January 7, 1800–March 8, 1874
Vice President: None
First Lady: Abigail Fillmore

14 FRANKLIN PIERCE
Served: 1853–1857
Political Party: Democratic
Lived: November 23, 1804–October 8, 1869
Vice President: William R. King
First Lady: Jane Pierce

15 JAMES BUCHANAN
Served: 1857–1861
Political Party: Democratic
Lived: April 23, 1791–June 1, 1868
Vice President: John C. Breckinridge
First Lady: Harriet Lane (Buchanan's niece)

16 ABRAHAM LINCOLN
Served: 1861–1865
Political Party: Republican
Lived: February 12, 1809–April 15, 1865
Vice Presidents: Hannibal Hamlin, Andrew Johnson
First Lady: Mary Todd Lincoln

17 ANDREW JOHNSON
Served: 1865–1869
Political Parties: Democratic (Union)
Lived: December 29, 1808–July 31, 1875
Vice President: None
First Lady: Eliza Johnson

18 ULYSSES S. GRANT
Served: 1869–1877
Political Party: Republican
Lived: April 27, 1822–July 23, 1885
Vice Presidents: Schuyler Colfax, Henry Wilson
First Lady: Julia Grant

19 RUTHERFORD B. HAYES
Served: 1877–1881
Political Party: Republican
Lived: October 4, 1822–January 17, 1893
Vice President: William A. Wheeler
First Lady: Lucy Hayes

20 JAMES A. GARFIELD
Served: 1881
Political Party: Republican
Lived: November 19, 1831–September 19, 1881
Vice President: Chester A. Arthur
First Lady: Lucretia Garfield

21 CHESTER A. ARTHUR
Served: 1881–1885
Political Party: Republican
Lived: October 5, 1829–November 18, 1886
Vice President: None
First Lady: Mary Arthur McElroy (Arthur's sister)

22 GROVER CLEVELAND
Served: 1885–1889
Political Party: Democratic
Lived: March 18, 1837–

June 24, 1908
Vice President: Thomas A. Hendricks
First Lady: Frances Cleveland

23 BENJAMIN HARRISON
Served: 1889–1893
Political Party: Republican
Lived: August 20, 1833–March 13, 1901
Vice President: Levi P. Morton
First Lady: Caroline Harrison (died 1892)

24 GROVER CLEVELAND
Served: 1893–1897
Political Party: Democratic
Lived: March 18, 1837–June 24, 1908
Vice President: Adlai E. Stevenson
First Lady: Frances Cleveland

25 WILLIAM MCKINLEY
Served: 1897–1901
Political Party: Republican
Lived: January 29, 1843–September 14, 1901
Vice Presidents: Garret A. Hobart, Theodore Roosevelt
First Lady: Ida McKinley

26 THEODORE ROOSEVELT
Served: 1901–1909
Political Party: Republican
Lived: October 27, 1858–January 6, 1919
Vice President: Charles W. Fairbanks
First Lady: Edith Roosevelt

27 WILLIAM HOWARD TAFT
Served: 1909–1913
Political Party: Republican
Lived: September 15, 1857–March 8, 1930
Vice President: James S. Sherman
First Lady: Helen Taft

28 WOODROW WILSON
Served: 1913–1921
Political Party: Democratic
Lived: December 28, 1856–February 3, 1924
Vice President: Thomas R. Marshall
First Lady: Ellen Wilson (died 1914), Edith Wilson

29 WARREN G. HARDING
Served: 1921–1923
Political Party: Republican
Lived: November 2, 1865–August 2, 1923
Vice President: Calvin Coolidge
First Lady: Florence Harding

30 CALVIN COOLIDGE
Served: 1923–1929
Political Party: Republican
Lived: July 4, 1872–January 5, 1933
Vice President: Charles G. Dawes
First Lady: Grace Coolidge

31 HERBERT HOOVER
Served: 1929–1933
Political Party: Republican
Lived: August 10, 1874–October 20, 1964
Vice President: Charles Curtis
First Lady: Lou Hoover

32 FRANKLIN D. ROOSEVELT
Served: 1933–1945
Political Party: Democratic
Lived: January 30, 1882–April 12, 1945
Vice Presidents: John Nance Garner, Henry A. Wallace, Harry S. Truman
First Lady: Eleanor Roosevelt

33 HARRY S. TRUMAN
Served: 1945–1953
Political Party: Democratic
Lived: May 8, 1884–December 26, 1972
Vice President: Alben W. Barkley
First Lady: Bess Truman

34 DWIGHT D. EISENHOWER
Served: 1953–1961
Political Party: Republican
Lived: October 14, 1890–March 28, 1969
Vice President: Richard M. Nixon
First Lady: Mamie Eisenhower

35 JOHN F. KENNEDY
Served: 1961–1963
Political Party: Democratic
Lived: May 29, 1917–November 22, 1963
Vice President: Lyndon B. Johnson
First Lady: Jackie Kennedy

36 LYNDON B. JOHNSON
Served: 1963–1969
Political Party: Democratic
Lived: August 27, 1908–January 22, 1973
Vice President: Hurbert Humphrey
First Lady: Lady Bird Johnson

37 RICHARD M. NIXON
Served: 1969–1974
Political Party: Republican
Lived: January 9, 1913–April 22, 1994
Vice Presidents: Spiro T. Agnew, Gerald R. Ford
First Lady: Pat Nixon

38 GERALD R. FORD
Served: 1974–1977
Political Party: Republican
Lived: July 14, 1913–December 26, 2006
Vice President: Nelson Rockefeller
First Lady: Betty Ford

39 JIMMY CARTER
Served: 1977–1981
Political Party: Democratic
Lived: October 1, 1924–December 29, 2024
Vice President: Walter F. Mondale
First Lady: Rosalynn Carter

40 RONALD REAGAN
Served: 1981–1989
Political Party: Republican
Lived: February 6, 1911–June 5, 2004
Vice President: George H. W. Bush
First Lady: Nancy Reagan

41 GEORGE H. W. BUSH
Served: 1989–1993
Political Party: Republican
Lived: June 12, 1924–November 30, 2018
Vice President: Dan Quayle
First Lady: Barbara Bush

42 BILL CLINTON
Served: 1993–2001
Political Party: Democratic
Born: August 19, 1946
Vice President: Al Gore
First Lady: Hillary Clinton

43 GEORGE W. BUSH
Served: 2001–2009
Political Party: Republican
Born: July 6, 1946
Vice President: Dick Cheney
First Lady: Laura Bush

44 BARACK OBAMA
Served: 2009–2017
Political Party: Democratic
Born: August 4, 1961
Vice President: Joe Biden
First Lady: Michelle Obama

45 DONALD TRUMP
Served: 2017–2021
Political Party: Republican
Born: June 14, 1946
Vice President: Mike Pence
First Lady: Melania Trump

46 JOE BIDEN
Served: 2021–2025
Political Party: Democratic
Born: November 20, 1942
Vice President: Kamala Harris
First Lady: Jill Biden

47 DONALD TRUMP
Served: 2025–
Political Party: Republican
Born: June 14, 1946
Vice President: JD Vance
First Lady: Melania Trump

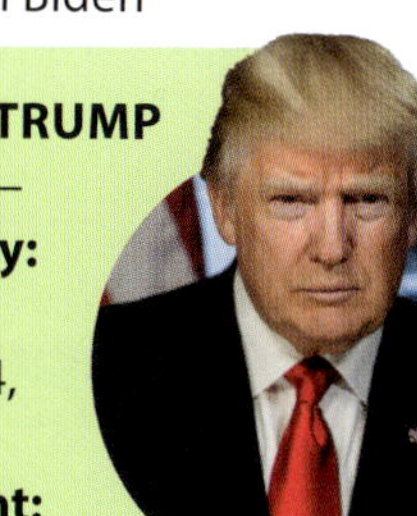

First Ladies

See how much you know about these presidential partners.

Grace Coolidge

1 What was one of Grace Coolidge's pets called?

A. Dan the dog
B. Rebecca the raccoon
C. Prissy the pig
D. Calvin the cat

2 Which first lady was known as the "secret president" after her husband suffered a stroke?

A. Anna Harrison
B. Abigail Fillmore
C. Edith Wilson
D. Lou Hoover

Eleanor Roosevelt

3 Which of the following was an accomplishment of Eleanor Roosevelt?

A. She hosted her own radio show.
B. She held press conferences for female reporters.
C. She invited Black singer Marian Anderson to sing at the Lincoln Memorial during a time when many states were segregated.
D. All of the above

4 Which ghost has *not* been spotted or heard in the White House, according to legends?

A. Mamie Eisenhower playing cards
B. Dolley Madison protecting the Rose Garden
C. Abigail Adams hanging laundry in the East Room
D. A mysterious opera singer and piano player

5 Which two first ladies were born outside the United States?

A. Betty Ford and Mary Todd Lincoln
B. Edith Roosevelt and Abigail Adams
C. Melania Trump and Louisa Adams
D. None of the above—like presidents, first ladies must be born in the United States.

6 Which first lady continued to hold a paying job while she was in the White House?

A. Jill Biden, a teacher
B. Laura Bush, a librarian
C. Hillary Clinton, a lawyer
D. Jackie Kennedy, a reporter

7 Who did Ida McKinley often write letters to?

A. Annie Oakley
B. Susan B. Anthony
C. Harriet Beecher Stowe
D. Amelia Earhart

Ida McKinley

8 What Guinness World Record did Michelle Obama help set?

A. Most Vegetables Grown in a Backyard Garden
B. Tallest Snow Person
C. Longest Line Formed by People Holding Hands
D. Most Jumping Jacks in a 24-Hour Period

Michelle Obama

9 Which first lady sometimes joined her husband at the battlefield?

A. Bess Truman
B. Mary Todd Lincoln
C. Dolley Madison
D. Martha Washington

10 Lady Bird Johnson made a train tour through the South to gather support for the Civil Rights Act of 1964. What was her train called?

A. The Lady Bird Special
B. The Johnson Express
C. The Flying Lady Bird
D. The Civil Rights Tour

Answers on page 200

GAME

Park Puzzle

Put these national parks in order of the date they were established.

VIRGIN ISLANDS NATIONAL PARK
St. John, US Virgin Islands
Established by President Dwight D. Eisenhower

NEW RIVER GORGE NATIONAL PARK AND PRESERVE
West Virginia
Established by President Donald Trump

YELLOWSTONE NATIONAL PARK
Idaho, Montana, Wyoming
Established by President Ulysses S. Grant

GRAND CANYON NATIONAL PARK
Arizona
Established by President Woodrow Wilson

BIG BEND NATIONAL PARK
Texas
Established by President Franklin D. Roosevelt

Answers on page 200

Metric Conversions and Time Zones

CONVERTING TO METRICS

US MEASUREMENT	METRIC MEASUREMENT
Length	
1 inch (in)	25.4 millimeters (mm)
1 inch (in)	2.54 centimeters (cm)
1 foot (ft)	30.48 centimeters (cm)
1 yard (yd)	0.91 meter (m)
1 mile (mi)	1.61 kilometers (km)
Area	
1 square inch (in^2)	6.45 square centimeters (cm^2)
1 square foot (ft^2)	0.09 square meter (m^2)
1 square yard (yd^2)	0.84 square meter (m^2)
1 square mile (mi^2)	2.59 square kilometers (km^2)
1 acre	0.40 hectare (ha)

US MEASUREMENT	METRIC MEASUREMENT
Weight	
1 ounce (oz)	28.35 grams (g)
1 pound (lb)	0.45 kilogram (kg)
1 ton (2,000 lb)	0.91 metric ton (t)
Volume	
1 teaspoon (tsp)	4.93 milliliters (mL)
1 tablespoon (tbsp)	14.79 milliliters (mL)
1 fluid ounce (fl oz)	29.57 milliliters (mL)
1 cup (c)	0.24 liter (L)
1 cubic inch (in^3)	16.39 milliliters (mL)
1 pint (pt)	0.47 liter (L)
1 quart (qt)	0.95 liter (L)
1 gallon (gal)	3.79 liters (L)
1 cubic foot (ft^3)	0.03 cubic meter (m^3)
1 cubic yard (yd^3)	0.76 cubic meter (m^3)

CONVERTING FAHRENHEIT TO CELSIUS

32 degrees Fahrenheit (32°F) equals 0 degrees Celsius (0°C). Use math to convert one to the other. (It's OK to use a calculator.)

TO CONVERT FAHRENHEIT INTO CELSIUS:
Subtract 32 from the Fahrenheit temperature. (F minus 32)
Multiply that number by 0.56.

TO CONVERT CELSIUS INTO FAHRENHEIT:
Multiply the Celsius temperature by 1.8. (C x 1.8)
Add 32 to that number.

TIME ZONES

HAWAI'I–ALEUTIAN

ALASKA

PACIFIC

MOUNTAIN

CENTRAL

EASTERN

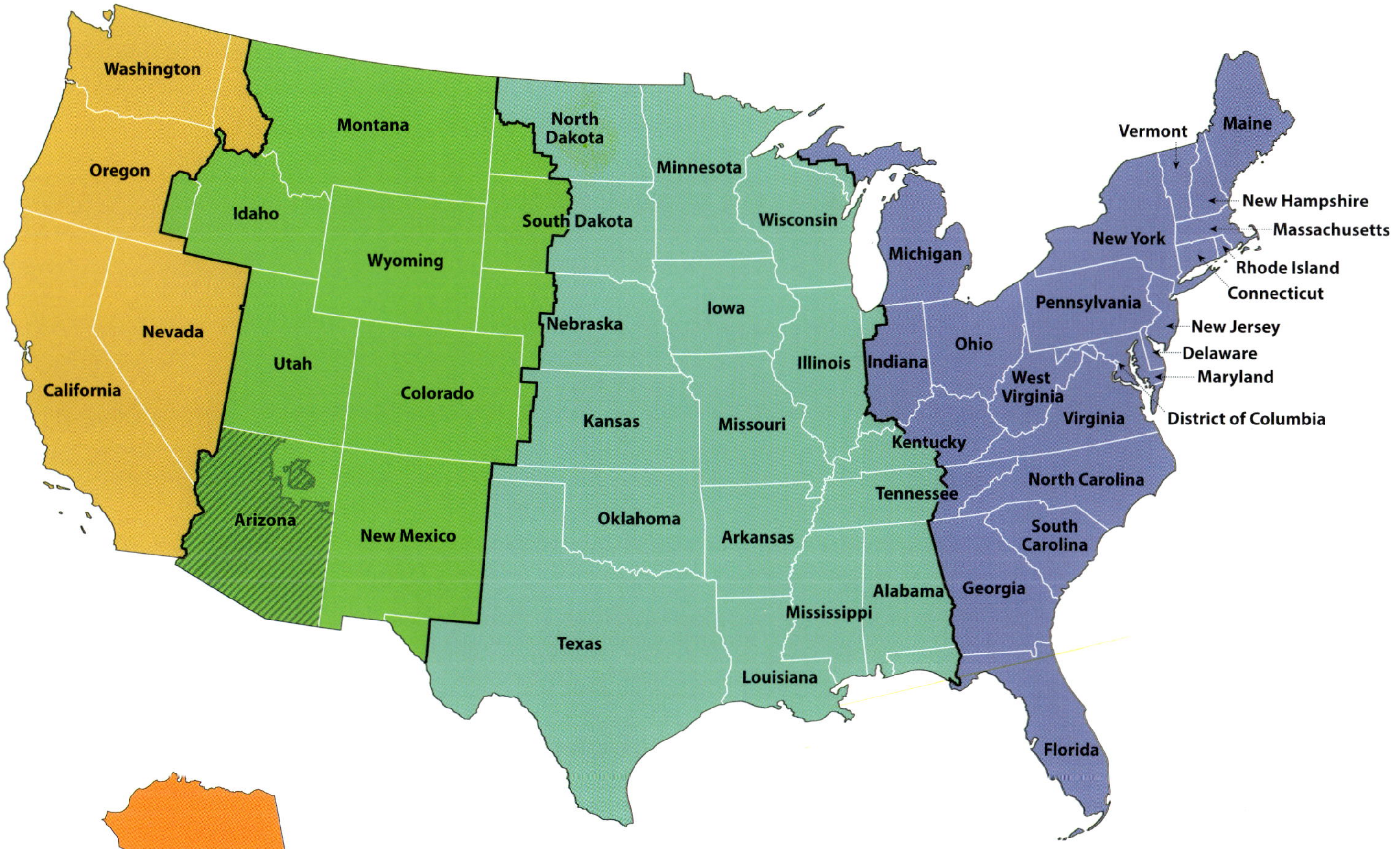

Alaska and Hawai'i are not shown in actual position or to scale.

A time zone is a zone on the globe that extends from pole to pole and is approximately 15° longitude wide. This standardizes times all over the world and allows everyone to know what time it is anywhere, which is important for business and transportation.

If you laid a world map flat on a table, the very center is something called Coordinated Universal Time, or UTC. This is the basis for all time zones worldwide. The time zone to the east of the UTC is one hour ahead of it, and the time zone to the west is one hour behind it. That keeps going all around the world.

So if it's 8 p.m. UTC time, it will be 2 p.m. in Dallas, Texas, six zones west of the UTC—and, therefore, six hours behind. It will be 3 p.m. in Miami, Florida, which is one zone to the east of Dallas, and, therefore, one hour ahead. One zone to the west of Dallas, in Denver, Colorado, it will be 1 p.m.

The United States has six time zones:

- Eastern, UTC minus 5 hours
- Central, UTC minus 6 hours
- Mountain, UTC minus 7 hours
- Pacific, UTC minus 8 hours
- Alaska, UTC minus 9 hours
- Hawai'i-Aleutian, UTC minus 10 hours

Answers

PAGES 30–31

Game: Spot the Not

MEDIA LITERACY

GAME

Spot the Not

See if you can tell the difference between the AI-generated photo and the real one.

You might have used AI (**artificial intelligence**) on platforms like ChatGPT to help you with research, or on Canva to create cool photos. But it's important to understand when something has been generated by AI, especially when it comes to the news. **AI-generated** content can be inaccurate, or it could even have been created just to trick you.

Play this game to see if you can spot the AI-generated images.

1a 1b 2a 2b 3a 3b 4a 4b

COOL AI HACK!

If you're not sure about a photo on the Internet, ask an adult to help you do a reverse search. You might be able to find the original source of the photo and determine if that source is credible. Another clue that the photo is AI-generated is that it won't show up as much in a search.

POWER WORDS

AI-generated *adjective:* when an AI platform has created something new based on patterns and data it's learned

artificial intelligence *noun:* a computer program that has been taught to use millions of pieces of information and images to think like a human—and then keep learning

Answers on page 200

30 TIME FOR KIDS 2027 ALMANAC 31

1B is AI-generated. The shadows and clouds are illustrated.
2A is AI-generated. She has extra fingers and her hand merges with her foot.
3A is AI-generated. The landscape is almost too perfect and appears cartoonish.
4B is AI-generated. The statue is too short.

PAGE 38

Quiz: Brain Busters

1, B; 2, C; 3, D; 4, A; 5, A; 6, C; 7, B; 8, D

PAGE 48

Game: Festival Fun

1. The Bahamas
2. India
3. Venice, Italy
4. Buñol, Spain
5. Thailand
6. Shetland Islands, Scotland
7. Oaxaca, Mexico

PAGES 98–99

Quiz: Hot Spots

1, C; 2, C; 3, B; 4, A; 5, D; 6, C; 7, B; 8, D; 9, D; 10, B; 11, A; 12, D; 13, A; 14, C; 15, C; 16, B

PAGE 134

Game: Double Trouble

ENTERTAINMENT AND CULTURE

GAME

Double Trouble

See if you can spot the 15 differences in these two photos of Katseye performing at the 2025 Kids' Choice Awards. (The real picture is on the top.)

Answers on page 200

134 TIME FOR KIDS

PAGE 144

Game: Dino Derby

1, *Titanosaurus*; 2, *Ankylosaurus*; 3, *Nigersaurus*; 4, *Maiasaura*; 5, *Tyrannosaurus*; 6, *Microraptor*; 7, *Spinosaurus*

PAGE 164

Game: Unbreakable

1. Hockey player Wayne Gretzky has 2,857 career points.
2. Basketball player Caitlin Clark had 769 points in her rookie season.
3. Baseball player Rickey Henderson has 1,406 career stolen bases.
4. Soccer player Mia Hamm has 147 assists.
5. Gymnast Simone Biles has 23 World Championship gold medals.
6. Football player Emmitt Smith has 18,355 career rushing yards.
7. Tennis player Serena Williams has 23 Grand Slam titles in the Open Era (before women were paid for playing).
8. Swimmer Michael Phelps has 28 Olympic medals.

PAGE 196

Quiz: First Ladies

1, B; 2, C; 3, D; 4, A; 5, C; 6, A; 7, B; 8, D; 9, D; 10, A

PAGE 197

Game: Park Puzzle

1. Yellowstone, established March 1, 1872
2. Grand Canyon, established February 26, 1919
3. Big Bend, established June 12, 1944
4. Virgin Islands National Park, established August 2, 1956
5. New River Gorge, established January 20, 2021

Credits

TIME and TIME for Kids articles have been adapted by TFK Editors.

World Maps derived from Equal Earth, made with Natural Earth data. United States maps from Adobe Stock. Cartographic editing by Mike Boruta.

Cover: (top left) Paramount Studios, (left) Ezra Shaw/Getty Images, (bottom left) Vladimir Borzykin/Getty, (center) pcruciatti/Adobe Stock, (top right corner) Sensvector/Adobe Stock, (top right) Liam McBurney/PA Images/Alamy, (right) Picture Office/Adobe Stock, (bottom right) Martin Heyn/Getty. **Interior:** 1: (top left) 103tnn/Adobe Stock, (bottom left) quantic69/Getty, (bottom) Maridav/Getty, (top right) johnandersonphoto/Getty, (bottom right) Conny/Adobe Stock. 3: (top right) FlixPix/Alamy, (top center right) titipong8176734/Adobe Stock, (bottom center right) Stasique/Adobe Stock, (bottom right) yodiyim/Getty. 4: (top left) ikate25/Adobe Stock, (center left) Georgijevic/Getty, (bottom) aphotostory/Adobe Stock. 5: (top) coldsnowstorm/Getty, (center right) Freder/Getty, (bottom right) xavierarnau/Getty. 6: (top) zhengzaishanchu/Adobe Stock, (center left) Lustre Art Group/Adobe Stock, (bottom) Scott Bufkin/Adobe Stock. **Chapter 1:** 7: FlixPix/Alamy. 8: (bottom left) NASA/Charles Beason, (bottom right) NASA. 8–9: SpaceX. 10–11: Justin Setterfield/Staff/Getty. 11: Annegret Hilse/Special Olympics World Games Berlin 2023/Getty. 12: Anne Frank Fonds Basel/Contributor/Getty. 13: (center) DREAMWORKS ANIMATION/Photo 12/Alamy, (bottom right) BFA/Walt Disney Studios/Alamy. 14: Colossal Biosciences. 14–15: (top) leonello/Getty, (bottom) Clive Rose - Gran Turismo/Gran Turismo via Getty. 15 (center) Moncherie/Getty. 16: Kevin Mazur/Getty Images for iHeartMedia. **Chapter 2:** 17: titipong8176734/Adobe Stock. (top left) 18: SOUTH CAROLINA AQUARIUM UNDER SCDNR MTP 2024-0004, (bottom left) RICH CAREY/GETTY IMAGES. (left) L. Sullivan/USFWS, (center) MJ_Prototype/Getty, (right) Wirestock/Getty. 20: Wirestock/Getty. 20–21: Al Carrera/Getty. 21: johnandersonphoto/Getty. 22: (left) Nataba/Getty, (bottom left) Conny/Adobe Stock, (top) balhash/Getty, (bottom right) mzphoto11/Adobe Stock. **Chapter 3:** 23: Stasique/Adobe Stock. 24–25: Eva-Katalin/Getty. 26: DAVID DEHOYOS FOR NASA. 27: vchalup/Adobe Stock. 28: Chip Somodevilla/Getty Images. 28–29: fstop123/Getty. 29: (left) leezsnow/Getty, (right) National Archives. 30: (top left) Oleksandrum/Adobe Stock, (top right and bottom left) AI, (bottom right) bondarillia/Adobe Stock. 31: (top left and bottom right) AI, (top right) Karlos Lomsky/Adobe Stock, (bottom left) Kaesler Media/Adobe Stock. 32: (left) Pixel-Shot/Adobe Stock, (right) Irina Shats/Adobe Stock. **Chapter 4:** 33: yodiyim/Getty. 34: Stasique/Adobe Stock, (center right) pushkaash/Adobe Stock. 35: Refluo/Shutterstock. 36–37: JuiceBros/Getty. 38: (left) Konstantin Yuganov/Adobe Stock, (bottom) simonkr/Getty, monkeybusinessimages/Getty. **Chapter 5:** 39: ikate25/Adobe Stock. 40: (top left) ShunTerra/Adobe Stock, (bottom left) hurricanehank/Adobe Stock, (right) Lightfield Studios/Adobe Stock. 41: (center left) duckycards/Getty, (bottom left) Jeff Whyte/Adobe Stock, (top right) LarsSchmidtEisenlohr/Adobe Stock, Event Horizon Telescope (EHT). 42: (top) IQ art_Design/Shutterstock, (top left) Rozaliya/Adobe Stock, (top center) arachi07/Adobe Stock, (top right) Minakryn Ruslan/Adobe Stock, (bottom left) Manutsawee/Adobe Stock, (bottom center) byjeng/Adobe Stock, (bottom right) Tatsiana/Adobe Stock. 43: (top) khaledSaifulllah/Adobe Stock, (top left) byjeng/Adobe Stock, (top center) Igor Kali/Adobe Stock, (top right) bigjo/Adobe Stock, (bottom left) inge/Adobe Stock, (bottom center) ikonacolor/Adobe Stock, (bottom right) Aleksandr Volkov/Adobe Stock. 44: (left) M-image/Adobe Stock. 44–45: (top) Dragan/Adobe Stock, (bottom) ssstocker/Adobe Stock. 46: Bastiaan Slabbers/Getty. 46–47: Harshal/Adobe Stock. 47: (top) csfotoimages/Getty, (right) eve orea/Adobe Stock, (bottom) Ali Trisno Pranoto/Getty. **Chapter 6:** 48: (top left) JackF/Getty, (center left) AndrewJ/Adobe Stock, (bottom left) ferrantraite/Getty, (top right) Jack Tamrong/Adobe Stock, (top center right) vichinterlang/Getty, (bottom center right) SvetlanaSF/Getty, (bottom right) RelaxFoto.de/Getty. 49: Georgijevic/Getty. 50: (top left) Josh Bryan/Adobe Stock, (bottom left) Erman Gunes/Adobe Stock, (top center right) photology1971/Adobe Stock, (top center right) runrun2/Adobe Stock, (center right) ullstein bild/Contributor/Getty, (bottom right) sakkmesterke/Adobe Stock. 51: Dina Litovsky for TIME. 52: (top) Jo Whaley for TIME, (bottom) NEMO. 53: Jo Whaley for TIME. 54: (top) Bimotal, (bottom) Kangsters. 55: (left) Jo Whaley for TIME, (top) Rakuten Kobo, (bottom) TOSY. 56–57: karelnoppe/Getty. 57 (all) TFK. 58: (left) Earth Pixel LLC./Adobe Stock, (top) Earth Pixel LLC./Adobe Stock, (bottom) pcruciatti/Adobe Stock. **Chapter 7:** 59: aphotostory/Adobe Stock. 60-63: Natural Earth. 64–96: Максим Лебедик/Adobe Stock. 67: (top right) G7 Stock/Adobe Stock. 71: (top right) filipbjorkman/Adobe Stock. 72: (top center) filipbjorkman/Adobe Stock, (bottom right) Beibeinside/Adobe Stock. 75: (bottom left) stringerphoto/Adobe Stock. 87: (top left) Beibeinside/Adobe Stock. 92: (top right) ikonisto/Adobe Stock. 95: (bottom center) Yanniklab/Adobe Stock, (bottom left) Douglas Sacha/Getty. 96: (bottom) titoOnz/Getty. 97: (bottom left) Brent Hofacker/Adobe Stock, (top) Nikcoa/Adobe Stock, (right) SHARKY PHOTOGRAPHY/Adobe Stock. 98: (left) andyKRAKOVSKI/Getty, (bottom) Wangkun Jia/Getty, (top) Gannet77/Getty. 99: (left) dennis/Adobe Stock, (top) lucky-photo/Adobe Stock, (bottom) mirecca/Adobe Stock. 100: (top) Alex Liew/Getty, (bottom) Sergey Ryzhov/Adobe Stock. **Chapter 8:** 101: coldsnowstorm/Getty. 102: (left) MNStudio/Adobe Stock, (bottom) xiaoying shi/Getty, (right) piyaset/Getty. 103: (top left) Bertrand Godfroid/Getty, (bottom left) Luis Diaz Devesa/Getty. 104: shufu/Adobe Stock. 104–105: Mike Mareen/Adobe Stock. 105: (center) COURTESY CALTECH, (portraits) TFK. 106: (center) Minverva Studio/Adobe Stock, (bottom) designua/Adobe Stock. 107: Satoshi Kina/Adobe Stock. 108: Bryan Gailey/Adobe Stock. 109: S Quintans/Adobe Stock. 110: (bottom center) Alex/Adobe Stock, (bottom) AndriiSlonchak/Getty, (top) Richard/Adobe Stock, (right) Michael/Adobe Stock. 111: (top left) Ken Griffiths/Getty, (bottom left) Lukas/Adobe Stock, (top right) Christopher Thienel/Getty, (bottom right) Lauren/Adobe Stock. 112: (top left) mozgova/Adobe Stock, (bottom left) Alexey Seafarer/Adobe Stock, (top right) Petr Caska/Adobe Stock, (bottom right) Татьяна Мордкович/Adobe Stock. 113: (top left) Galyna Andrushko/Adobe Stock, (bottom left) Chris/Adobe Stock, (top right) slowmotiongli/Adobe Stock, (bottom right) Rocky89/Getty. 114: (top left) RRA/Adobe Stock, (bottom left) Vadim_Orlov/Adobe Stock, (top right) Stéphane Bidouze/Adobe Stock, (bottom right) Dmitriy/Adobe Stock. 115: (top left) 25ehaag6/Getty, (bottom left) Jakub/Adobe Stock, (top right) Mark Baldwin/Adobe Stock, (bottom right) Gary/Adobe Stock. 116: Courtesy Scott Lange. 117: (left) COURTESY HARPER CARROLL, (top) COURTESY ELIZABETH FETHERSTON, (bottom) GLORIA BARRON PRIZE FOR YOUNG HEROES. 118: (left) vgajic/Getty, (top right) Petra Richli/Adobe Stock, (bottom) Gorodenkoff/Adobe Stock. **Chapter 9:** 119: Freder/Getty. 120–121 and 122: (top) Kevin Winter/Getty Images. 122: (bottom) Jeff Kravitz/FilmMagic/Getty. 122–124: Frogella.stock/Adobe Stock. 122–123: Christopher Polk/Billboard via Getty Images. 123: (top) Alberto E. Rodriguez/Getty Images for Disney/Pixar, (bottom) Steve Granitz/FilmMagic/Getty. 124: (bottom) Geisler-Fotopress GmbH/Alamy, (right) Emma McIntyre/Getty Images for Nickelodeon. 124–125: Amazing Illustration/Adobe Stock. 125: Kevin Winter/Getty Images. 126: (bottom) Kevin Winter/Getty Images for The Recording Academy, (top) Kevin Mazur/Getty Images for The Recording Academy. 126–127: agrus/Adobe Stock. 127: JYP Entertainment/Penske Media via Getty Images. 128: (right) *Chooch Helped* by Andrea L. Rogers, illustrated by Rebecca Lee Kunz, published by Levine Querido. 128–129: Tatiana Maksimova/Getty. 129: (left) Atheneum/Caitlyn Dlouhy Books, (right) Esther Hildebrandt/Adobe Stock. 130: Dimitrios Kambouris/Getty Images for The Met Museum/Vogue. 131: (top) Gilbert Flores/Variety via Getty Images, (bottom) Dia Dipasupil/Getty Images. 132: (top) Liam McBurney/PA Images/Alamy, (bottom) Taylor Swift Productions/Silent House/Album/Alamy. 133: (all) TFK. 134: Kevin Winter/Getty Images. **Chapter 10:** 135: xavierarnau/Getty. 136: (top left) AlenKadr/Adobe Stock, (bottom left) Roman Tiraspolsky/Adobe Stock, (top right) vladischern/Adobe Stock, (bottom center) Steve Cukrov/Adobe Stock, (bottom right) ahirao/Adobe Stock. 136–137: HstrongART/Shutterstock. 137: (bottom) vladischern/Adobe Stock, (left) AlenKadr/Adobe Stock. 138: (bottom) NASA, (top) COURTESY ANDREA CARTER. 139: (top) ARTHUR MORRIS/GETTY IMAGES, (center) MAEGAN LANHAM/TEXAS PARKS AND WILDLIFE DEPARTMENT. 140: MARK STEBNICKI. 141: (top) COURTESY ASHLEY RUIZ, (bottom) COURTESY IF/THEN® COLLECTION. 142–143: magemasher/Adobe Stock. 144: (top left) Lewisroland/Adobe Stock, (bottom left, top center, and top right) Daniel Eskridge/Adobe Stock, (bottom center) warpaintcobra/Adobe Stock, (center right) Michael Rosskothen/Adobe Stock, (bottom right) warpaintcobra/Getty. **Chapter 11:** 145: zhengzaishanchu/Adobe Stock. 146: (bottom) NASA, (top) Aerial_Views/Getty. 147: (top and bottom left) KEEGAN BARBER/NASA, (right) NASA. 148–150: NASA, ESA, CSA, STScI. 151: (top) ESA/Webb, NASA, CSA, M. Barlow, (bottom) NASA, ESA, CSA, STScI. 152–153: NASA/JPL. 154 (left) NASA/Johns Hopkins University Applied Physics Laboratory/Carnegie Institution of Washington, (bottom) NASA, ESA, STScI., (right) NASA/JPL. **Chapter 12:** 155: Lustre Art Group/Adobe Stock. 156–157: TIMOTHY A. CLARY/AFP via Getty Images. 157: Matthew Stockman/Getty Images. 158: (top) Luke Hales/Getty Images, (bottom) Harry How/Getty Images. 159: (bottom) David Becker/NBAE via Getty Images, (top) Joel Auerbach/Getty Images. 160: Richard Heathcote/Getty Images. 161: (bottom) Fernando Leon/ISI Photos/Getty Images, (top) Alex Slitz/Getty Images. 162: (left) © Walter G Arce Sr Grindstone Medi/ASP/Alamy, (top) PA Images/Alamy, (bottom) Ulrik Pedersen/CSM/Alamy. 163: (left) YUTAKA/AFLO SPORT/Alamy Live News, (top) Ulrik Pedersen/NurPhoto/Alamy, (bottom) Jonathan Tenca/CSM/Alamy. 164: (top left) Yohei Osada/AFLO SPORT/Alamy Live News, (bottom left) UPI/Alamy, (top center) Adam Stoltman/Alamy, (center) Allstar Picture Library Ltd/Alamy, (bottom center and top right) Zuma Press, Inc./Alamy, (center right) Duncan Grove/Alamy Live News, (bottom right) Naoki Nishimura/AFLO SPORT/Alamy. **Chapter 13:** 165: Scott Bufkin/Adobe Stock. 166–167: TingDesign/Adobe Stock. 168–196: Poligrafistka/Getty. 168: (top) George Dodd/Getty, (bottom) Martina/Adobe Stock. 169: (top) Drone Dood/Adobe Stock, (bottom) Ray Tan/Getty. 170: (top) Gloria Moeller/Adobe Stock, (bottom) Teri/Adobe Stock. 171: (top) Jennifer/Adobe Stock, (bottom) yvonne navalaney/Adobe Stock. 172: (top) Gabriele Maltinti/Adobe Stock, (bottom) David A. Dobbs 2017/Adobe Stock. 173: (top) Maridav/Getty, (bottom) alexmisu/Adobe Stock. 174: (top) Leonid Andronov/Adobe Stock, (bottom) William Reagan/Getty. 175: (top) SeanPavonePhoto/Adobe Stock, (bottom) scottevers7/Adobe Stock. 176: (top) Sherman Cahal/Adobe Stock, (bottom) SeanPavonePhoto/Getty. 177: (top) Philippe Gratton/Getty, (bottom) Kurt Holter/Adobe Stock. 178: (top) DenisTangneyJr/Getty, (bottom) Sue Smith/Adobe Stock. 179: (top) Tindo/Adobe Stock, (top right) Willard/Getty, (center) Ruslan/Adobe Stock, (bottom) chandler_borries/Adobe Stock. 180: (top) SeanPavonePhoto/Adobe Stock, (bottom) JeffGoulden/Getty. 181: (top) Zack Frank/Adobe Stock, (bottom) Michael Ver Sprill/Getty. 182: (top) C.Echeveste/Adobe Stock, (bottom) sparhawk4242/Getty. 183: (top) Tom/Adobe Stock, (bottom) mandritoiu/Adobe Stock. 184: (top) Chansak Joe A./Adobe Stock, (bottom) eqroy/Adobe Stock. 185: (top) Kevin/Adobe Stock, (bottom) GracedByTheLight/Getty. 186: (top) Gleb Tarassenko/Adobe Stock, (bottom) djwoody/Adobe Stock. 187: (top) Olga/Adobe Stock, (bottom) f11photo/Adobe Stock. 188: (top) braddailey/Adobe Stock, (bottom) 4kclips/Adobe Stock. 189: (top) chrisjscoggins/Adobe Stock, (center) Utah.gov, (bottom) LightPhoto2/Adobe Stock. 190: (top) Ron and Patty Thomas/Getty, (bottom) quasarphotos/Adobe Stock. 191: (top) Jeremy Edwards/Getty, (bottom) Kristina Blokhin/Adobe Stock. 192: (top) KeenaiPhotography/Getty, (bottom) Steve Swope/Adobe StockRF. 193: (left) cdwheatley/Getty, (top) mandritoiu/Adobe Stock, (top right) Camp Photo/Getty, (center right) PhotoSpirit/Adobe Stock, (bottom right) SUNGKYU/Adobe Stock, (bottom) cdwheatley/Getty. 194–195: (all) Library of Congress. 196: (top left and right) Library of Congress, (bottom left) Pictures Now/Alamy, (bottom) Library of Congress. 197: (top left) cdwheatley/Getty, (bottom left) Paul/Adobe Stock, (top right) Donna Bollenbach/Adobe Stock, (center right) Andrew S./Adobe Stock, (bottom right) Patrick/Adobe Stock. 198: Berit Kessler/Adobe Stock. 199: TingDesign/Adobe Stock. **Back Cover:** (top left) yodiyim/Getty, (center left) titipong8176734/Adobe Stock, (bottom left) eve orea/Adobe Stock, (top right) warpaintcobra/Adobe Stock, (bottom right) NASA, ESA, CSA, STScI.

Index

M

N

O

P

Q

R

S